HANSARD SOCIETY SERIES IN
POLITICS AND GOVERNMENT

Series Editor
F.F. Ridley

D0221966

HANSARD SOCIETY SERIES IN POLITICS AND GOVERNMENT

Edited by
F.F. Ridley

1. THE QUANGO DEBATE, edited with David Wilson

2. BRITISH GOVERNMENT AND POLITICS SINCE 1945: CHANGES IN PERSPECTIVES, edited with Michael Rush

3. SLEAZE: POLITICIANS, PRIVATE INTERESTS AND PUBLIC REACTION, edited with Alan Doig

4. WOMEN IN POLITICS, edited with Joni Lovenduski and Pippa Norris

5. UNDER THE SCOTT-LIGHT: BRITISH GOVERNMENT SEEN THROUGH THE SCOTT REPORT, edited with Brian Thompson

6. BRITAIN VOTES 1997, edited with Pippa Norris and Neil T. Gavin

7. PROTEST POLITICS: CAUSE GROUPS AND CAMPAIGNS, edited with Grant Jordan

8. PARLIAMENT IN THE AGE OF THE INTERNET, edited by Stephen Coleman, John Taylor and Wim van de Donk

9. DEMOCRACY AND CULTURAL DIVERSITY, edited by Michael O'Neill and Dennis Austin

The Hansard Society Series in Politics and Government brings to the wider public the debates and analyses of important issues first discussed in the pages of its journal, *Parliamentary Affairs*

Democracy and Cultural Diversity

Edited by
Michael O'Neill and Dennis Austin

Series Editor
F.F. Ridley

OXFORD UNIVERSITY PRESS
in association with
THE HANSARD SOCIETY FOR
PARLIAMENTARY GOVERNMENT

OXFORD
UNIVERSITY PRESS

Great Clarendon Street, Oxford OX2 6DP

Oxford University Press is a department of the University of Oxford.
It furthers the University's objective of excellence in research, scholarship,
and education by publishing worldwide in

Oxford New York

Athens Auckland Bangkok Bogotá Buenos Aires Calcutta
Cape Town Chennai Dar es Salaam Delhi Florence Hong Kong Istanbul
Karachi Kuala Lumpur Madrid Melbourne Mexico City Mumbai
Nairobi Paris São Paulo Singapore Taipei Tokyo Toronto Warsaw

with associated companies in Berlin Ibadan

Oxford is a registered trade mark of Oxford University Press
in the UK and in certain other countries

Published in the United States
by Oxford University Press Inc., New York

A catalogue for this book is available from the British Library

Library of Congress Cataloging in Publication Data
(Data available)

ISBN 0–19–929000–8

Printed in Great Britain
by Headley Brothers Limited, The Invicta Press,
Ashford, Kent and London

ACKNOWLEDGEMENTS

The editors wish to record their gratitude to those who have contributed to the publication of *Democracy and Cultural Diversity*. We owe particular thanks to Professor Fred Ridley, general editor of the series in which the book appears. His good counsel never failed. We thank, too, the contributors who responded promptly to our invitation to write and who endured our revision to their text. It fell to Sandra Odell in Nottingham to turn a variety of emendations into a cogent manuscript.

The Foreword contributed by John Wakeham expresses the essence of the project and we are obliged to him, given the many calls on his time, for agreeing to write. We are also beneficiaries of the splendid assistance given by Gill Mitchell and the Oxford University Press.

We owe more than we can put into words to Margaret Austin and Wendie O'Neill, guardians of our sanity and time.

Michael O'Neill, Screveton
Dennis Austin, Macclesfield
February 2000

CONTENTS

CONTRIBUTORS TO THIS VOLUME

Dennis Austin is Emeritus Professor and Fellow in the Institute of Development Policy and Management, University of Manchester

Richard Bellamy is Professor of Politics at the University of Reading

Clive Church is a Jean Monnet Professor in European Studies at the University of Kent

Martin Dent is a Fellow at Keele University

Alain Gagnon is Professor of Political Science at McGill University, Canada

Montserrat Guibernau is Lecturer in Government and Politics at the Open University

Anirudha Gupta is Emeritus Professor at the Jawaharlal Nehru University, New Delhi, India

Michael O'Neill is Senior Lecturer in Politics and Jean Monnet Fellow in European Integration at Nottingham Trent University

Andrew Rigby is Director at the Centre for the Study of Forgiveness and Reconciliation, Coventry University

David Seah is Assistant Professor of Public Administration at the National University of Singapore

Desmond Thomas is a Tutor in the Education Department at the New Bulgarian University, Sofia

Donna Lee Van Cott is Assistant Professor of Political Science at the University of Tennessee, USA

Darren Wallis is Lecturer in Politics at Nottingham Trent University

FOREWORD

Belief in parliamentary rule is not abstract but comes from the experience of states which, despite deep-seated divisions, have succeeded in ensuring democratic government. Few countries are so fashioned as to be entirely uniform. Most have societies that are divided by language, religion, race, or regional identities, and the task of reconciling such differences is never easy. Despotic rule may succeed for a time in suppressing dissent but, when it fails, the resulting explosion of anger and rebellion is all the greater. The hope, therefore, is that by providing open channels of expression, democratic parliamentary rule can be therapeutic. Freely conducted elections, debate in parliament, constitutional safeguards and institutional arrangements for the protection of minorities can all play their part. The fears of minorities and the grievances of those excluded from politics need to be met, and democratic government offers at least the possibility of moving politics along a peaceful path. If persuasion fails, it is unlikely that force can heal social decisions and is more likely to exaggerate them. Speaking in the House of Commons in November 1947, Winston Churchill remarked that: 'No one pretends that democracy is perfect or all-wise. Indeed, it has been said that democracy is the worst form of government except for all those other forms that have been tried from time to time.' That is certainly part of the conviction that societies are best governed when they are ruled with the consent of their citizens.

The essays which follow examine this prescription in a number of countries across the world. Some are large—India. Others are quite small—Malaysia, Ghana, Belgium. Some are divided by the political legacies of an immensely difficult history, as in the Lebanon, Slovakia, and Spain, others by different communities of origin, as in Switzerland, Mexico, and a number of Latin American states. Countries as well established, as well versed in the arts of parliamentary democracy as Britain and Canada have struggled with the problem of democratic reform to meet the demands of a changing society. The picture that emerges from these interesting accounts illustrates the difficulties, but also encourages the hope that provident government can steer a course between competing pressures, bridge ethnic and other potentially explosive divisions if they put their trust in institutions of consent rather than coercion and in discussion rather than force. After all, what are parliaments for if they do not succeed in managing affairs by talking and persuading?

The Right Honourable Lord Wakeham

Introduction: Democracy and Cultural Diversity

BY DENNIS AUSTIN AND MICHAEL O'NEILL

THE questions raised by this book are not whether democratic institutions can survive conflict between opposed communities but whether they are the best way in practice to moderate their rivalry. Can parliaments, elections and constitutions bridge differences of race, religion and region? The chapters which follow this brief Introduction offer grounds for hope. They cover a range of states in which divided societies are shown in a positive mode — cooperating peacefully and democratically across communities in Switzerland, managing relations between provincial jealousies in Canada, facing up to caste and communal hatreds in India, and taking sensitive note of minority grievances in Central and South America. There are no accounts of failure although several of these country by country studies describe how delicately balanced many governments are between success and disappointment. Indeed, success itself is often ambiguous in the sense that ethnic and religious tensions may slacken only to tighten again. Scholars can record the changes but not foresee the outcome. That enigmatic library of Babel with its 'detailed history of the future' has not yet opened its doors and governments hopeful of reducing communal unrest by democratic measures must tread a narrow path. The studies in this account extend from mature parliamentary states to those which have only recently begun to claim democratic credentials but in none of them has reform been easy.

They are established democracies or struggling to become democracies, a familiar pattern today. Insofar as there is a spirit of the age — always an elusive concept — it is reflected in the movement towards the democracy of parliaments and elections. The explanation is not hard to find. The defeat of fascist dictators, the collapse of Soviet rule and the failure of many military regimes to do more than impose a corrupt order has left a vacuum. Modern day Germany, Italy, Spain and Portugal, and a minority of countries in eastern Europe, each in its own way, testify to the renewal of democratic practice. Nor were earlier attempts at a tutelary democracy by Britain extinguished in a number of former dependencies. The consequences are that a growing list of regimes have adopted a more open politics. The states under review are those in which democratic usage has had its effect in diminishing communal and religious unrest – linguistic rivalries in Belgium, ethnic competition in Ghana, minority fears in Malaysia – and supporting longstanding federal arrangements in Canada and Switzerland. But it would be silly not to acknowledge that when the enmity between rival communities is deep and a willingness to try persuasion is absent, the hope of peaceful reform has to be abandoned. The history of Northern Ireland is a grim testimony to the difficulties of reconciliation. Democratic rule is presently inconceivable among the warring states in the Caucasus or in face of tribal hatreds in central Africa. In such circumstances governments turn to other means of control, some reluctantly others more willingly. The politics of Sri Lanka were once peacefully conducted in a seemingly idyllic setting. The hills stood leafy guard over the towns and temples of the island but beneath the surface calm lay passion and conflict. The government in Colombo tried to keep alive the institutions of parliament through frequent elections but when negotiations between Sinhalese and Tamils failed, the army was sent into the northern Jaffna peninsula against Tamil insurgents. The violence still has no end in sight.

The contrast between democratic practice and armed suppression is not always contingent on events. When men behave cruelly that is because they are men. Constitutions, parliaments and legal safeguards can offer a framework for tolerance and justice but they cannot enforce good behaviour. To be able to trust such arrangements we need to give hope a long lead for all too often 'man has been a wolf to his fellow men'. When we also consider the abject conditions which much of the world's population has to endure, we cannot be over optimistic. Yet the examples looked at later do show that plural societies can succeed in keeping ethnic differences within constitutional bounds. Violence and aggression may well be innate qualities — biosomatic atavisms? — in at least the male of our species but they are not, on the evidence from these dozen or so states, either irrepressible or incapable of being channelled by peaceful constitutional ways. Government is a difficult but not an impossible art.

All the contributors take for granted the nation state as the necessary arena of reform. Are they right to do so? Several critics have pointed to the weakness of modern governments when confronting challenges not only from discontented communities but from interests more powerful than themselves. Nation states which were the centre of a world order now face new actors (for which the shorthand is globalisation) and few other than the most powerful can play the decisive role once allotted them. Many are ceasing to be the sole motors of wealth creation which lies with the corporate ownership of capital; some are losing the loyalty of their citizens. In answer to global pressures, nationalism has paradoxically both narrowed its appeal and lost its hold on events within its own borders. Whether the world is in transition from the familiar pattern of states to an indiscernible map no one can say: what is certain is that societies are restless and governments are troubled by the unrest. What hope, therefore, is there that inadequate states, as they limp their way into the new century, can meet the problem of local nationalisms and ethnic conflict?

The argument has gained ground in recent years and cannot easily be dismissed. The expanding contours of the economic world no longer fit the political map of nation states, the problem being not so much one of status or stature but capacity. Some states cannot cope. They are overwhelmed by their own history particularly in the former communist world where internal dissent and the sheer misery of daily life has paralysed governments from Russia to Kyegyzstan and in south-eastern Europe. Other states are divided — indeed, fragmented — to the point almost of non-existence. They are 'fictive states', shadowy entities which move in and out of reality and exist only as a name on the membership of international organisations. For such states, the future that beckons is bleak and forms no part of the chapters which follow.[1] The tension between communities may also reach breaking point, the fracture coming from the very processes intended to give expression to local opinion. In 1947 the Indian subcontinent was torn apart. In 1992 the Czechs and Slovaks parted company. The break may be violent as in India, or peaceful as in Czechoslovakia, but separation marks a failure of institutions and leaders to avoid the pain of divorce.

The examples actually chosen are more robust. They struggle with but also manage ethnic conflict. Of course states are not eternal. There was a time when empires, churches and feudal loyalties provided the protection which the nation state later provided. Perhaps it too will be superseded but, for the present, in the absence of alternatives, states are still the indispensable condition for the way in which society conducts its affairs, sustaining the legal means of exchange, offering a framework of security and providing an international identity. They are the only entities capable of doing so. They are also the arena where political arguments are debated and, when possible, resolved. Because some western governments are uneasily poised between old sovereignties and new institutions that is no cause to doubt the reality of states elsewhere in the world. They are indeed the avowed end of many dissident groups whose aim is not to abolish but to reshape the map of nation states to their own ends. To say, therefore, that states have to face both local and global pressures is simply to recognise that the task of governing modern societies must constantly respond to periodic shifts of scale.

Very often, changes to the architecture of government begin when the appeal of ethnicity crosses the boundary between culture and politics. Whether the outcome should envisage a world of fewer or greater number of states is part of the debate. There was never of course a stable map of the world despite the hopes of the European founder states at that famous Peace of Westphalia three centuries ago. Wars, revolutions, industrial change, the break-up of empires and the increasingly global reach of national economies have repeatedly rearranged the jigsaw. The chapters by Michael O'Neill for Belgium and Britain and by Alain Gagnon for Canada show how the pressure for change has rearranged the structure of government in all three countries. Regional and ethnic nationalism has certainly grown in the protective shadow of wider structures such as the European Union and the North American Free Trade Area—taking advantage of the weakness of established states, buffeted and hollowed out by the force of transnational finance and trade. But how wrong were the early critics of subnationalism! The 'people without history' whom Marx and Engels once ridiculed have reappeared with a vengeance, although ethno-nationalism too is in constant flux, adding to the vulnerability of the international world. The claims to sovereignty by local communities have grown and slackened according to circumstance. The irony is that local nationalisms are more likely to seek expression under democratic regimes if only because constitutional governments are concerned to take seriously civic rights and the bargaining processes of politics characteristic of parliamentary rule. Few, if any, democracies are immune from the need to manage diversity. If, however, a reasoned order is to exist, the link between ethno-nationalism and parliamentary democracy is vital since without the bargaining and compromise, and all the unheroic virtues of democratic politics, ethnic nationalism may run to excess, to end, at the worst, in the charnel house of ethnic cleansing.

A minority of countries in these chapters have also had to confront the danger of social breakdown. They are democracies scarred by violence—India, Mexico, Nigeria, Lebanon. Others have emerged from long periods of conflict, Malaysia being an obvious example. The scale of the problem can be seen in India. Anirudha Gupta describes the horrors of communal conflict without losing confidence in the capacity of Indian democracy to meet the challenge from those intent on violence. The size of the task should not be underestimated when communities turn savagely against each other.

Ethnic conflict is bloody, quick to erupt, destructive. It is also purposeful. Even the communal violence of a mob may not be altogether frenzy. In October 1984 news spread through the Indian capital of the assassination of Indira Gandhi at the hands of her Sikh bodyguard, and '. . . a mob spread out into different parts of Delhi. Sikhs were dragged from buses, taxis, cars, autorickshaws, two wheelers and cycles. Their vehicles were burnt and at some point frenzied mobs threw their drivers into the flames. We did not find any grief on the part of those who were participating in the looting and burning. Attempts to pacify them by the peace marchers met with derisive laughter. Listening to the raucous exultation and looking at their gleeful faces, one would have thought it was a festival but for the arson, murder and looting that was going on.' (Report of Joint Inquiry into the Riots in New Delhi 1984, *New Delhi Press*, 1984.)

Such capacity for hate makes savages of us all. But there is method even in this degree of madness. The frenzy of those who kill or maim will have behind it calculations of profit not only among those who loot and murder but among politicians who fuel their anger. Emotion, appetite and purpose are rarely distinct. Even the assassin who plans, watches and then strikes shares the emotion of his or her community. The Tamil Tigers' leader from Sri Lanka must surely have been gripped by a form of madness when in May 1991 she killed Rajiv Gandhi and sacrificed her own life so coolly, so deliberately, yet demonically — bowing down before him — when she exploded her bomb. In the face of such terrible events, men and women look for safety not from a government they distrust but from their own community. For violence disturbs. It disturbs daily life and catches society in a net of fear. It may come suddenly as a shout in the street or the spread of rumour, then the looting of villages and the killing of men, women and children: death will come from mortars, grenades, rifles, scythes and sticks. Governments respond in equal measure, often with added ferocity. As the terror spreads, the state turns to emergency methods of control, suspending constitutional rule, meeting force with force until slowly, increasingly, almost inexorably, the institutions of a free society are eroded. Then it is that the poison of violence enters the main stream of politics.

Why does it happen? There are general explanations rooted in social deprivation and the pressure of population on scarce resources, including land and jobs. We have to take account of the end of the Cold War and the removal of restraints on local nationalism — a danger offset by the cessation of proxy wars between the former Super Powers. The obvious explanation of ethnic violence is of course nationalism, the ethnic nationalism of those struggling to be free and an irredentist nationalism among those determined to control. Western societies today are less approving of such emotion, fearing its power of unreason, but the rest of the world is as nationalist now as Europe was yesterday, and so persistent an emotion must have some merit of advantage. The elective affinities of nationalism are never simple, but for many of its believers it is a true *zeitgeist*, challenging and in many societies displacing religion in men's affections. The nationalism which leads to ethnic cleansing is grotesque, but patriotism too has its claim on our loyalties. Citizens owe a duty to the state which protects them; and when nationalism is non-xenophobic, evoking pride in one's country without contempt for others, its virtues are self-evident. The plain fact is, men need to belong — and to feel a sense of belonging — and nationalism breathes life into the legal-rational state: it gives society its soul. The problem is that it can be two sided. It can divide as well as unite; the difficulty arises when nationalism narrows its appeal to an allegiance defined by the community of one's origins or by an exclusive faith. Then those left out are resentful. They look for alternatives and the troubles begin. Those of us who are at ease in a national society may condemn such emotions as atavistic or dismiss them as tribal; but they are characteristic of our age, and Ernest Gellner was surely right to link nationalist and subnationalist movements throughout the world to 'modernisation': to an increase in population, urban growth, advances in technology and a mass literacy. The argument has been enlarged recently by Benedict Anderson who writes of nations as imagined acts of self-creation, shaped by cultural roots and reflecting the persistent need by men and women to see themselves as a people in history who require a national story.

The nationalist interpretation of ethnic unrest certainly matches the world of the twentieth century. Far from being eroded, nationalist demands have multiplied. There are also many more states today and few are single societies. They date from an age when governments were predatory and incorporated their neighbours or from a time when immigrants arrived in substantial numbers to add to the native population. States that were once an acceptable framework of order for a variety of people then became targeted by those who demand a new flag, a new anthem, a new government and control of their own resources. Grievances can spread quickly today and those who endured in silence or who might have been scarcely aware that they had collective cause to complain, learn soon enough to engage in mass forms of protest. There are almost two hundred UN members today and few doubt but that more will arrive.

The examples looked at in these studies do not, however, hold so pessimistic a view of a world about to splinter. They are generally more hopeful. They acknowledge the danger of conflict between rival communities and between governments and minorities but they also describe the various ways in which societies can struggle to meet the difficulties of pluralism. Democratic institutions and procedures, they say, can ease the tension in communal division. They write of states, each very different in the problems it faces, which have tried — not always successfully — to keep ethnic or religious or linguistic rivalries within constitutional bounds. Some — Switzerland for many decades, the United Kingdom in recent years — take pride in their diversity, believing that differences of culture contribute not to the weakness but the vibrancy of a national identity. Some — Belgium, Canada, Nigeria, Mexico, Spain and states in South America — are trying to move forward to new arrangements. Darren Wallis, for instance, examines the particular tensions that accompany democratic transition in a country where ethnic differences are sharpened by prejudice ; Montserrat Guibernau discusses how longstanding antagonisms can be muted by socioeconomic change. Others — war-torn societies in the Middle East — search for ways of healing that are both pluralist and democratic, though memories are long and mistrust is deep.

If, however, there is a general precept to be drawn from these accounts it is the need to be cautious. Plural societies pull in different directions and need all the help they can get, not only from democratic practice but from constitutional forms and legal safeguards. The complexity of the problem can be seen in the variety of the remedies adopted. No one case is quite like another. Yet a common theme does emerge, namely, that despite the difficulties, even in states as divided as Belgium and the Lebanon or India and Nigeria, governments can reach an accommodation with aggrieved communities if those involved are minded to do so. If the will is there, a way can be found. Circumstances will shape the remedy but, in order to succeed, a readiness must be present. The chances of success are then likely to be governed by the advantages perceived on all sides to the divide. There must be bargains and they must be proportionate.

That the circumstances and rewards will vary is clear: more difficult to assess is their effect.

1. How critical is the mix of ethnic, religious or regional elements? Anirudha Gupta reaches the surprising conclusion that more is better than few in order to maximise the cross-currents of a society which lacks room for bargaining when too starkly divided. India as a 'gigantic muddle' can operate a multiple set of alliances in an ever changing kaleidoscope. (The contrast would be Greek–Christian–Cypriots *versus* Turkish–Muslim–Cypriots across a single frontier). On the other hand, the limits to multi-ethnicity were seen in the former Yugoslav Federation: bargaining failed, war and secession followed. Asghar Ali Engineer's assessment in his study of Indian elections of the arithmetic of ethnic conflict has significance beyond his own continent: 'Those areas which have a minority Muslim population of 15 to 40% tend to be riot prone if only because, in a ballot-box orientated democracy, minorities with decisive votes tilt the balance and arouse hostility.' Numbers matter. So does the relative weight of constituent states or regions. Hence, Martin Dent's comments on Nigeria which, though plagued by communal strife, now has a fair balance of population between its 36 states, and that may enable the country to move towards some measure of ethnic peace under its newly established civilian government. Ghana, as Dennis Austin shows, has already taken a similar route, and not for the first time Nigeria may follow its smaller neighbour towards a greater tolerance of regional, tribal loyalties. In similar vein, Andrew Rigby reviews Lebanon's unique consociational arrangements, and David Seah examines how the particular ethnic mix of Malaysia has tested the will of local elites to strike a balance between rival communities.

2. The inadequacy of elections. The ballot box sustains parliamentary rule but, as the case studies show, elections can also produce permanent minorities — the seed-bed of ethnic unrest. To use a homely metaphor, the democracy of elections stirs the political pot, adds new ingredients and draws them together. That may give a greater weight of movement to politics but when voters line up behind ethnically contentious issues, the danger of communal

conflict is heightened. In many plural societies the graph of violence rises prior to elections. The pot boils over. The legitimacy of elections needs, therefore, to be placed in the context of constitutional safeguards and judicial restraints of the kind described in subsequent chapters.

3. Political leadership. Carlyle's declaration that history is the biography of great men is no longer accepted — the sociologists have been at work — but perhaps Hegel too is right: 'the great man is the one who ... actualises his age'. The reflective influence of a leader can be decisive. Churchill modestly disclaimed his role during the war — 'the nation had the lion's heart, I had the luck to give the roar' — but one wonders who else could have roared to such effect. The cult of personality, primarily of wicked leaders, was raised to extraordinary heights in the twentieth century — Lenin, Hitler, Stalin, Kim IP Sung — and one cannot dismiss the effect of cruel or corrupt leaders.

   In what sense do they 'actualise their age'? One difference, important to our theme, is the extent to which non-democratic groups look for a monopoly of power whereby leader, party and state are welded together — *ein volk, ein reich, ein führer.* What gets squeezed out is any room for civil society and the free activity of men and women. There are other leaders, however, of a different character. It was said of Jawaharlal Nehru that part of the make-up of his mind was a 'disposition to find solutions consistent with some sense of free politics'. When such a disposition exists, leaders and elites can certainly influence events, not least by striking bargains and making compromises between opposed communities in divided societies. There is also a critical difference between those who fear defeat and those who merely resent it. Democratic governments may try to cling to office, but although hurt by defeat in parliament or at the polls they do not suffer more than a sense of loss, whereas the apprehension of non-democrats is that defeat will strip them of wealth and dignity if not of life. Hence their desire for total control and maximum security — a hope rarely, if ever, attainable.

4. Constitutional arrangements. One can start with Donna Lee Van Cott's interesting analysis of legislative reforms in Latin America. They are now extensive and encouraging in their protection of local communities. She discusses, inter alia, declaratory statements and preambles which encode, so to speak, provisions affecting the rights of minorities, for even to recognise plurality goes some way towards providing for its expression. The problem of indigenous ethnic communities, as in Ecuador, Colombia, Guatemala, Nicaragua, Panama etc is not peculiar to Latin America. There are aboriginal peoples in Canada, north-east India and in Malaysia for whom provision has been made. Alain Gagnon describes how

the concept of aboriginal people as 'First Nations' has been given greater prominence in Canada in recent years. The constitutional measures adopted to meet the grievances of excluded communities will be described later as an indication of the way in which dominant groups can take democratic account of minorities. Richard Bellamy discusses the question in his interesting inquiry into theories relating to culturally diverse societies.

The question is not simply one of native rights. Minority interests differ widely in degrees of sophistication, cohesion and economic standing. They include prosperous bourgeois societies as well as untutored aboriginal groups. For their rights to be catered for, each requires a government based on consent. The means of reform (discussed later) are equally varied — qualified representation at national and regional level, ways of exercising the vote to give minorities a voice, regional devolution, an equitable share of national resources, judicial safeguards and protection of cultural identities, enshrined in law, in respect of language, education, employment, freedom of worship and so on. The particular problem of language — the 'pedigree of nations' — is described by Desmond Thomas for Slovakia where the position of minorities blocks any easy path of reform.

5. Federalism is the classic case of constitutional engineering and answers to the need for a balanced representation whereby those who accept the authority of the state can also preserve a distinct autonomy. Clive Church reviews the success of the Swiss 'paradigm' in these particular terms. Historical arguments over the nature of sovereignty within a federal unity may seem arcane today although the debate has been reopened in western Europe: the fact remains that federalism as a shared power has enabled many of the world's states to be governed that might otherwise be dismembered. It has helped to reconcile Flemings and Walloons in Belgium; Ibo, Hausa, Tiv, Yoruba and adjacent communities in Nigeria; Hindus and non-Hindus, Bengali, Punjabi, Tamils and very many others in India. It is now contemplated by some for Italy, Spain and (perhaps) the United Kingdom. Federal structures can also evolve. The Federated Malay States were enlarged to bring in East Malaysia across the sea. The Nigerian Federation grew threefold from the 12 designed by General Gowon in the 1960s to the present 36. Whether Europe, or western Europe, or some of western Europe, will take a federal form as well as a single currency, a Court of Justice, a Commission and a parliament, is something only the Library at Babel can reveal.

6. Interference from abroad. Ethnic rivalries have no respect for international boundaries. Very often one side or the other seeks support from beyond the state, as during the Chinese insurrection in Malaysia and among various factors in the Lebanon. Even the

existence of a near or distant Patron can heighten tension as by
France in Quebec or by Pakistan among India's Muslims, or Tamil
Nadu in Sri Lanka, or between neighbouring states in Africa
where boundaries are a nonsense and communities on both sides
of a frontier are familial. Divided by enmities within and by
hostile governments north and south, Lebanon has suffered the
fate of many small states alternately bullied and cosseted by more
powerful neighbours. How lucky are island states, although
Cyprus is divided as much by Athens and Ankara as by Nicosia
and Famagusta. We write of 'interference' as harmful but in recent
years one has also seen 'interference' on the side of the angels in
relation to 'aid and good governance', diplomatic pressure for
human rights to be respected and offers of arbitration by leaders
external to a domestic dispute — Northern Ireland being an obvious example.

What can one say in conclusion to this Introduction? First, the case
studies which follow are evidence not simply of good intentions but of
achievements by a number of democratic and would-be democratic
governments in managing relations between citizens of different ethnic
origin or community persuasion. The record is there as evidence that
such societies can work together. The problems are set out for each
country and they are by no means simple. There is often a hard choice
between doing too much and conceding too little in respect of competing claims. Breakdown or deadlock is always possible, as in Northern
Ireland, or the see-saw history of civilian–military governments in
Ghana, or the mixed fortunes of reform in Mexico and the Lebanon.
But the problems can be overcome by governments and societies
determined to succeed.

Secondly, *Parliamentary Affairs*, in which these chapters originally
appeared, is committed to 'parliament' as an essential element in
democratic government. That is irrefutable, but our examples show that
parliaments — and even elections — do not ensure democratic practice.
Parliament in Nigeria, for example, has often been occasional and
perfunctory. Democratic rule by majority needs to be buttressed, therefore, as safeguards against its own excess, by institutions which are
semi-detached from politics: a constitution, a Supreme Court, a Bill of
Rights, an independent judiciary, an unbiased administration. Such
restraints are needed particularly where leaders begin to use democracy
(as in Malaysia) to abuse democracy, or where majority rule rides
roughshod over minorities.

Thirdly, there is no one blueprint for managing ethnic or religious
conflicts. Constitutional democracy is not a construct that can be
shipped from one country to another as a sort of political flatpack. The
tailoring has to be local and it has to be unhurried. A pluralistic
constitutional state takes hold only by practice: it functions only by the

daily practice of its virtues. Hence the variety of the examples offered in these separate accounts of states sustained by good leaders, good judgment and, very often, by good luck.

Fourthly, ethnic conflict is, at first reading, an internal danger of mismanaged states. As such, it might be thought to be of less consequence than the great events of history in wars and revolutions. Very often, ethnic unrest can in fact be restrained; but it can also spread to neighbouring states, and when it is genocidal it evokes a general anxiety. After all, it was ethnic violence in the Balkans and great power interests which led to 1914. It was the supposed plight of ethnic Germans in Sudetenland which became one of the causal links of the Second World War. And who can deny the immense and lasting significance of Hitler's ethnic cleansing?

Fifthly, the essence of all the following chapters is simple: fairness. At the centre of the arrangements for democratic rule over diverse societies is a perceived justice under fair policies of administration, revenue allocation and control. Fairness ought also to exclude corruption — 'the infallible symptom of constitutional liberty', according to Edward Gibbon. But readers will know that when fairness and justice fail, the alternative is the injustice and inequity of undemocratic rule by military rulers and party dictators. Repression can hold an ethnically mixed society together for a long time, as under Stalin in Russia, Tito in Yugoslavia, Suharto in Indonesia and Mobutu in Zaire. Dictators often, alas, die in office: but when repression fails, the consequences are severe. A constitutional democracy, on the other hand, has a longer life span than a single leader, and by opening the safety valves of dissent helps to ensure its own safety.

---

1 The recent indictment of post-communist reform in Russia is exceptionally severe. The UN Development Report by Anton Kruiderink describes how, across the former communist empire, a 'growing human insecurity is at the source of human violence, and when democracy becomes equated with misery, its hope will turn into disillusionment. There will be many volatile societies coming our way'. The former Soviet Union has 'unraveled in traumatic manner. The target of these imploding societies is Russia which continues to stutter from one crisis to another'. The statistics of health, education, expectation of life, disease and the diminished status of women are grim, the consequence is that such states are 'incapable of producing the democratic instruments needed'. (A full summary is given in *The Times*, 23 August 1999.)

Canada: Unity and Diversity

BY ALAIN-G. GAGNON

AT the threshold of the new millennium, the debate over citizenship can be characterised as one of tension between universalism and particularism. The former alludes to homogenising bases of citizen allegiance, while the latter points to the increasing fragmentation of identities. This polemic can be discerned in the increasing politicisation of identity-based demands within states which challenge the modern Jacobin conception of national citizenship. In pluri-national states, consisting of territorially based socio-cultural groups, federalism is still widely hailed as a successful pathway towards reconciling the conflicting ends of unity and diversity.[1]

Conceptualising the idea of 'federal citizenship' requires that federalism be understood as a particular sentiment within which the asymmetry of allegiances in a single state is fostered. In other words, a balance between unity and diversity must be understood as the correlate of a 'federal spirit' and as a precondition for the reconciliation of plural sentiments of belonging. Striking a federal balance, institutionally, *is* accepting federalism as ideology. The framing of citizenship, and any subsequent plurality, thus accepts an asymmetry of sentiments of belonging within a single state.[2]

Reconciling politicised socio-cultural conflicts in multi-national states does not stop short at federation. Rather, the management of such conflicts calls for a deeper understanding of the evolution of 'federalism' in particular cases.[3] The Canadian case, which is among the most propitious for reconciliation, is telling of the difficulties in arriving at a federal balance. Indeed, the continuing legacy of Pierre Trudeau's pan-Canadian vision serves only to further processes of fragmentation already under way through an excess of universalism.

The quest for universalism

The historical foundations of Canadian self-government, with the advent of the British North America Act in 1867, are marked by two fundamental features. First, the plurality of identity was acknowledged and second, a federal solution was regarded as a means by which to achieve unity.

Prior to the enactment of the British North America Act, the landscape of identity within the British Dominion of North America was marked by two lines of cleavage. The colony was divided into several distinct politico-administrative units which fostered particular regional bases of allegiance — the Province of Canada, Nova Scotia, New Brunswick, Prince Edward Island and Newfoundland. Additionally, two distinct socio-cultural groups — English-and French-Canadians — were distinguished by language, ethnic origin and religion. The position of the Aboriginal nations was not considered.

The cleavage deepened with the arrival of Loyalists — English patriots defeated by the American revolutionaries — and came to supplant the prior 'Canadian' identity which flourished under the French regime. As such, a distinction between English- and French-Canadians took form. With the Constitutional Act of 1791, a superficial recognition of the two communities saw the Province of Canada divided into Lower and Upper Canada, the French-Canadian petty bourgeoisie controlling the assembly of Lower Canada. However, although the legislative process operated under a system of representative government, the British authorities denied the communities the principle of responsible government, depriving them of the political and economic power to which they would have access in a non-colonial relationship. This situation, along with the economic crisis, culminated in the French-Canadian rebellion of 1837–38. The uprising ultimately failed, and the reaction of the British authorities was to adopt measures for the assimilation of the French-Canadian population: English became the sole official language of the Province of Canada and the legislative assemblies were merged and accorded the same number of parliamentary seats, in effect leading to a situation of underrepresentation for the more populated territory of Lower Canada. Several factors, however, impeded the desired goal of assimilation.[4]

The Confederation Agreement of 1867 was a product of the growing fragmentation of identity and the simultaneous need for unity. From the start, the Canadian federation was founded on the conflicting imperatives of unity and diversity. This polemic was reflected by the positions of prominent political actors at the time. On one side some, like John A. MacDonald, sought union as a means by which to forge the creation of an indivisible Canadian nation with strong central institutions. Contrasting this view were those who interpreted Confederation as a 'compact', or a 'treaty' between the ethno-linguistic communities or between the original colonies. In Simeon and Robinson's words, 'Confederation was primarily a device for the preservation and development of its member communities . . .'[5] The contradictory visions underpinning the union have had significant repercussions. Prince Edward Island and Newfoundland did not endorse the compromise and persistent strands of opposition endured in Nova Scotia, New Brunswick and Quebec. This dissension regarding the interpretation of the agreement led to conflicts which would plague the country well after its origins. The constitutional space granted to collective identities in Canada began under controversial and badly defined terms, and the consequences of such ambiguity became heightened when linguistic matters came to the forefront of federal-provincial relations.

The exclusion of a historical account of the place of Aboriginals in Canada during this period reflects the fact that they were to a large extent disregarded as a constituent collective identity, and left on the margins of the system. They had remained autonomous until confederation, the British having recognised Aboriginal entitlements under the Royal Proclamation of 1763. While attempts to 'civilise' Aboriginals were undertaken under a system of reservations, it was not until 1857 that protection gave way to the objective of assimilation. This objective clearly surfaced with the transfer of the fiduciary role to the Canadian government in the British North America Act. Once the precedent was set, the process of assimilation continued to prevail through the period under review. Only the means have varied. By the 1960s, the Aboriginal population was mired in an advanced state of socio-cultural disintegration.

The latter half of the nineteenth century was marked by regional resistance to the centralising efforts of John A. MacDonald, and by the declining presence of French outside Quebec. On the linguistic front, the provisions of the Act proved to be lacking in the protection of the French language. Article 133, which dealt with bilingualism, was limited in its application to parliaments, the central and Quebec judiciaries, and provided no linguistic recourse for French-Canadians living outside Quebec. The consequences were apparent: 'The abolition of education rights for the francophone minorities in New Brunswick (1871), the Northwest Territories (1892) and Ontario (1912), the hanging of Louis Riel (1885), the elimination of French from the Manitoba legislature (1890) all confirmed the systematic opposition in English-Canada to the extension of French language rights . . .'[6] In provinces dominated by English-Canadians, a convergence gradually took place, resulting in the territorial expansion of British imperialism at the expense of regional allegiances. Among French-Canadians, the waning of French outside the territory of Quebec became a source of resentment and contributed to a nationalist movement based on demands for the recognition of duality in the form of bilingualism and biculturalism, backed by a defensive inward-looking identity. The first half of the twentieth century saw the growing polarisation of two nationalisms. English-Canadians were increasingly influenced by the prominence of British imperialism and French continued its decline in the provinces. At the same time, French-Canadian nationalism was consolidating its position as the guarantor of French-Canadian rights, more readily willing to politicise their demands. Their opposition to the Boer War and the two conscription crises attest to this. In short, the 'two solitudes' came to be more and more exclusive as distinct poles of allegiance.[7]

The period 1945 to 1968 witnessed a gradual transformation of the symbolic order in Canada. Following the grant of Dominion states under the 1931 Statute of Westminster, the social fabric of the country was challenged by the ever-present threat of American cultural intrusion and the recently landed flow of immigrants. Canada found itself in an identitive void as a basis for unity. While Canada distanced itself from Great Britain, several initiatives were undertaken constitutionally to assert a pan-Canadian identity. Cultural and scientific institutions were established, a law of citizenship enacted (1946), the Supreme Court of Canada displaced the Judicial Committee of the Privy Council in London as the highest court of appeal in the country (1949), and a national flag was adopted in 1965. Moreover, the influence of postwar Keynesianism in the Western world was conducive to an unprecedented expansion of the central government, resulting in the encroachment of spending powers into traditionally provincial areas of jurisdiction. Jane Jenson contends that the latent effect of Keynesian policies on the symbolic order of Canada was to quell regional loyalties in favour of individual welfare, and class identity came to supersede regional considerations as the basis for policy in Canada.[8]

Such developments coincided with profound transformations in Quebec society, as critics of the clerico-nationalist ideology of Premier Duplessis gained ground. Two currents, related by their rejection of the inward-looking nationalism espoused by Duplessis, were particularly influential. The first group, centred on the journal *Cité Libre*, rejected nationalism as reactionary and promoted the development of a pan-Canadian identity which respected differences. The objectives of this group were to strengthen the central government as a bulwark against Quebec nationalism which they associated with Duplessis' parochialism. The second group, which was neo-nationalist, sought to redefine French-Canadian identity around the activities of the Quebec state and territory by combining the notion of a 'civic identity' with a cultural and linguistic basis.[9] Both movements were instrumental in the election of Jean Lesage's Liberals in 1960 and the subsequent modernisation of the Quebec state.

It is in this context that Lesage's government began pressing demands for autonomy, and an independence movement burgeoned in Quebec. The strain on Canadian federalism was recognised by the central government and an inquiry into a redefinition of the federal agreement culminated in the Royal Commission on Biligualism and Biculturalism in 1963. Its mandate was to 'recommend the required measures in order for the Canadian federation to develop along the principle of equality between the two founding nations, while taking into account the contribution of the other ethnic groups'. By 1968, it was up to the Liberal government of Pierre Trudeau to judge the merits of the report of the Commission.

In the final analysis, the legacy of the British North America Act lies in its ambiguity and its failure to curtail fragmentation. In the 1960s, a map of allegiances would run as follows: the majority of English-Canadians were divided between their British roots, the new Canadian symbols and regional loyalties which were in regression; the recently arrived immigrants began to demand some formal recognition of their differences, as contributing members of Canadian society; French-Canadians came to identify with the Quebec state—a Quebec-centred citizenship—and differentiated themselves on the basis of language and culture, moving further away from French-Canadians outside Quebec; finally, Aboriginals were caught in a bind, establishing a historically-based expression of their identity while subject to the prospect of outright termination of their separate existence. In short, the Act harboured conflict regarding the nature of federalism and its relation to constituent identities. The Canadian project of nation-building succeeded in displacing British and regional alliances, but many of the conflicts accrued from the provisions of the British North America Act lingered. Pierre Elliott Trudeau became Prime Minister of Canada in 1968 with the conviction of redefining Canadian federalism and to eliminate its ambiguities. That was his deepest motive, and it is to his vision and legacy that we now turn.

The road to fragmentation

Trudeau is arguably the most important figure in the history of Canadian federalism. As co-founder of *Cité Libre*, he was in the forefront of all the dissent aimed at Duplessis through the 1950s. Against the increasing visibility of the Quebec nationalist independence movement in the 1960s, and the autonomist nationalism of the Lesage government, Trudeau turned to the idea of universalism as the ideal upon which to construct Canadian federalism. Trudeau considered any form of nationalism as reactionary, based on emotion and detrimental to the openness of universal values. He defended federalism as a bulwark against the model of the nation-state which he associated with a closed particularism.[10] Upon achieving the position of Prime Minister, as a member of the Liberal Party of Canada, Trudeau's thought on nationalism would form the basis of the central government's views on the country's definition of identity and its relation to the institutional configuration of the federation well after the end of his tenure.

In the evolution of Trudeau's ideas, one notes an inconsistency between his career as an intellectual and his views while in office. As a political theorist, he defended the principles of universalism and reason as the just bases of organisation for states. In the early sixties, he contends that 'Now the history of civilisation is a chronicle of the subordination of tribal 'nationalism' to wider interests.'[11] The organising principle of the nation-state was seen as a force which impeded his notion of progress. While the idea of a 'nation' in the sociological sense is acknowledged by Trudeau, he considers the allegiance which it generates—emotive and particularistic—to be contrary to the idea of cohesion between humans, and as such creating fertile ground for the internal fragmentation of states and a permanent state of conflict. With this normative backdrop, Trudeau defends the idea of a 'juridical nation'—a political entity founded on rationality—as the basis for common purpose and peace. This was Trudeau's solution for the coexistence of diverse collective identities within a single state. Moreover, such acceptance of diversity was thought to be conducive to converging values between states and to the eventual recognition of universalism. In short, federalism was seen as the foremost instrument upon which to build the 'juridical nation' which embodies the application of reason in politics. In his words, 'in the last resort the mainspring of federalism cannot be emotion but must be reason'.[12]

The practicality of politics, however, tempered Trudeau's emphasis on reason as the pillar of his political thought. Trudeau adopted a strategy of pan-Canadian nation-building—the construction of a Canadian sense of allegiance—as a means by which to achieve his universalistic vision. With the end of unifying Canadians, he appealed more and more to nationalism and emotion. His nationalism, however, was distinguished by the fact that it was to be based on 'universalisable' values which surfaced in the Liberal Party's 1968 electoral platform under the slogan of a 'just society': individual liberty and the equality of opportunity necessary for its exercise. The platform was focused on the development of the individual, and sought to foster allegiance in favour of the 'juridical nation'. As such, any allegiance to a particularistic, collective status founded on historical, cultural or territorial legitimacy was rejected. The ideal of individual autonomy was to be guaranteed from coast-to-coast by the central state invested with a sense of moral righteousness in the framing of citizenship status.[13]

Upon Trudeau's election, the situation in Quebec seemed increasingly precarious: the expectations of francophones were heightened by the preliminary report of the Bilingual/Bicultural Commission; the Front de Libération du Quebec had been gaining force since its inception in 1963; the 1996 Quebec election saw two small parties for independence receive close to 9% of the votes; and René Lévesque began to assemble various democratic forces for independence. This was the context facing Trudeau's government in its attempt to reform Canadian federalism. At least three key policies related to identity-building were initiated: the White Paper on the Aboriginal question, the Official Languages Act and multi-culturalism, and the constitutional entrenchment of a Charter of individual rights and freedoms.

The White Paper on the Aboriginal question

The White Paper on the Aboriginal question revealed the extent to which Trudeau's ideas could not incorporate socio-cultural plurality. In July 1969, he ignored the position expressed by the assembly of Aboriginals; he proclaimed the legal provision of 'special status' for

Indians to be discriminatory (to Indians themselves and to other Canadians). The Aboriginals sought a revision of their status within the federation, whereas Trudeau suggested that they be recognised as Canadians like all others, which in effect implied the termination of reserved territories and the invalidation of the treaties for which they had attempted to gain recognition. Moreover, in adopting such a position, the federal government was seeking to abdicate its fiduciary role with respect to the collective entitlements of Aboriginals. Such an episode revealed the individualist convictions of Trudeau, his disregard for any 'special status' which he interpreted as a symbolic ally to the Quebec nationalist cause and a lack of concern for the economic, demographic and political weakness of the First Nations. Having sparked much dissent by those principally interested, the White Paper was abandoned in 1971. However, its latent effect was an unprecedented endeavour to create formal avenues of mobilisation by the Aboriginals. In S.M. Weaver's words, 'The White Paper became the single most powerful catalyst of the Indian nationalist movement, launching it into a determined force for nativism (sic) — a reaffirmation of a unique cultural heritage and identity.'[14] Henceforth, Aboriginal identity would gain momentum as an autonomous collective force in any discourse concerning the country's recognition of citizenship status and in the defining features of Canadian federalism.

The Official Languages Act and multi-culturalism

As early as 1969 Trudeau disregarded the report of the Commission, and sought to foster 'national unity' by adopting a policy of bilingualism at the pan-Canadian level. As such, the government decoupled the notions of bilingualism and biculturalism following Trudeau's suggestion to the Commission in 1963 that it limit the inquiry essentially to the language issue. For Trudeau, adopting cultural duality as a defining feature of the federation meant recognising special status for Quebec which, from his standpoint, would constitute a step towards independence. While the Commission continued to emphasise biculturalism, it nevertheless shared Trudeau's adoption of the 'personality' principle rather than a strict 'territorial' scheme in matters of linguistic sovereignty. Eric Waddell highlights the individualistic inclinations of the Commission's 1967 volume entitled *The Official Languages*:

Hence, the commissioners came down in favour of integral coast-to-coast bilingualism at the very time when Quebec was abandoning such an option. At the same time they admitted to the problems inherent in the application of such a concept and proposed four levels of intervention: that French and English become the official languages of the Parliament and Government of Canada; that New Brunswick and Ontario imitate Quebec in becoming officially bilingual; that bilingual districts be established throughout the country in areas where the minority is sufficiently numerous to be viable as a group; and that the federal capital area should accord equal status to French and English.[15]

Such recommendations corresponded to Trudeau's vision of rational-ism, individualism and universalism. As Trudeau stated in 1968, 'if minority language rights are entrenched throughout Canada then the French-Canadian nation would stretch from Maillardville in BC to the Acadian community on the Atlantic coast'.[16] The following year Tru-deau's government adopted such recommendations in the Official Lan-guages Act. Apart from the two official language minorities, the law was generally received with criticism. The reactions of English-Canada were negative, and the results of bilingual districts are modest to this day, as provincial resistance to the provisions of official bilingualism has been the norm. Opposition was also intense among francophone Quebecers, except for matters concerning bilingualism in central insti-tutions. Indeed, many Franco Quebecers came to believe that nothing short of territorialisation of language regimes and the recognition of particular status of Quebec as an autonomous collectivity or as a sovereign nation would allow them to survive and flourish. The effects of the British North America Act were clear for Quebecers: French held an economically inferior position in their province and its salience declined significantly in other provinces. Bilingualism was not the answer to such developments, and the idea of asymmetry came to represent a more realistic avenue for promoting an equal status for French language and culture. These sentiments were reflected by the Gendron Commission and various linguistic laws which later formally declared French to be the official language of Quebec. In short, the federal law was counter-productive — rather than fulfilling its goal as a unifying device, it stirred up nationalism in Quebec and regionalism in the West.

The reaction to the federal government's response to the cultural question was more controversial. In 1971 the Trudeau government adopted a policy of multi-culturalism, countering the defining principle of biculturalism recommended by the Commission. Indeed, the mandate of the Commission was in large degree interpreted by neo-Canadians (those who had recently arrived) as one predicated on eventual assimi-lation. The decision of Trudeau's government to bypass a bicultural definition of the country in favour of multi-culturalism was interpreted by Quebec autonomists as a strategic move designed to override their national aspirations. France Giroux summarises this line of criticism:

The partial recognition of ancestral rights reveals, a contrario, a refusal to recognise the Quebec nation . . . Without attributing a hierarchical set of rights [for Quebec] vis-à-vis the rights of cultural communities, the representatives of the federal government attempt . . . to confuse the criteria of legitimacy of group demands within a multi-national state. As such, demands by national minorities, those of cultural communities, and those of the majority group are regarded, without being defined or explicitly taking into consideration the criteria of legitimacy attributed to a nation which allow for a viable and effective democratic order . . . In effect, without valid criteria for inclusion and exclusion, all demands become acceptable; thus it becomes possible to pit group demands against one another and to transform pluralism into a zero-sum game.[17]

National identity in Quebec, as a pole of allegiance, was relegated to the same formal space in the federation as other ethno-cultural groupings. The central government justified this policy by using the language of individual rights with the hope that it would foster more universal grounds for allegiance and act as a counter-nationalism to Quebec and Aboriginal allegiances. It was, in effect, a competing vision for society.[18]

Indeed, Will Kymlicka contends that Canadian multi-culturalism, while seemingly respectful of differences on the surface, is actually homogenising (in a federal context) due to its failure to distinguish between 'ethnic' minorities and 'national' communities.[19] He notes that the fundamental difference between the two is that the former seek inclusion, while the latter seek self-determination. Trudeau's policy failed to recognise this distinction, sharing with the US assimilationist model a certain homogenisation or universalisation of identity, albeit through cultural relativism. Kymlicka argues that the US reluctance to recognise minority nations is a direct result of its assimilationist model and its fear that such recognition will undermine any base for unity. Canada's response stems from similar fears. However, the Canadian strategy was to elevate the status of cultural communities to the same level as national minorities. Both strategies are universal, both are bound by nation-building projects in the name of unity, and both fail in any significant way to recognise group-differentiated rights as a federal principle.

The effects of the policy were again counter-productive. By forging a common identity throughout Canada based on the 'sum of its parts', it was hoped that the identity marker for unity could be universal—the recognition of all cultures equally, within a regime of individual rights and bilingualism. In this way, adherence to particular cultural attachments could be voluntary for all individuals, while Canada's symbolic order was to be based on the negation of any particular cultural definition. However, multi-culturalism incited Canadians to identify with self-enclosed collectivities, to the detriment of a pan-Canadian sense of cohesion. Canadian identity came to be defined by the recognition of cultural differences. Such a definition imposes no limits to the diversity of identities in the larger society, encouraging a multiplicity of allegiances and practices which are often incompatible. This is a direct result of the policy's predilection towards cultural relativism. The fact that poly-ethnic cultures are recognised, a priori, in a vacuum of time and space tends towards ghettoisation and fragmentation in terms of allegiance to a larger polity. Neil Bissoondath argues this point forcefully, labelling the phenomenon 'cultural apartheid'.[20] The contention here is that multi-culturalism in effect defines culture provisionally — in a static sense — and prohibits full social interaction as a basis for unity. This is the result of recognising cultures in juxtaposition, one with another, without any expectation that they may contribute to the overall direction of the larger society in an evolutionary interplay of ideas. Moreover, in opposing the idea of potentially converging cultures, the policy of multi-culturalism served to undermine the justification for a policy of bilingualism.

The constitutional entrenchment of a Charter of Rights and Freedoms

For the Trudeau government, the patriation of the Canadian constitution and the entrenchment of a charter of individual rights and freedoms represented the final act in establishing universal bases of identity across Canada. The project failed in 1971, in 1975–76, and again in 1978–79 due to provincial dissent regarding an acceptable amending formula, the contents of the Charter and a new division of powers. After the defeat of those wanting independence in the Quebec referendum of 1980 — when Trudeau promised that there would be 'change' regardless of the result — the drive for patriation gained momentum. Mired in a legal dispute with eight provinces in Autumn 1981, Trudeau managed to split the unified front of the provinces and patriation took place, despite Quebec's unwillingness formally to consent to the agreement. In terms of identity, the provisions with the most resounding consequences ran as follows: the amending formula affirmed the principle of provincial equality for some major changes, disregarding Quebec's traditional right of veto in constitutional amendments. (Henceforth, the convention of provincial consent for constitutional amendment was replaced by a scheme which required merely two/thirds of the provinces representing at least 50% of the population.) The Charter also protected classically conceived notions of individual rights (Articles 2–15(1)), accorded special status, to be defined at a later date, to the Aboriginals (Articles 25 and 35), and entrenched the policies of the Official Languages (Articles 16–20, 23) and multi-culturalism (Article 27); finally, the constitution confirmed the principle of equality of economic opportunity (Article 36).

The consequences of the 1982 episode served merely to further the tendencies of fragmentation. With regard to the Aboriginal population, the 'to be defined' clause simply led to future tension in negotiations. The Trudeau government increased the expectations of the First nations while never fully intending to include any notion of special status in the constitution which would correspond to the Aboriginals' demand for the recognition of an inherent right to self-government. Indeed, the Penner Committee's recommendation which promoted the idea of an inherent right was rejected by Trudeau. In 1983 and 1984, two provincial conferences concerning the question of Aboriginal rights resulted in an impasse. Still today, no ruling is in sight, and the Aboriginal nations are faced with a dearth of available institutional channels with which to assert their will for an inherent right to self-determination. For a good number of Aboriginals, such developments have rendered Canada a mere instrument.

The Constitution Act of 1982 was also detrimental to relations between francophone Quebecers and Canadians outside Quebec. Both the autonomists of the Quebec Liberal Party and the sovereignists of the Parti Québécois considered patriation without Quebec's consent to run counter to federal conventions established since the founding of the country and hence illegitimate. In the hearts and minds of Quebecers, the outcome of the 1982 constitutional negotiations represented a 'breach of trust'. Tully echoes the Quebec position, arguing that 'what lies at the bottom of the Canadian federation is neither a unifying constitution nor a common vision, but the multiplicity of activities of multilateral negotiation itself'.[21]

In terms of content, besides multi-culturalism and bilingualism, two complementary principles were deemed problematic and counter to Quebec's aspirations. First, the principle of numeric equality of the provinces was rejected by Quebec. The view in Quebec was that the principle of equality entails an understanding that the distinct political communities in Canada enjoy *equal capacity* to meet their aspirations. This would entail a recognition of the principle of duality, as well as some institutional leeway for asymmetry. Second, Quebec rejected the principle of individual rights on a pan-Canadian basis as it would in effect override the prerogatives of the National Assembly, and poten-tially the rights of territorially-based socio-cultural collectivities, a pillar of Quebec's interpretation of federalism. Again, Tully states this posi-tion most aptly:

When the Quebec Assembly seeks to preserve and enhance Quebec's character as a modern, predominantly French-speaking society, it finds that its traditional sovereignty in this area is capped by a Charter in terms of which all its legislation must be phrased and justified, but from which any recognition of Quebec's distinct character has been completely excluded. The effect of the Charter is thus to assimilate Quebec to a pan-Canadian national culture, exactly what the 1867 constitution, according to Lord Watson, was established to prevent. Hence, from this perspective, the Charter is 'imperial' in the precise sense of the term that has always been used to justify independence.[22]

Contrary to settling the question of Canada's identitive landscape, the constitutional reforms of 1982 failed to curb the growing dissension. The Meech Lake (1987) and Charlottetown (1992) accords sought to reintegrate Quebec into the constitutional agreement but in both cases the Trudeau forces intervened vigorously to keep the tenets of the 1982 package intact. While their point of view triumphed, a latent effect was to revitalise the convictions of autonomist and sovereign nationalists in

Quebec. Indeed, in the aftermath of the failed Meech Lake Accord, the Quebec government established the Commission for the Political and Constitutional future of Quebec. The problem, according to the Commission, is that:

Theoretically, the Canadian federal union could have continued to change in constitutional and political terms while respecting both the aspirations of Quebecers and those of other Canadians. In practice, the overall conception of Canada and the federal regime which now predominates seems rigid and clearly oriented towards the quest for uniformity and the negation of differences. Renewing the Canadian federation, while acknowledging and respecting Quebec's differences and needs, unequivocally means a thorough calling into question of the order of things in Canada.[23]

As Simon Langlois contends, the homogenising pressures of the Trudeau vision fed Quebec's desire to constitute a francophone 'global society' — a society whereby Franco Quebecers could assign to their language and culture a majority status in all spheres of activity — launched by the creation of a parallel network of institutions.[24] Pan-Canadianism represented the negation of this francophone space in North America.

Among the Anglophone majority outside Quebec, the Charter's impact was received more favourably. The principles of provincial equality, multi-culturalism and the normative emphasis on individual rights have been consolidated as the main tenets of Canadian political culture, leaving no room for traditional federal principles based on the recognition of particularistic status. While Quebec has enjoyed some de facto asymmetry in the past, through bilateral negotiations with the federal government, the position of the rest of Canada has hardened with the effects of the Charter, and the possibility of entrenchment has been rendered more difficult.

Conclusion

The policies enacted by Trudeau and by the Chrétien governments (1993–97, and 1997 onwards) have not succeeded in achieving a balance between unity and diversity. The idea of a 'juridical nation' has not prompted allegiance to a pan-Canadian identity. Identity is not easily reconstructed around procedural principles without a prior sense of belonging by the citizens of a particular socio-cultural collectivity. They have been relatively successful at displacing regional identities, yet have failed to incorporate Aboriginal and Quebec sentiment. Indeed, the identities in question are not only distinct in a sociological sense, but in many respects espouse incompatible visions and traditions. The persistent constitutional impasse attests to this. Canada finds itself composed of a plurality of conflicting identities which are less willing today to negotiate and exercise channels of dialogue than was the case in 1968. In this environment, Canada is but an instrument to its constituent socio-cultural identities, resulting in a growing fragmentation of identities—a diametrical effect to Trudeau's intended goal of forging a universal basis of allegiance across the country. In this context, Article 36 on the equality of economic opportunity and the associated politics of redistribution represent an unconvincing thread for unity, particularly with the waning of the welfare state.

The Canadian experience provides valuable lessons with regards to the need to strike a balance between unity and diversity in framing 'federal citizenship'. As has been shown, federal citizenship must involve the recognition of constituent socio-cultural entities, avoiding a discourse which places self-determining collectivities in a straight-jacket. Questions of identity are inherently political in character, involving power relations which must be understood through a historical perspective. As such, efforts to reconstruct the character of multinational societies through sweeping measures which neglect considerations of time and space invariably deny federal principles and undermine the bases of allegiance to the federal state. In other words, procedurally-defined universal ideals are not sufficient to overcome socio-historical conditions or to forge unity. Federalism as ideology presupposes an ambiguity as to the ends of negotiations between federated entities which provides space for conflict management, and more generally, for politics. It is in this political space that the balance between unity and diversity resides, allowing constituent collectivities the means by which to exercise their self-determining prerogatives. Trudeau's universalism was predicated on a denial of this space altogether: it envisaged a 'termination of politics' and the resolution of conflicts associated with shared allegiance. The lesson to be drawn is that the result of such an approach is to heighten rather than impede processes of fragmentation. Federal citizenship—a balance between unity and diversity—requires an appreciation of the spaces between rival identities (including the power relations implied) not measures which attempt to 'solve' politics in a federal state per se.

1   The research assistance of Raffaele Iacovino is gladly acknowledged. For a survey of this theme see M. Forsyth, 'Towards the Reconciliation of Nationalism and Liberalism' in G. Laforest and D. Brown (eds), *Integration and Fragmentation: The Paradox of the Late Twentieth Century*, Kingston: Institute of Intergovernmental Relations, 1994; W. Kymlicka and J.R. Raviot, 'Vie commune: aspects internationaux des fédéralismes', *Études internationales*, December 1997; A-G. Gagnon, 'The Political Uses of Federalism' in M. Burgess and A-G. Gagnon (eds), *Comparative Federalism and Federation: Competing Traditions and Future Directions*, Harvester and Wheatsheaf, 1993.

2   For a converging conceptual definition of a 'federal balance' and its application to citizenship status, see S.V. LaSelva, 'Reimagining Confederation: Moving Beyond the Trudeau–Lévesque Debate' in *The Moral Foundations of Canadian Federalism. Paradoxes, Achievements and Tragedies of Nationhood*, McGill-Queen's University Press, 1996.

3   The methodology employed here uses historical sociology. This allows for an assessment of political processes inclusive of collective identities as spatio-temporal 'constructions' which manifest themselves through power relationships and are constantly changing. See R. Simeon and I. Robinson, *State, Society and the Development of Canadian Federalism*, University of Toronto Press, 1990, and 'The Dynamics of Canadian Federalism' in J.P. Bickerton and A-G. Gagnon (eds), *Canadian Politics*, Broadview Press, 3rd edn, 1999.

4   In 1848, the reformists from Canada East (previously Lower Canada) allied with those of Canada West and responsible government was granted. In the same period, the provision making English the sole official language was repealed. Moreover, by the 1950s the equalisation of seats in parliament favoured the residents of Canada East due to their growing minority status. Finally, the ideology of survival propagated by the increasing elite status of the clergy constituted another obstacle to assimilation. French-Canadian identity was closely linked to religious faith.

5   See R. Vipond, *Liberty and Community: Canadian Federalism and the Failure of the Constitution*, State University of New York, 1991.

6   E. Waddell, 'State, Language and Society. The Vicissitudes of French in Quebec and Canada', in A. Cairns and C. Williams (eds), *The Politics of Gender, Ethnicity and Language in Canada*, University of Toronto Press, 1986, p. 75.

7   See J.P. Bickerton, A-G. Gagnon and P. Smith, *Ties that Bind: Parties and Voters in Canada*, Oxford University Press, 1999, especially ch. 6.

8   See I. Robinson and R. Simeon, 'The Dynamics of Canadian Federalism', op. cit, and J. Jenson, 'Citizenship Claims' in K. Knop et al, *Rethinking Federalism: Citizens, Markets and Governments in a Changing World*, University of British Columbia, 1995, pp. 107–8.

9   On the differences between traditional and neo-nationalist, see M. Behiels, *Prelude to Quebec's Quiet Revolution. Liberalism versus Neo-Nationalism 1945–1960*, McGill-Queen's University Press, 1985. On the distinction between different conceptualisations, or expressions of identity in Quebec see D. Karmis, 'Identities in Quebec: Between 'la souche' and automisation' in Quebec Studies Papers, McGill University, June 1997.

10 See P.E. Trudeau, *Memoirs*, McClelland and Stewart, 1993, and 'New Treason of the Intellectuals', and 'Federalism, Nationalism and Reason', in *Federalism and the French-Canadians*, Macmillan, Toronto, 1968.

11 *New Treason of the Intellectuals*, op. cit., p. 156.

12 P.E. Trudeau, 'Federalism, Nationalism and Reason', pp. 194–5.

13 P.E. Trudeau, 'The Values of a Just Society' in T.S. Axworthy and P.E. Trudeau (eds), *Towards a Just Society, The Trudeau Years*, Viking, 1990. For the mythology and revisionist history which followed the ideology of the 'just society' see W.J. Norman, 'The Ideology of Shared Values: A Myopic Vision of Unity in the Multi-nation State' in J. Carens (ed), *Is Quebec Nationalism Just?*, McGill-Queen's University Press, 1995; and A-G. Gagnon et F. Rocher, 'Pour prendre congé des fantômes du passé' in A-G. Gagnon and F. Rocher (eds), *Répliques aux détracteurs de la souveraineté du Québec*, VLB Éditeur, 1992.

14 For the arguments advanced by Trudeau at the time see S.M. Weaver, *Making Canadian Indian Policy: The Hidden Agenda 1968–1970*, University of Toronto Press, 1981, pp. 53–6; J. Tully, *Strange Multiplicity: Constitutionalism in an Age of Diversity*, Cambridge University Press, 1995. See also J.R. Miller, *Skyscrapers Hide the Heavens*, University of Toronto Press, 1989; F. Abele, 'The Importance of Consent: Indigenous People's Politics in Canada' in J. Bickerton and A-G. Gagnon (eds), op. cit.

15 E. Waddell, 'State, Language and Society', op. cit., p. 91.

16 P.E. Trudeau, cited in K. McRoberts, 'English-Canadian Perceptions of Quebec', in A.G. Gagnon (ed), *Quebec: State and Society*, Nelson Canada, 2nd ed, 1993, p. 122.

17 F. Giroux, 'Le nouveau contrat national est — il possible dans une démocratie pluraliste? Examen comparatif des situations français, canadienne et québécoise', *Politique et Sociétés*, 16/3, p. 141. Our translation.

18 G. Bourque et al, elaborate, 'The ideology (. . .) Defines itself in its relation to the territorial state; it circumscribes a community of belonging to the state within a country — Canada. It thus privileges, clearly, national dimensions of the production of the community, even though the discourse struggles to find a coherent representation of the Canadian nation. This Canadian nationalism finds its full significance in its opposition to the 'counter-nationalism' of Quebec and the Aboriginals'. See G. Bourque, J. Duchastel and V. Armony, 'De l'universalisme au particularisme: droits et citoyenneté' in J. Ayoub, B. Melkevik and P. Robert (eds), *L'amour des lois*, Presses de l'Université Laval/l'Harmattan, 1996, p. 240. Our translation.

19 See W. Kymlicka, 'Citizenship and Identity' in J.P. Bickerton and A-G. Gagnon (eds), op. cit.

20 See N. Bissoondath, *Selling Illusions: The Cult of Multi-culturalism in Canada*, Penguin Books, 1994. Bissoondath argues that the dynamic nature of cultural sources of meaning are neglected under the Canadian policy, resulting in the stagnant 'folklorisation' or 'commodification' of cultural production, reducing culture to 'a thing that can be displayed, performed, admired, bought, sold or forgotten (. . .) [it is] a devaluation of culture, its reduction to bauble and kitsch', (p. 83).

21 J. Tully, 'Diversity's Gambit Declined' in C. Cook (ed), *Constitutional Predicament: Canada After the Referendum of 1992*, McGill-Queen's University Press, 1994, p. 162.

22 J. Tully, 'Let's Talk: The Quebec Referendum and the Future of Canada', Austin and Hempel Lectures, Dalhousie University and University of Prince Edward Island, 1995, p. 8.

23 *Report of the Commission on the Political and Constitutional Future of Quebec*, Quebec, March 1990, pp. 47–8; A-G. Gagnon and D. Latouche, *Allaire, Bélanger, Campeau et les autres: les Québécois s'interrogent sur leur avenir*, Québec Amérique, 1991, ch. 1.

24 S. Langlois, 'Le choc de deux sociétés globales' in L. Balthazar, G. Laforest and V. Lemieux (eds), *Le Quebec et la restauration du Canada, 1980–1992*, op. cit., pp. 101–3.

Mexico: Political Management of Diversity

BY DARREN WALLIS

'The Indian world of Mexico offers an opposition between the visible
and the invisible. The modern history of Mexico . . . has powerfully
conspired to make the Indian population invisible.'
(Carlos Fuentes, *A New Time for Mexico*, 1998)

The Zapatista rebellion that erupted in the southern state of Chiapas
on 1 January 1994 was largely unanticipated and, initially at least,
violent and bloody. It also brought Mexico's Indian population a degree
of national and international visibility that it had rarely experienced
since the conquistadores arrived in the early sixteenth century. Questions of Indian autonomy and rights, constitutional protection for
indigenous ways — especially those relating to justice and education —
and the position of indigenous groups in Mexican social and political
life have since been debated with a renewed intensity. Issues of
land ownership and distribution that appeared to have been closed by
the agrarian reform of 1992 have re-engaged activists and policy
makers.

The fact, however, that it took an armed rebellion to force these
issues up the political agenda says much about the nature of Mexican
politics, and the characteristic regime response to demands from below.
Mexico differs from many of the other cases under consideration in
that it has had an authoritarian regime in power for most of this
century. Successive governments utilised techniques of cooptation, clientelism and bureaucratic control alongside repression to keep demands
from indigenous and other marginalised groups low down the agenda,
and to keep opposition movements divided through selective concessions. Although many analysts today argue that the Mexican system
was never as unambiguously monolithic as its stereotype suggests, it did
manage to keep the indigenous question effectively hidden for long
periods. In this sense, the rebellion in Chiapas represents decades of
frustration at political marginalisation when the promised 'fruits of the
revolution' failed to materialise.

Nevertheless, the management of ethnic diversity has presented the
regime with many conundrums dating back to the early post-revolutionary period. In this account, we look at the mechanisms used by the elite
to deal with the issues arising from the high degree of ethnic pluralism
exhibited by Mexico's population. Policy in the immediate post-revolu-

tionary period was defined by Indígenismo — an emphasis on the role, purpose and significance of the Indian population for the wider Mexican society. Despite such rhetorical devices, however, and the creation of many government-backed indigenous institutions, policy quickly moved in the direction of national integration, with assimilation promoted through cooptation and bureaucratic control. This provided for a high degree of political stability, but was to prove unsustainable over the long run. From the 1970s onwards, there was an increase in autonomous indigenous organisation, a phenomenon that was tied up with a general increase in social movement activity in Mexico and Latin America.

Such pressures from below, combined with a loss of state capacity and resources, led to a reconsideration of the ethnic question in the late 1980s, culminating in a 1991 constitutional amendment defining the nation as multi-ethnic. For many indigenous groups, this amendment did not go far enough, either in seeking to promote indigenous autonomy, or in its capacity to begin to address underlying economic concerns, especially in a period of neo-liberal restructuring. The gap between indigenous demands and the government's policy responses rapidly widened to produce the Zapatista rebellion. As we shall see, the Zapatistas and related movements pose fundamental questions relating to Mexico's national development, questions that neither the government, nor the opposition, nor indeed Mexican public opinion have yet resolved satisfactorily. The management of ethnic diversity, in short, has become increasingly problematic in Mexico in the 1990s; to date, the government has papered over the cracks, but the pressures are likely to continue to increase.

The population

Mexico's native population is defined by the Instituto Nacional de Estadística, Geografía e Informática as those speaking an indigenous language. On this basis, the 1990 census indicated that some 7.9% of Mexico's population was indigenous. But many argue that this definition is restrictive (it excludes children under the age of five, for example) and their estimates put the Indian population at closer to 15% of the total, or approximately 13 million people. As well as being substantial, the population is also very diverse. According to the Instituto Nacional Indigenista (INI) there are some 59 significant Indian groupings. Some are small and regionally concentrated; others, like the Nahuas, are much larger (over 1.5 million people) and geographically diffuse. A large number of indigenous languages and dialects exists, cultural traditions vary and there is a degree of heterogeneity in religious practice.

Diversity ends, however, when the economic situation is considered. Although indigenous groups are to be found in nearly every Mexican state, they are mainly concentrated in the more rural states in the central and southern regions. Despite some advances, Indians remain campesinos (peasants) and they generally score worse on basic indices of development than any other group. In an obvious sense, therefore, debates on indigenous rights, autonomy and culture are bound up with social justice. As Alexander Dawson has suggested, 'Indians . . . existed clearly within the framework of a nation in which their cultural 'otherness' was really only a matter of economic problems created by their oppression'.[1] This situation has changed little through to the present day. Separating these issues has a certain academic utility, but not in terms of everyday resistance to exploitation: basic necessities are still denied to millions of native people and the emergence of indigenous concerns, in Chiapas and elsewhere, has been fundamentally inter-twined with economic questions.

Indígenismo

The Mexican revolution (c. 1910–17) and its immediate aftermath brought Indian questions to the forefront of the political agenda. In the colonial period, Indians had been subject to overt coercion: millions had perished or were forced into slavery. Indians remained marginalised following independence. Whilst frequent rebellions against central state control took place, assertions of Indian autonomy were generally unsuccessful, and the civil war pitted Indian against Indian under both Liberal and Conservative leadership. Later, dubious 'scientific' theories, imported from Europe, provided a rationale for the continued margin-alisation of the inferior 'primitive'. Such theories were to remain popular even amongst many revolutionary Indígenistas, who used them as a basis to justify education and assimilation programmes.

Rough estimates suggest that one third of the Mexican population at the turn of the century was indigenous, and the contribution of Indians to the popular struggle was often critical, though their involvement was frequently contingent, localised and temporary, and rarely involved grandiose ideological objectives. Nevertheless, such activity raised the profile of the ethnic question and farmed a basis for the rise of Indígenismo in the period after 1917. Most obviously, the Revolution's commitments to land reform and social justice required an analysis and resolution of the 'Indian question', which most observers viewed as inexorably bound up with the problems of peasant society.

After the revolution, official discourse concerning the position of the Indian changed from the nineteenth century view of the 'savage' or 'barbarian' to a position that exalted the glories of Mexico's Indian heritage. The murals of Siquieros, Orozco and Rivera, for example, celebrated the glories of the Indian past and helped to revitalise contem-porary Indian culture. Government publications such as *El Maestro Rural* — the official voice at the forefront of the government's education drive — eulogised Indian social, economic and political practice, and often emphasised the superior social organisation, degree of social peace and 'spiritual values' of Indian communities. Indeed, for many, 'far from being primitive or barbaric, Indian cultures and cultural institutions provided models for the Mexican future' and the promotion of indigenous consciousness in this earlier period played an important role in later struggles between Indian groups and the state.[2]

Changes in discourse were matched by institutional developments, which gave greater opportunities for the promotion of indigenous demands and concerns, and which helped to shape government policy, but it was in the area of rural policy under President Cárdenas that the biggest advances were made. Despite the progressive measures contained in the 1917 Constitution, land reform had proceeded only slowly during the 1920s and 1930s, and in states such as Chiapas the latifundista system remained largely intact. This situation changed dramatically under Cárdenas, when large scale land expropriations took place and the distribution of land to indo-campesino communities reached levels not experienced before or since. To take but one illustration, of the total land distributed between 1915 and 1940, fully two-thirds was distributed under Cárdenas between 1934 and 1940. As Jan Rus observes, for many Indians, the real revolution was 'the time of Cárdenas . . . the period when the benefits of 'the new Mexico' — among them agrarian reform, labour unions, and an end to debt contracting and peonage — finally reached out to include them as well'.[3]

Yet despite these positive measures, Indígenismo experienced contradictory pulls. According to Stephen Morris, one strand of Indígenismo emphasised that 'a sense of glory regarding the Indian past has long been an important part of the nation's identity', and this was used to promote Indian values, culture and organisation. Another strand, by contrast, viewed 'the Indian and Indian culture as not truly Mexican, but rather as impediments to the unification of the nation and obstacles to its political, economic and cultural development'.[4] Here, eulogising the Indian past and stressing Indian virtues may have served as no more than legitimising façades to facilitate policies of assimilation and national integration.

Certainly much of the discourse in the government's mass education programme of the time emphasised ways in which Indians could be integrated into the mestizo nation. The thousands of rural school teachers sent forth to educate the masses in the 1920s and 1930s were promoting a particular view of national development through assimilation, even if many of them were to develop strong pro-indigenous sympathies. This was not a programme of segregation of Indians, nor of their unequivocal and instant conversion to the modern world, but it was a programme for 'the education of the "other" so as to integrate himself . . . [into a] "national synthesis".'[5]

Over time, this universal, homogenising and uniform policy of national development became dominant over Indígenista programmes in favour of local autonomy and cultural independence. Official endorsement of Indian cultural values was largely confined to those that demonstrated modernising and integrationalist tendencies, and Indígenista institutions distinguished between the 'primitiveness' of those unprepared for citizenship against the 'Mexicanness' of those who demonstrated such a capacity. As Dawson states: 'This was an inclusive notion of citizenship, in that it could include Indians from a variety of cultures in a multi-ethnic nation, but it was restrictive in that it demanded a certain modernistic orientation from those subjects who would be awarded full citizenship.'[6]

Even under Cárdenas, therefore — the most explicitly pro-indigenous of Mexico's presidents — Indígenismo was a means to an end, not the end itself. Again, Dawson reminds us that: 'The Cardenista state saw the idea of any sort of substantial or permanent Indian autonomy as anathema to its concept of the modern nation-state. Though the nation might be multi-ethnic, in this perspective it had to find a way of including even those Indians who wished to be excluded.'[7]

The means to this end was usually through new forms of political domination. Thus, even as land distribution proceeded apace under Cárdenas and the material conditions for many Indian communities improved, so the burgeoning corporate state began to replace old mechanisms of political control. That this was often done through Indígenista and campesino organisations (developed to promote and protect indigenous and peasant concerns) was not coincidental: it was a standard Cardenista technique for managing popular political involvement, and was to remain a key part of the way in which the Mexican regime maintained its dominance over the next sixty years. Lawrence Whitehead captures this centralising tendency well: '. . . it was generally by political as opposed to directly military means that central control was asserted. One example was the strenuous efforts made by Cárdenas to reach the Indian population — partly through indigenismo, but more critically through rural education and agrarian reform. A permanent consequence was the growth of Federal power, as the Indian question became the preserve of national government, and could be used to prize open hostile local cacicazgos ['bosses']. The federalisation of the Indian question often meant the substitution of local patrones — landlord, cacique, priest, labour contractor — by new, bureaucratic bosses, agents of indigenista or agrarian programmes.'[8]

If the development of these new forms of political domination were largely seen as an acceptable trade off for the material gains that the Cárdenas administration brought, they were to become increasingly problematic once these benefits began to dry up, as they did after 1940. The Mexican revolution began to consolidate; it moved to the right and never returned to survey the heights that Cárdenas had climbed. For indigenous groups, the years after 1940 were marked by low levels of economic reform and high levels of political control. Institutional developments and rhetoric occasionally gave a nod in the direction of indigenous concerns, but did little to address the fundamental questions of economics and culture.

The development of indigenous resistance

The period from 1940 to 1970 is generally seen as a political and economic 'golden era' for the regime. Economic growth, combined with low inflation, provided the necessary resources to keep the different revolutionary constituencies on board; the political system consolidated its 'co-opt and control' policies. From the 1970s onwards, however, the regime became subject to a greater degree of contestation from both opposition parties and new social movements of various hues. This reflected a dual dynamic. In the first place, there was a loss of state capacity arising from perennial economic crises, culminating in the debt crisis of the 1980s and the economic collapse of late 1994. Without resources to distribute to its supporters, the ruling PRI could no longer guarantee their loyalty, and various sections of Mexican society began to look to the opposition for solutions.[9] As a response to the pressures that it faced, the government attempted a policy of controlled democratic reform, which gradually slipped from its grasp to the point where the PRI can now no longer guarantee election victories, as evinced by its losses in the Chamber of Deputies and Mexico City during the 1997 elections.

Secondly, autonomous group activity from below became more pronounced from the 1970s onwards. Many of these were groups rooted in ethnic identity and language, giving them a distinctive cultural angle in addition to their articulation of economic concerns. As many observers commented, ethnic identity, a vision of history and a people's culture were now being used to counter the dominant ideology and organise resistance.[10] Several case studies confirm the development of indigenous struggles long before the protests of the 1990s.[11] Various 'democratic openings' from the early 1970s onwards — openings that were subject to reverses, admittedly — provided an environment in which indigenous groups felt confident in airing their grievances.

The fact remains, however, that many such struggles were localised and particular. Despite democratic reform and challenges to its authority, the PRI remains in power, and economic distribution, far from spreading, has actually retrenched. In terms of specific political arrangements, the government under President Salinas (1988–94) made a concession to indigenous pressures in 1991, with an amendment to Article 4 of the Constitution, formally recognising the multi-ethnic basis of the nation, but this amendment did not go nearly far enough for many indigenous groups. Indeed, because such groups demanded 'more specific and far-reaching changes', the implementing legislation was not enacted.[12] Mexico's indigenous population has become better organised and more vociferous, and the political system provides better and more frequent opportunities for them to present their case, but the ability to shape policy remains disappointing. This gap between promise and fulfilment helps to explain the explosion of protest from 1994 onwards, which touched not only Chiapas but many other southern and central states as well, and which has often been violent and bloody. Increased expectations and frustrated hopes have been familiar stories for a number of years.

We should, nevertheless, be wary of asserting that policy has been wholly negative. There are difficulties in assessing whether many policies are, in general, beneficial to the indigenous population, and whether indigenous organisations are able to shape such outcomes. For example, the National Solidarity programme (Solidaridad)[13] under President Salinas was an internationally-touted poverty-relief programme, which helped to offset some of the economic and political costs arising from economic restructuring. Solidaridad targeted marginalised communities with poverty relief through the development of basic infrastructure utilities, and support for projects involving various specified groups, such as women, children and the native population. Government subsidies matched local inputs, and an underlying principle was that communities developed and ran their own projects. Critics identified an implicit political agenda — large amounts of Solidaridad funding went to traditional PRI areas where the party had performed badly in 1988 — but there were also clear benefits. The budget of INI, for example, increased 18-fold during the first three years of the policy, allowing it to 'transform itself from a service provider into an actual economic development agency'.[14] Moreover, pressure for bargaining involving indigenous communities became dominant. Two years after the establishment of regional Solidarity funds — the principle economic programme for Indian groups — between one-quarter and one-third were being consolidated under indigenous organisation control. Because Solidaridad was so strongly associated with the disgraced Salinas administration, there has been a tendency to bury its achievements along with his — and its — failings. Nevertheless, the programme clearly had an impact on the economic and political lives of many indigenous groups that was not always negative.

Developments of this nature managed to keep something of a lid on the growth of opposition, but the underlying trends made protests almost inevitable. Thus, the general impact of economic restructuring has seen a worsening of income distribution and poverty, whilst specific political concessions to indigenous groups qua indigenous groups have remained hollow. Similarly, many organisations formally charged with representing Indian interests have continued to pursue a policy of trying to alter federal government policy, whilst indigenous groups themselves have begun to claim a more local, cultural autonomy. For much of the post-revolutionary period, indigenous protest had been moderated by the generally successful articulation of two key state-society mediations — 'lo

nacional' and 'lo popular'. The former entailed a sense of national
independence (especially vis-à-vis the United States); the latter emphasised programmes of distributive justice. Both provided the principal
linkages between the government and the population in the absence of a
third key mediation, liberal citizenship. In the modern period (c. 1985
onwards), however, 'lo nacional' and 'lo popular' have largely been
dismantled by neo-liberal administrations with no 'sufficiently secure
mediation of citizenship' to replace them.[15] In other words, the population has been exposed to the winds of neo-liberalism without the
windshield of effective citizenship; it has, therefore, increasingly
attempted to articulate its own meanings of citizenship, often couched in
terms of indigenous identity and sometimes constructed outside of
Western, liberal precepts. It is in this context that we should view the
rebellions of 1994 and afterwards.

The Chiapas rebellion

The Zapatista rebellion has remained high on the national agenda since
1994, partly because of sporadic violence, partly because it captured
the imagination as the 'first rebellion of the twenty-first century'. The
extensive use of the internet by the rebels also attracted considerable
attention, at the same time as it minimised government control of rebel
communiqués. From our perspective, a key feature of the rebellion was
its timing: it broke out on 1 January 1994, the day that the North
American Free Trade Agreement (NAFTA) came into force, and just
two years after a constitutional amendment had effectively reversed the
communal land ownership programme. Both policies were likely to
have an adverse, almost devastating, impact on rural communities,
especially those involved in the production of crops such as maize, for
which there was no prospect of domestic producers competing with
large-scale producers in North America. The rebellion, therefore, artic-
ulated the fears of many sections of Mexican society over the implications of economic restructuring. Subsequently, the Zapatistas organised
an international conference to protest against the effects of neo-liberalism, and there is little doubt that their criticisms in this area met with a
good degree of sympathy.

Such concerns, however, also went hand-in-hand with a set of
demands relating to the position of the Indian in society, which emphasised the need for cultural autonomy, self-government and an explicit
constitutional recognition of indigenous rights. Morris captures these
emphases well: 'Voicing demands for local autonomy, an end to racism,
respect for indigenous traditions and customs and . . . the right to
educate their young in their native language, the insurgents of Chiapas
have raised the consciousness of the nation's indigenous, offered them
a vehicle for political mobilisation, while at the same time challenging
traditional Mexican (mestizo) views regarding the Indian and the nation
. . . In other words . . . Chiapas makes it more difficult for the mestizo

to view him/herself as part of an indigenous Mexico, when to the indigenous s/he clearly represents the "other".'[16]

It is the interplay between these economic and cultural concerns that provides the biggest challenge to the prevailing modernisation model of national development. In Morris' words, Chiapas forms part of a 'post-Cold War reality that features a broad-based resurgence of ethno-nationalism and national resistance to globalisation'.[17] Although the armed phase of the rebellion was relatively short-lived and unsuccessful, the rebels have subsequently been able to construct important alliances not only with other indigenous groups but with various social movements pursuing democratic reform.

The Zapatistas early on organised a National Democratic Convention, and a political front — the FZLN — emerged as the complement to the armed revolutionaries, the EZLN. They were also instrumental in fostering the development of the National Plural Indigenous Assembly for Autonomy (ANIPA), which began to consider constitutional amendments for promoting indigenous autonomy from 1995 onwards, and the creation of the Congreso Nacional Indígena (CNI), which held its first national conference in late 1996, declaring 'Never again a Mexico without us'. Such developments not only raised the profile of indigenous organisations but pushed discussion of the constitutional position of Indians up the agenda of reform.

By 1996, the Chiapas rebellion and the government response to it had oscillated between violence and negotiation. In truth, the violence of the early days never fully resurfaced, but sporadic interludes of rebel activity matched government offensives, and claims of human rights abuses were common. For long periods, an atmosphere of mutual distrust pervaded the relationship between the government and the rebels, and 'talks about talks', or talks concentrating on mutual guarantees and dealing with military issues, took precedence over talks dealing with substantive matters. Although a National Commission for Intermediation (Conai) under Chiapas archbishop Samuel Ruíz was recognised in April 1995, the government continuously attempted to deny its legitimacy and to negotiate directly. (Ruíz resigned from Conai, which then folded in June, 1998). More successful in an intermediary role was the Comisión de Concordia y Pacificación (COCOPA), also established in 1995. The rebel leaders held frequent talks with COCOPA (which has undergone three 'renovations' since 1995) on substantive issues relating to indigenous rights and welfare, the most significant step being the agreement reached at San Andrés Larrainzar on 'Indigenous culture and rights' early in 1996.[18] The underlying principles of the new relationship between the state and the indigenous communities were stated to be pluralism, sustainability, and 'integrality' of public policy towards Indians. A number of specific statements were developed, the most significant of which were: an explicit recognition of Indian peoples within the general constitution; full participation and political representation, especially through greater decentralisation of executive, legislative and judicial powers; the protection, promotion and diffusion of various indigenous cultures; the development of education that takes advantage of indigenous knowledge, traditions and forms of organisation; a guarantee of basic necessities and the development of production and employment; and protection of indigenous migrants.

In terms of specific policy changes, these principles were translated into a broad range of demands. They can be listed briefly as follows: (1) indigenous representation in local and regional legislatures and government; (2) separate judicial norms for the resolution of internal conflicts; (3) guarantees for indigenous forms of social organisation and development of cultural diversity; (4) recognition of indigenous communities as separate entities in public law; (5) the right to develop separate forms of government in municipalities where Indians formed a majority, and for state legislatures to have greater latitude in determining which powers and resources should be devolved to such administrations; (6) changes to Article 4 of the constitution, legitimising a separate Indian presence and practices, and Article 115, reforming the federal relationship and allowing for greater municipal autonomy; and (7) respect for separate languages, religious practices and medicine.

Taken together, these demands implied a far reaching reform in the relationship between the Mexican state and the indigenous population. Whilst the agreement did not match many demands for a fourth level of government for indigenous communities alongside federal, state and municipal governments, it did imply a redrawing of many municipal boundaries, a greater degree of representation for indigenous groups at municipal and state levels, and a consequent increase in indigenous control over resources and decision making. Developments in subnational politics have been integral to the struggle for democracy in Mexico in the 1980s and 1990s, and the concessions won through the Chiapas rebellion would potentially help to promote democratic procedures and practices at the local level, whilst continuing the struggle for greater democracy at the federal level.

Moreover, the proposed reforms were likely to have a significant impact on the relationship between the indigenous and non-indigenous populations. The federalisation of the Indian question had largely removed it as a day-to-day issue for much of the mestizo population. San Andrés would now give the issue a greater degree of immediacy for the general population, but it would also challenge many existing power relationships favouring mestizos. Chiapas may have opened much of the population's eyes to the plight of indigenous communities, and generated a high degree of sympathy, but it remains an open question how mestizos will react to any enforced changes in their municipal arrangements and to the allocation of executive and legislative positions to indigenous groups qua indigenous groups. Attitudes amongst the general population cannot be said to be either unambiguously positive or sympathetic. Moreover, there is open hostility to Indian autonomy from many quarters. In states such as Chiapas, the federal government has a 'low state presence', and 'real power is exercised through extra-legal means, including private armies' — usually run by landowners who have much to fear from any increase in the power of indigenous groups.[19] Examples of conflicts, human rights abuses and massacres involving such groups abound, and it is not clear that the federal government has either the inclination or the ability to overcome such reactionary forces. The Zedillo administration has been forced into a number of concessions with hard line governors, and there are real limits to the capacity of the current administration to impose its will on significant parts of the territory.

The San Andrés agreement was formally presented to President Zedillo late in 1996. Despite the government's agreement in the negotiations and in formal statements it backtracked on translating them into constitutional and legislative changes. The government claimed that the proposals 'lacked "juridical precision"' and should not be allowed to 'fracture the constitutional order'.[20] In August 1997 the government explicitly stated that its concerns over the proposals related directly to the challenge that they posed to sovereignty and national unity. Despite the rebellion and the momentum for change, the modernisation model of national development was still a key driving force. But although government tactics involved delay and obfuscation, it could not avoid the issue altogether. By early 1998 the pressure to implement the San Andrés agreements had started to build, partly at least in response to the substantial evidence of human rights abuses and persecution in the south, especially in Chiapas and Oaxaca. In February of that year, the Interior Minister Labastida stated that the government was willing to consider legislation based upon the San Andrés accord, and plans were developed for a revised version of an Indian Rights and Culture bill. COCOPA took the lead in developing specific proposals: it reiterated support for policies allowing indigenous communities greater autonomy in choosing government representatives, in protecting traditional forms of justice and guaranteeing respect for indigenous culture in areas such as education.

Then, on 15 March 1998, the government presented its own bill to congress. It incorporated some of the proposals agreed at San Andrés, but it did not provide for the creation of an 'exceptional regime' for indigenous groups. Rather, greater legislative and judicial autonomy at the municipal level, alongside measures enhancing participation and representation, were added to the policy of administrative devolution popular since the 1980s. Thus: 'indigenous autonomy is most complete where Indians comprise the majority of a municipality; states are directed to take the concentration of indigenous populations into account when drawing or redrawing municipal boundaries or electoral districts in order to maximise such instances.'[21]

Despite the growth in indigenous protest, therefore, and despite the government's decreased ability to dominate the national agenda, policy has been piecemeal and reactive, and has fallen short of the demands of many indigenous groups. Opposition parties and congressional representatives are pushing for more wide-reaching reforms that will embed the position of the native population in the constitution and in everyday political life. Implementation of the government's own proposals, much less that of any more radical agenda, remains an open question. In this sense, San Andrés represents a crossroads in the democratisation of the Indian question in much the same way as 1988 represented the crossroads in the democratisation of federal elections. The government was forced to do something, but it did so reactively, half-heartedly and with an underlying objective of maintaining many existing power relationships. It took more than the 1988 election to democratise federal elections in Mexico, and it will take more than the San Andrés accord to democratise the Indian question and fully meet the demands of Indian communities.

That a 'new, indigenista paradigm' has emerged in the 1990s is undeniable, as is the much greater degree of popular and elite awareness of the issue. It took an armed rebellion, however, to awaken the government to these issues, and current policy falls some way short not only of indigenous demands but of the minimal compromises reached at San Andrés. Mexico has taken no more than a small step on the road to the type of autonomy arrangements increasingly developed elsewhere in the region.

Conclusions

The struggles in Chiapas, Oaxaca and elsewhere in the south, couched in terms of indigenous rights, autonomy, democracy and justice, have presented a new set of constitutional conundrums to government and its policy makers. Initial responses included an agreement to incorporate the International Labour Organisation's Convention on Indigenous and Tribal Peoples into Mexican law, followed by the 1991 constitutional amendment and the concessions in the San Andrés agreement of 1996. Nevertheless, government obfuscation and its attempt to pre-empt the opposition and indigenous groups with the watered-down bill of 1998 suggest that the preferred model of uniform national development is still dominant. Donna van Cott may be right when she argues that the Mexican arrangements constitute a 'territorial autonomy regime' with 'powers that are not typical of autonomous arrangements elsewhere in the world',[22] but they are still minimal, nascent and contested. Indigenous autonomy along the Bolivian, Nicaraguan or Colombian lines is still to be conceded.

We also have to be wary of placing too great an emphasis on the strength of indigenous movements. Cultural rebellion has been localised and limited, and has not as yet widened to other areas. Indigenous groups need to fully develop a consciousness of ethnicity 'for itself' as well as 'of itself' in order to affect wider change.[23] Something like this has occurred on a small scale, but it will have to become yet more prevalent if political arrangements for managing Mexico's diverse population are to move beyond the concessions made in 1991 and 1998. In addition, many groups have disputed the Zapatistas' right to speak on behalf of all indigenous groups. As van Cott has argued, the negotiations between the government and the Zapatistas: 'suffer[ed] the birth defect of having been negotiated by an armed group of a few thousand Indian and non-Indian combatants claiming to represent an heterogeneous national indigenous population of several million, rather than by the dozens of indigenous political organisations existing in the country.'[24]

The point is well made. It is true that other indigenous groups were later involved — COCOPA took care to look beyond the Zapatistas, and the National Indigenous Congress has sought to foster an indigenous identity at the national level. Nevertheless, the argument that the process has been driven forward by a small and not necessarily representative group is valid. It may be, therefore, that as long as such organisational and ideological constraints remain, policy towards the Indian population will be at best incremental. It is also more likely to be by concessions wrung from a reluctant government than by any constitutional root and branch settlement. Yet the movement towards a more representative control through congress, and towards a greater recognition of Indian rights, seems likely to continue. Politics in Mexico have rarely been calm — the Zapatista rebellion was one more violent episode in a turbulent history — but it is also true that Mexican politics are built out of the past and that what happened in 1994 cannot be undone. The problems highlighted by the rebellion are now part of the pattern of Mexican government and politics. How the pattern will be woven or unravelled remains unknown, but existing pressures from within Mexican society, and from the region and the world, ensure that change will come.

1   A. Dawson, 'From Models for the Nation to Model Citizens: *Indigenismo* and the 'Revindication' of the Mexican Indian, 1920–40', *Journal of Latin American Studies*, 30, 1998, p. 295.

2   Ibid., p. 287.

3   J. Rus, 'The "Comunidad Revolucionaria Institucional": The Subversion of Native Government in Highland Chiapas, 1936–1968' in G. Joseph and D. Nugent (eds), *Everyday Forms of State Formation: Revolution and the Negotiation of Rule in Modern Mexico*, Duke University Press, 1994, p. 265.

4   S. Morris, 'Reforming the Nation: Mexican Nationalism in Context', *Journal of Latin American Studies*, 31, 1999, p. 374.

5   G. Palacios 'Post-revolutionary Intellectuals, Rural Readings and the Shaping of the 'Peasant Problem' in Mexico: *El Maestro Rural*, 1932–34', *Journal of Latin American Studies*, 30, 1998, p. 321.

6   Dawson, op. cit., pp. 307–8.

7   Ibid., p. 306.

8   L. Whitehead, 'State Organisation in Latin America since 1930' in L. Bethell (ed), *The Cambridge*

History of Latin America. Volume VI: Latin America since 1930: Economy, Society and Politics, Cambridge University Press, 1994, p. 24.

9 The PRI's full title is the Institutional Revolutionary Party.

10 P. Brown, 'Cultural Resistance and Rebellion in Southern Mexico', *Latin American Research Review,* 33, 1998, p. 228.

11 See the case studies in Joseph and Nugent, op. cit., and W. Cornelius et al, *Subnational Politics and Democratization in Mexico,* Center for US–Mexican Studies, UCSD, 1999.

12 N. Harvey, 'Rural Reforms and the Zapatista Rebellion: Chiapas, 1988–1995' in G. Ortero (ed), *Neoliberalism Revisited: Economic Restructuring and Mexico's Political Future,* Westview Press, 1996, p. 202.

13 This programme became known as the Alliance for National Welfare under President Zedillo.

14 J. Fox, 'The Difficult Transition from Clientelism to Citizenship: Lessons from Mexico' in *World Politics,* 46, 1994, p. 170.

15 N. Harvey, 'Resisting Neoliberalism, Constructing Citizenship: Indigenous Movements in Chiapas' in Cornelius et al, op. cit., pp. 244–5.

16 Morris, op. cit., p. 375.

17 Ibid., p. 369.

18 San Andrés contained a 'General Agreement' on areas for discussion of Indian rights and culture, and three more specific documents relating to a 'General Pronouncement' on rights and culture, 'Political Commitments' towards specific policies in the same area, and an agreement relating to the case of Chiapas, which looked for the incorporation of the general, federal principles into the constitution and government of the state of Chiapas. See *Acuerdos de San Andrés sobre 'Derechos y Cultura Indígenas',* 8 January 1996.

19 Harvey, op. cit., p. 260.

20 Morris, op. cit., p. 375.

21 D. van Cott, 'Rejecting Secession: Ethnicity-based Autonomy Arrangements in Latin America', paper for the *American Political Science Association,* Boston, 1998.

22 van Cott, op. cit., p. 16.

23 Brown, op. cit., p. 229.

24 van Cott, op. cit., p. 15.

Latin America: Constitutional Reform and Ethnic Rights

BY DONNA LEE VAN COTT

ONLY a decade ago, the title of this article might have elicited derision from political scientists specialising in Latin America. First, because social scientists have tended to view the region's politics in class-based terms and to disregard the ethnic and cultural bases of political conflict. Second, because the region's new constitutions have been as frequent as they have been meaningless. The average life span of Latin American constitutions is less than 20 years. More than 200 have been written in the 150 years since independence, with a fresh constitution typically accompanying each change of power. Their ephemeral nature and illegitimacy have exacerbated the tendency of political scientists to dismiss constitutions in many non-Western societies on the grounds that they fall short of Western standards.

In the 1990s, scholars of the region must rethink their assumptions about Latin American politics and constitutions. They must make sense of a new, more political wave of constitutional reform in which once-marginalised groups are mobilising for particular rights. Among the most successful are indigenous peoples whose proposals have been incorporated in most of the new constitutions. They comprise approximately 10% of the region's population, ranging from less than 1% of the total population in Brazil to approximately 30–45% in Peru and Ecuador, and more than 60% in Guatemala and Bolivia. Twelve groups have more than a million members which together constitute 73% of the region's total indigenous population; roughly 200 groups have less than 1,000 members. Indigenous communities have always resisted domination and forced integration but only in the 1970s did they form organisations capable of sustained political action on behalf of their constituents above the local level.

The political conjuncture presented by public debates on constitutional reform in the 1990s provided the perfect philosophical and practical context for indigenous peoples to put forward their claims. Constitution-making is a symbolic act in which the people (or peoples) give their consent to the institutions and values that define the terms of their self-government. Prior to the recent constitutional debates in which they took part, indigenous peoples were excluded from the process of constituting the states of Latin America. They now have the opportunity to participate autonomously. Their representatives took part in constituent assemblies in Colombia, Ecuador, Nicaragua, Paraguay and Venezuela. A member of Guyana's Amerindian Peoples Association was elected vice-president of that country's Constitutional Reform Commission in 1999. The inclusion of the formerly excluded during these crucial political moments lends much-needed legitimacy to the new constitutions.

This chapter argues that a distinctive constitutional model has emerged in Latin America in countries with proportionately significant indigenous populations as well as those where Indians have a more 'symbolic' presence. The scope of new indigenous rights and recognition is discussed in the first section below. A particular focus is on the cases of Colombia and Bolivia which are the oldest and most implemented of the reforms. In two countries where indigenous rights have been recognised, separate (albeit lesser) recognition has also been extended to African American populations. A discussion of these rights follows. In section two there is an explanation of why Latin American states adopted the new model of multi-cultural constitutionalism in the 1990s.

Ethnic rights in new constitutions

After the liberal reforms of the late nineteenth century, references to indigenous peoples were removed from the region's constitutions. They began to reappear during the 1960s and 1970s in conjunction with agrarian reform, but these generally referred to Indians as campesinos (peasants). After 1979, several Latin American countries recognised language and cultural rights: Ecuador and Peru did so during the transition to democracy of that year; Guatemala did so in 1985 as that country shifted to civilian rule. Argentina, Bolivia, Brazil, Colombia, Mexico, Nicaragua, Panama and Paraguay provided some recognition of indigenous languages and cultures in the 1980s. As Iturralde explained (in the Journal *Alteridades* in 1997), the mere recognition of indigenous culture and language did not encounter much resistance from the legal and political establishment; more contentious were claims for official status or parity for indigenous languages, culture and religion alongside those of the dominant culture. The attainment of official status for indigenous languages did not come until the latest wave of constitutional reform, as part of the new multi-cultural constitutional model.[1]

Although they vary on a number of dimensions, ten new Latin American constitutions share at least three of the five elements of what can be called the 'multi-cultural model': (1) formal recognition of the multi-cultural nature of their societies and of the existence of indigenous peoples as distinct, sub-state social collectivities; (2) recognition of indigenous peoples' customary law as official, public law; (3) collective property rights with restrictions on the alienation or division of communal lands; (4) official status for indigenous languages in territorial units where they are settled; and (5) a guarantee of bilingual education. All but one of these ten constitutions (Nicaragua) were replaced or radically reformed after 1990. Only one replaced in this decade (Uruguay) lacks at least three elements of the model. (Uruguay's indigenous population of some 4–5,000 Indians was exterminated by the mid-twentieth century.) An additional two constitutions incorporated the model when they ratified ILO's Convention 169 on indigenous peoples, discussed below.

Formal recognition. Eight Latin American constitutions contain sections, usually near the beginning of the document, recognising the multi-ethnic, pluri-cultural and/or multi-lingual nature of their societies. For example, Bolivia's first article begins, 'Bolivia free, independent, sovereign, multi-ethnic and pluri-cultural . . .'; Ecuador's first article begins, 'Ecuador is a pluri-cultural and multi-ethnic state.' The Colombian and Peruvian constitutions declare the state's duty to recognise and protect the ethnic and cultural diversity of the nation. The Nicaraguan and Paraguayan constitutions use this type of language in more than one instance. Argentina's charter, while not explicitly recognising the ethnic diversity of its population, acknowledges the 'ethnic and cultural pre-existence of indigenous peoples'. Equally important is explicit recognition of indigenous peoples as distinct substate entities with their own forms of social and political organisation (provided in Bolivia, Brazil, Colombia, Ecuador, Guatemala, Mexico, Nicaragua, Paraguay, Peru and Venezuela). In Argentina, Bolivia, Brazil, Chile (by statute), Colombia, Costa Rica (by statute), Mexico and Peru, constitutions recognise the juridical personality of indigenous communities, thereby giving them the legal capacity to sue in courts and to enter into private or public contracts.

Symbolic language is cheap and may appear meaningless to those unfamiliar with the region or the aspirations of its indigenous populations. But it is an astounding development. Prior to the incorporation of these sentiments, official rhetoric proclaimed the homogeneous nature of Latin American societies, based on the assumption that the distinctive cultural traits and identities existing in colonial Latin America had been integrated into a new hybrid type through miscegenation and assimilation. Indigenous organisations successfully discredited this version of history in the 1980s and now demand official recognition of their existence as distinct peoples. For a movement that is as much about dignity and identity as it is about the improvement of material circumstances, symbolic recognition is significant. In Colombia, moreover, what may appear to be mere rhetoric has been interpreted by the nation's Constitutional Court as a mandate of higher rank than most other constitutional rights.

Several constitutions (Bolivia, Colombia, Ecuador, Mexico, Nicaragua, Panama, Peru) extend symbolic awareness to recognising and guaranteeing the existence of indigenous forms of social organisation.

Bolivia and Colombia go one step further by recognising the public and authoritative nature of these forms of organisation. In Ecuador and Guatemala, decentralisation and territorial reorganisation schemes, designed in conjunction with constitutional reforms affecting indigenous peoples, provide for this practical possibility since they allow local jurisdictions to be created according to ethnicity and language. The incorporation of ethnically defined social and territorial units ruptures the uniformity and universality of public administration at the local level and represents a break from the region's liberal tradition.

Recognition of customary law. As in post-communist countries, the constitutional debates in Latin America centred on the lack of fit between formal, legal guarantees of citizenship and a reality in which many are unable to access mechanisms to redress their grievances. In addition to codifying the regime of ethnic rights discussed here, most Latin American countries have overhauled their judicial systems in ways that are similar to contemporary reforms in Eastern Europe, for example, the adoption of constitutional courts, human rights ombudsmen, and independent councils to police the judicial profession.[2] These efforts have been assisted by a 14-country project on judicial reform sponsored by the Inter-American Development Bank. According to the Bank's specialist on judicial reform, the '17 constitutional reforms now under way in the region aim, almost without exception, to strengthen the judiciary and uphold citizens' rights'. Among the most important reforms are those to codes of criminal procedure which regulate Indians' access to and treatment by police and the justice system. Bolivia, Guatemala and Paraguay — countries where language and illiteracy are major barriers to access — are incorporating orality and translation into court proceedings.

The recognition of indigenous customary law is particularly important given concern throughout Latin America about the problem of weak judiciaries, the impunity of public officials and the inaccessibility of the justice system to disadvantaged groups. Indigenous communities seek recognition of customary law in large part due to the inaccessibility and weakness of the state's own justice administration. Reform, therefore, is crucial to improving indigenous peoples' access to justice and protecting their rights. Seven states — Bolivia, Colombia, Ecuador, Nicaragua, Paraguay, Peru and Venezuela — recognise the official and public nature of customary law and the jurisdiction of indigenous authorities over internal community affairs. Mexico is committed to doing so, pursuant to an accord between the government and the (mostly) Mayan armed rebel group EZLN (Zapatista Army of National Liberation). Signatories of ILO Convention 169 are committed to this recognition. In all cases, the scope of indigenous jurisdiction is limited by the constitution and ordinary laws of the country, although some states actually allow a broader reach in practice. In effect, the new constitutions formally recognise what has been the practice in the region since colonial times when the weak presence of the state in rural areas left a legal vacuum in which indigenous communities were relatively free to resolve internal disputes. Even in modern times, indigenous communities that retain their traditional authority structures commonly handle internal matters themselves and refer serious crimes, or those involving outsiders, to state courts where they are available. The innovation is that indigenous authorities are given a public character and their decisions are recognised as public law.

Formal recognition requires that some mechanism of coordination be created between customary and state legal systems (customary law is now a form of state law, but the semantic distinction is useful for the purpose of clarity). In most cases, the constitutions recognising this right indicate that the particulars will be determined by a subsequent statutory law. The writer knows of no case where states have produced such a law, owing to a lack of consensus on the scope of indigenous law within the government and among indigenous organisations. Governmental efforts to do so were under way in Bolivia and Peru in 1999. Bolivia has also achieved some clarity through its new Code of Penal Procedure, which lets defendants choose whether indigenous or state jurisdiction will prevail and limits sanctions imposed by indigenous authorities to those not violating constitutional or international law.

In the absence of legislation, the Colombian Constitutional Court has produced a series of rulings that define the limits of customary law. In 1994 it ruled that state courts should use the following criteria in determining the application of indigenous law: first, cultural traditions are to be respected, depending on the court's judgment with respect to the extent that those traditions have been preserved; second, the decisions and sanctions imposed by indigenous tribunals must not violate fundamental constitutional or international human rights; and third, indigenous customary law has supremacy over ordinary civil laws that conflict with cultural norms, and over legislation that does not protect a constitutional right of the same rank as the right to cultural and ethnic diversity. A 1996 decision extended the scope of customary jurisdiction beyond indigenous territories in cases where a judge deems a defendant's level of cultural alienation to warrant this, the following year, a new ruling allowed a Páez Indian community to use corporal punishment as a sanction, arguing that only such a high degree of autonomy would ensure the survival of indigenous cultures.

Collective property rights. Collective property rights do more than secure indigenous communities' ownership of their traditional lands. They provide the material basis for the exercise of jurisdiction, a sine qua non of autonomy which is the larger goal of all indigenous movements in Latin America. Thirteen Latin American countries recognise the right of such communities to own property in common. In some cases this right was retained from colonial times; in others it was restored or reinforced by revolutionary governments. Costa Rica and

Panama recognised indigenous collective property rights in 1939 and 1953, respectively, long before it became a regional trend. In most cases, constitutions prohibit the alienation of collective title through mortgaging, non-payment of taxes, or sale. The Mexican and Peruvian governments went against the current trend by weakening these protections in 1992 and 1993. Brazilian Indians have the right only to collective use of their traditional lands which remain the property of the federal government. In many cases, collective property or even territorial rights are weakened by the inability of indigenous communities to exercise control over the exploitation of natural resources. Throughout the region, where legal systems were adapted from French and Roman law, the state retains subsoil rights. While many states are bound by international or national law to consult with indigenous communities about the exploitation of these resources, this is almost never accomplished to the satisfaction of the communities.

Language and education. Only in Paraguay does an indigenous language have official status comparable to Spanish. (Peru rescinded official status for Quechua in the 1993 constitution.) For unique historical reasons, Guaraní is widely spoken by non-indigenous Paraguayans. In Colombia, Ecuador, Nicaragua, Peru and Venezuela indigenous languages are official in zones where their speakers are settled. In Ecuador and Guatemala indigenous organisations are negotiating to redraw administrative borders according to linguistic criteria in order to provide a more participatory, culturally appropriate public services and development planning.

Seven constitutions guarantee bilingual education. Guatemala and Mexico are committed to incorporating this right into their pending reforms. (Other countries provide some bilingual education without a constitutional mandate.) The main obstacles to implementing this right are the lack of resources for education in the region, the lack of qualified bilingual teachers, and the opposition of teachers' unions to changes that impair their prerogative to negotiate their terms of employment.

Autonomy. In addition to the five rights enumerated above, the new multi-cultural constitutions incorporate a number of other special provisions affecting the indigenous population. The most important of these would be the creation of autonomous politico-territorial regimes based on ethnicity. Although indigenous organisations throughout the region are pressing for their establishment, they remain an exception to the model described here, since they typically encounter stiff resistance, particularly from provincial elites who dominate politics in rural areas and who view indigenous political autonomy as encroaching upon their prerogatives. Two such regimes predate the current wave of constitutional reform. Panama has recognised large regions of indigenous self-government (comarcas) since the 1920s, recognition that was codified in 1953. The state recognised three additional comarcas for other indigenous groups in 1983, 1996 and 1997. Nicaragua's creation of two multi-ethnic autonomous regions in 1987 — the fruit of five years of warfare between the Sandinista government and Miskitu Indians backed by the United States — inspired indigenous organisations throughout the hemisphere to press for similar rights.

In the 1980s, autonomy became the defining claim of indigenous movements and the centre-piece of their project to build 'multi-ethnic, pluri-cultural' states. It articulates the dual nature of their demand for the voluntary reconstitution of relations with the states and societies in which they live and their desire to preserve a territorial sphere in which the state and non-indigenous society cannot intrude while integrating more effectively and participatively into the wider state and larger society. As in other countries challenged by claims by communal groups for territorial autonomy this claim becomes more difficult to implement as indigenous populations increasingly become not only more urbanised but territorially integrated with non-indigenous groups. Constitution-makers must choose between conferring autonomy upon *territorial* entities where Indians constitute a majority (indirect consociation) or upon *population* groups (direct consociation): the latter is exemplified by Colombia's special indigenous senatorial district, by Chile's statutory National Indigenous Development Board and by the Saami parliaments created recently in Sweden and Norway. The concept of autonomy becomes more difficult where Indians constitute a majority. How can a state foster national unity and solidarity if a majority of the population and territory is autonomous of the state and non-indigenous society, or the majority of the territory is organised into 'exceptional' or anoma-lous administrative units? The realisation of the ideal of autonomy is also impeded by the lack of consensus among indigenous organisations within specific countries over the shape autonomy regimes should take, i.e. whether they should be confined to culture or take on a territorial shape. If the latter, should they be constructed at the community, municipal or a higher administrative level; and should they be mono- or multi-ethnic?

Only in Colombia has the aspiration for autonomy become a reality. The 1991 Colombian Constitution gave indigenous resguardos (exten-sive reserves governed by indigenous authorities) the status of munici-palities, with the right to share in annual resource transfers amounting to approximately US$ 61,000 per resguardo from the national govern-ment. These transfers are currently supervised by local municipal authorities because of the Colombian legislature's resistance to passing legislation converting resguardos into Indigenous Territorial Entities with the power to administer the resources themselves, as the constitu-tion requires.[3] Although Indians are less than 3% of the population, their resguardos cover approximately one-quarter of Colombian terri-tory, so their autonomous status is a significant territorial anomaly. Autonomy regimes are under discussion elsewhere. The 1998 Ecuador-ian constitution allows for the creation of indigenous and Afro-Ecuadorian administrative districts with powers comparable to autonomous governments. It remains to be seen how or whether this will be implemented in practice. Both Guatemala's 1995 Accord on Indigenous Rights and Identity and Mexico's 1996 San Andrés Accord,[4] recognise the right of indigenous communities to political autonomy, but there is no consensus within the indigenous movements in either country over the appropriate administrative unit for this autonomy. Both governments are attempting to hold autonomy below the level of a government unit with meaningful powers; indigenous organisations are split on whether autonomy should be exercised at the community (submunicipal) level, the municipal level, or across more extensive multi-ethnic regions. Canada's creation of an autonomous indigenous region called Nunuvut in 1999 may provide an influential model for future indigenous claims to autonomy, since Nicaragua's autonomous regions have been a failure.[5]

The creation of territorial autonomy regimes is facilitated by the shift in the new constitutions — and throughout Latin America — towards greater decentralisation of administrative and political powers to the municipal level. This is a phenomenon promoted by the multi-lateral development banks and international non-governmental organisations whose experts view decentralisation as a means toward greater responsiveness, efficiency and accountability of government while promoting democratic participation and values. For these reasons and others, decentralisation to local government was also launched in the post-communist constitutions: its success is important since effective decentralisation is a necessary, although insufficient, condition for local autonomy. As in eastern Europe, however, Latin Americans have been disappointed by the results. Resistance by local elites to relinquishing policy-making powers and corruption at the local level have limited the benefits. Given the way that indigenous groups are currently settled, and the opposition of elites to creating geographically extensive territories, it is likely that future experiments in indigenous autonomy — such as those being negotiated in Ecuador, Guatemala, and Mexico — will be at the municipal level.

Among the remaining political rights recognised by the new constitutions are special measures to guarantee indigenous representation in government. Colombia reserves two seats in the National Senate for indigenous representatives; The new Venezuelan constitution promises indigenous representation in the National Assembly. Indigenous comarcas in Panama elect their own representatives to the National Assembly and the constitution allows for electoral districts to be created to take into account the indigenous population. As of 1995, the Nicaraguan constitution allows for electoral districts to be drawn for the same purpose, as does the 1998 Ecuadorian constitution. Several constitutions exempt indigenous peoples from obligatory military or other public service, property taxes and income taxes.

African American rights. Communities of African descent in Latin America have been less inclined to mobilise to achieve special constitutional language or laws recognising a distinct black identity or set of rights.[6] Following the abolition of slavery in the nineteenth century, blacks lacked any special legal status or rights apart from the wider society. The exception to this rule is the case of some Maroon (runaway slave) communities which enjoyed a distinct, semi-autonomous legal status through treaties with colonial powers. The successor states to the colonial powers have tended to ignore these treaties and have resisted demands by Maroon organisations to recognise a distinct status based on historical treaty rights. Despite their legal equality, blacks endured social discrimination, were underrepresented in political office, and were trapped in rural or urban poverty. For the most part, where they have mobilised politically qua blacks it has been to demand equality, rather than recognition as a distinct group. The question of a special legal status for blacks is complicated in areas where they are biologically and culturally mixed with indigenous communities. For example, Miskitu and Garífuna Indians on the Atlantic Coast of Nicaragua, whose ancestors include indigenous peoples and blacks who migrated from the Caribbean, enjoy constitutional rights derived from their indigenous ancestry. Creoles — blacks lacking kinship with indigenous communities — living in the same area lack such rights. In Bolivia, the small group of blacks whose ancestors were brought as slaves to work in the mines have been assimilated into the Aymara indigenous community; the Bolivian government's indigenous affairs office lists Afro-Bolivians among the 'indigenous and original peoples'.

Despite this unpromising social and legal context, two states recognise blacks as distinct cultural communities. The first to do so was Colombia, whose 1991 constitution includes a Transitory Article recognising the collective property rights of black communities in the lands they inhabit in the Pacific Coast riverine region. It calls on the state not only to respect their traditional culture and distinctive identity but to promote their economic and social development. The rights applied to the riverine population may be extended to other parts of the country where black communities exist in similar circumstances. A separate constitutional article protects the rights of the predominantly black and English-speaking Raizal population in Colombia's archipelago of San Andrés, Providencia and Santa Catalina. A subsequent statutory law limited the rights of population movement and residence in the archipelago, regulated the use of land and ownership of property for the purpose of preserving the cultural identity of the Raizal population and the islands' natural environment, and guaranteed representation of Raizal communities in the departmental assembly. The rights accorded to the Afro-Colombian and Raizal populations are far less extensive than the regime of rights protecting indigenous peoples, reflecting their lack of representation in the National Constituent Assembly in which three indigenous delegates (two elected, one appointed) served, as well as the reluctance of the Colombian political elite to accept the idea of an ethnically distinct black population, a concept that continues to rankle.

The Colombian Constitutional Court broadened the constitution-makers' intentions with respect to Afro-Colombian identity and rights in a 1996 ruling. It argued that all Colombian blacks, although not organised according to the constitution's narrow definition of a black community as a traditional, river-based culture, are entitled to the protections and positive measures extended to ethnic groups under the constitution. They were victims in the past of social marginalisation 'which has had negative repercussions on their access to economic, social, and cultural opportunities'.[7] The ruling expands the scope of the population protected under the constitution. It applies the constitution's right to equality, and the state's duty to 'adopt measures favouring groups which are discriminated against or underprivileged', to blacks as a racial as well as an economically disadvantaged group; it also affirms the general interest of the public in promoting equality. The decision emphasised the socio-economic marginalisation of blacks, while maintaining a sensitivity to the possibility that blacks would recuperate Afro-Colombian cultures based on anthropological information and follow the path of indigenous peoples toward the (re)construction of ethnic identity.

The 1998 Ecuadorian constitution includes a far broader scope for Afro-Ecuadorian rights than its Colombian forerunner, although these rights are less ample than those for indigenous peoples. This may reflect the fact that in Ecuador indigenous and black organisations had a longer history of joint mobilisation prior to the 1998 constituent assembly debates. The constitution's section on 'indigenous peoples and blacks or Afro-Ecuadorians' contains the charter's most important statement with respect to ethnic rights. It recognises that 'indigenous peoples, which identify themselves as nationalities of ancestral roots, and black peoples or Afro-Ecuadorians, form part of the Ecuadorian State.' This language is interesting in that blacks are identified as *peoples*, a designation usually reserved by indigenous activists for Indians as distinct from the 'ethnic minorities' of the region. The term 'peoples' is preferred because it connotes a political community with the right to self-determination under international law. A set of 15 collective rights are recognised and guaranteed to indigenous peoples: they include but are not limited to the right to develop and strengthen their identity, and their spiritual, cultural, linguistic, social, political and economic traditions; to keep their tax-exempt, inalienable communally-owned lands; to be consulted with respect to plans to exploit natural resources on those lands and to participate in the benefits of that exploitation; to conserve their forms of social organisation and authority; to intellectual property rights over their ancestral knowledge; and to receive intercultural, bilingual education. The constitution states that the foregoing rights enunciated for the indigenous population shall apply to Afro-Ecuadorians 'to the extent they are applicable'. This language leaves the application of the indigenous rights regime to Afro-Ecuadorians open to interpretation. In addition to this section on collective rights, the chapter on the administrative divisions of the country allows for the creation of special territorial units encompassing indigenous and Afro-Ecuadorian populations. Provinces, municipalities, parishes and the 'organs of administration' are to have autonomous functions, as determined by law. Again, the devil is in the details.

The multi-cultural state

In no case in Latin America was the demand for special rights and recognition the most important reason for the decision to reform the political constitution. The impetus for constitutional change was dissatisfaction with the state and regime. In many cases, political elites, international experts and common citizens perceived states to be over-centralised and inefficient; in others, a persistent institutional stalemate between branches of government required constitutional adjustment. In all cases, judiciaries were weak and politically compromised, contributing to a deepening crisis of legitimacy. As in post-communist Europe, Latin American constitution-makers were concerned with the protection of rights and influenced by the international discourse on human rights in the late twentieth century. They were as susceptible as their European counterparts to the transmission of an 'international political culture', its absorption with political reconstruction and its marked preference for a narrow range of constitutional models.

Within the context of widespread dissatisfaction with the existing democratic model, the discourse of the indigenous rights movement provided a conceptual framework for elites to question the quality of the democracies they were consolidating, particularly with respect to the persistence of inequalities and political exclusion. Indigenous organisations offered an alternative vision of citizenship, one that incorporates collective rights and new modes of individual and collective participation — a vision that was nurtured by and framed within the contemporary international discourse on rights. Indigenous claims emphasise the inadequacy of citizenship in respect of individual and collective rights. In response, some Latin American countries recognised such demands but, as Iturralde argues, 'these reforms are attributable to the interest in reforming the state to adjust to new global conditions, more than out of the will to accept ethnic and cultural diversity as a sign of modernity'.[8] In the post-constitutional conjuncture, indigenous organisations are still struggling to strengthen that will.

They were able to participate in the international discourse on rights because they had begun organising in the 1970s. By the 1980s, when most Latin American countries shifted from authoritarian-military to elected-civilian government, indigenous organisations had proliferated and matured, and had created an inter-American network of advocacy and mutual support. Activity at the international level to codify indigenous peoples' rights gave additional impetus to their claims. The substantial revision in 1989 of the only international convention specifically addressing the rights of indigenous peoples — International Labour Organisation Convention 169, which revises the earlier Convention 107 adopted in 1957 — provided a specific instrument for ethnic organisations to demand a revision of state-indigenous relations and a model for revising them. The newer version eliminates its predecessor's integrationist language and emphasises the responsibility of states to ensure that policies affecting indigenous peoples are devised through a process of consultation and participation, although the precise meaning of these terms is contested by governments and indigenous organisations. The policies mentioned include land ownership, natural resource management, agrarian programs, employment, social security, health care, language rights and education. As Keck and Sikkink argue, public commitments to specified principles enable social movement organisations to embarrass governments by 'expos[ing] the distance between discourse and practice'.[9] A prominent organ of the inter-American indigenous rights movement states: 'The idea that a true democracy must be pluri-cultural is beginning to take hold in a number of Latin American countries. More than any other international document, the International Labour Organisation's Convention 169 represents this shift in attitude from an assimilationist perspective to one that respects and values Indigenous cultures.'[10]

As this passage suggests, a country's ratification of the convention and its adoption of the multi-cultural constitutional model are both the result of larger processes at the national and international level. Evidence from Bolivia, Colombia, Ecuador, Guatemala and Mexico indicates that the ratification of the convention provided a useful tool for indigenous organisations to mobilise behind a set of rights contained in the convention and to achieve their codification at a constitutional level. Ten Latin American countries have ratified ILO Convention 169.[11] In Colombia and Ecuador, the convention was ratified during constituent assemblies in which indigenous representatives served. In Guatemala, ratification immediately followed the conclusion of peace accords, pursuant to a provision in the accord on Identity and Rights of the Indigenous Peoples. In Mexico, indigenous organisations used the convention as a bargaining instrument to reach consensus with the government on the San Andrés accord.[12]

Conclusion

The new multi-cultural model of Latin American constitution-making provides a framework for the foundation and consolidation of political institutions in a region where politics has been subject more to the whims of individual power-wielders than to the rule of law. The full significance of the model remains to be seen, since most of the constitutions are too new for their effects to be known. Even in the oldest cases, political elites and private interests have obstructed the implementation of the new rights, particularly with respect to territorial autonomy. Given the weakness of ethnic organisations relative to other political interests, it will be difficult for them to sustain the pressure necessary to ensure the implementation of their new constitutional rights. In Colombia they have been assisted in part by the Constitutional Court, but the professional, independent jurists responsible for the Court's remarkable rulings do not exist in every country in the region.

As in post-communist Europe, prospects for the faithful implementation of the new multi-cultural constitutional model in Latin America are encouraged by 'positive externalities'. They include the existence of human rights instruments and the monitoring efforts of international governmental and non-governmental organisations. They are accompanied by positive developments common to states in both regions, such as the creation of constitutional courts and human rights ombudsmen, the attention of the independent media, and the existence of organised civil society groups willing and able to mobilise against efforts to curtail newly-won constitutional rights. As Pogany argues with respect to post-communist Europe, the impact of these pressures varies and 'their importance within a particular society will depend on a range of factors including the history of the country in question, its economic circumstances, the prevailing social and political culture and the presence of potentially divisive elements, such as sizeable national, ethnic, religious or linguistic minorities'.[13]

The presence of the latter, of course, need not be divisive. Latin American constitution-makers hope that ethnic diversity may actually promote national unity by drawing attention to the problem of political exclusion, emphasising the importance of rights to democracy, and infusing the political culture with the values of participation, inclusion and tolerance of diversity.

---

1   For a historical perspective on Latin American constitutionalism, see A. Borón, 'Latin America: Constitutionalism and Political Traditions of Liberalism and Socialism' in D. Greenberg, *Constitutionalism and Democracy*, Oxford University Press, 1993.

2   Latin American countries with constitutional courts include Bolivia, Chile, Colombia, Ecuador, Guatemala and Peru. In Argentina, Brazil, Mexico and Venezuela, existing supreme courts have been confined to considering constitutional questions.

3   Resguardos began receiving funds under Law 60 (1993) in 1994, when 12,046 million pesos (about US$ 12 million) were distributed to 439,267 Indians living on 364 recognised resguardos. Roughly US$ 15.5 million was transferred in 1995 (M.J. Cepeda, 'Democracy, State and Society in the Colombian Constitution', unpublished manuscript, 1995, p. 11). As a result of the creation of additional resguardos pursuant to the constitution, by March 1997 there were 442 resguardos and the Department of National Planning was awaiting approval of transfers of 27,000 million pesos (about US$ 61 thousand per resguardo). Interview with Raúl Arango, Unidad de Desarrollo Territorial, Departamento Nacional de Planeación, 30 January 1997.

4   The first is part of completed negotiations between the government and the URNG; the Mexican

accord is part of stalled negotiations between the government and the EZLN guerrillas. Meanwhile the government has offered its own constitutional reform proposal based on its interpretation of the San Andres accord.

5   The most important reasons are: resistance of the Nicaraguan government to relinquishing power; conflicts of interest among social groups in the regions; recent cataclysmic natural disasters; a failing national economy; and the hegemonic pretensions of the Miskitu.

6   For discussion of the difference between the situation of blacks and Indians in Latin America, see P. Wade, *Race and Ethnicity in Latin America*, Pluto Press, 1997. On Colombia's constitution and black rights, see K. Asher, *Constructing Afro-Colombia: Ethnicity and Territory in the Pacific Lowlands*, unpublished doctoral dissertation, University of Florida, 1998.

7   Sentencia T. 422 (1996). In this case, the representative of a local black organisation was denied a seat on the Santa Marta District Education Council on the grounds that the black population of the area did not constitute a distinct 'community' and lacked historical ties to the area and, thus, did not correspond to the definition of black communities under the constitution and the education law. That law allocates a seat to a representative of black community organisations and indigenous organisations.

8   Diego Iturralde Guerrero, 'Demandas Indígenas y Reforma Legal: Retos y Paradojas', 7 *Alteridades* 14, 1997, p. 91.

9   M. Keck and K. Sikkink, 'Activists Beyond Borders', *Transnational Advocacy Networks in International Politics*, Cornell University Press, 1998, p. 24.

10 Editorial, *Abya Yala News* 10, 4, 1997. The entire issue is devoted to the impact of ILO 169 in the hemisphere. See also, J. Dandler, *Indigenous People and the Rule of Law in Latin America*, Kellogg Institute: University of Notre Dame, 1996.

11 Non-Latin American countries signing the convention are Norway, Denmark and Holland. 27 countries ratified the older convention.

12 Interview with Mexican indigenous activist Margarita Gutierrez published in *Abya Yala News*, 10, 4, 1998.

13 I. Pogany, 'Constitution-making or Constitutional Transformation in Post-communist Societies?', *Political Studies XLIV*, 1996 p. 575.

Spain: Catalonia and the Basque Country

BY MONTSERRAT GUIBERNAU

AFTER 40 years of Franco's dictatorship, the 1979 constitution offered a new political framework within which Spaniards could organise their lives. One of the major issues facing the new regime was the national question, particularly in Catalonia and the Basque Country. The new constitution radically transformed the centralist non-democratic regime inherited from Francoism by creating the Autonomous Communities System. The lack of violence in the transition to democracy, the almost immediate acceptance of Spain by NATO and the European Community, and the rapid expansion of the economy prompted a dynamism that contrasted with the backwardness and conservatism of the Franco years. What remains to be decided is whether the momentum for change has reached a stop or whether there will be further reforms towards autonomy.

Catalonia

The tension between centralisation and various forms of cantonalism or federalism has been a constant problem faced by Spanish rulers. The joint rule of Ferdinand and Isabella (Reyes Católicos) from 1479 over Castile and the Crown of Aragon (of which Catalonia was its main element with Barcelona its capital), placed two very different areas under a common crown. The gulf between the two regions was enhanced by different political traditions and institutions. Although both kingdoms possessed parliamentary institutions (Corts), the Castilian Courts had never attained legislating power, emerging from the middle ages both isolated and weak, whereas Catalonia, Valencia and Aragon (forming the 'Crown' of Aragon) shared legislative power with the Crown and were well buttressed by laws and institutions derived from a long tradition of political liberty. Apart from sharing a common sovereign, neither Castile nor Aragon experienced radical institutional change.

In the event, the so-called equality of status between Castile and Aragon did not long survive the death of Ferdinand the Catholic. A growing gulf emerged between Castile and the other territories, including the state of Aragon. A radical shift in Castilian policy towards Catalonia occurred when Philip IV appointed the Count Duke of Olivares as chief minister in March 1621 with the object of creating a powerful absolutist state. In order to do so, Olivares abandoned any commitment to recognising internal diversity within the Spanish state. Rising tension between Castile and Catalonia climaxed with the Revolt of the Reapers (Revolta dels Segadors) in 1640, uniting Catalans against the harsh treatment of Castile. This event, often described as one of the earlier expressions of incipient nationalism in Europe, undoubtedly contributed to the rise of Catalan identity.

Catalonia maintained its rights and liberties until 1714 when, after a massive Franco-Spanish attack, Barcelona surrendered. Philip V ordered the dissolution of the Catalan institutions and Catalonia was subject to a regime of occupation. Catalan was forbidden and Castilian (Spanish) was proclaimed as the official language. The industrialisation of Catalonia in the nineteenth century was accompanied by major social changes, similar to those occurring in other European countries. This resulted, in turn, in the emergence of perceptible differences between Catalonia and the other regions of the Iberian peninsula, though parallel to the situation of the Basque Country. As the most economically developed part of a country, Catalonia found itself governed by an anachronistic and backward state in which political power resided with Castile. These differences have diminished but Catalan nationalists continue to make the case for residual differences.[1] Indeed, contemporary nationalism is merely the latest phase of a deep-rooted tradition of cultural separatism.

By the end of the nineteenth century, the influence of Romanticism inspired the Renaixença, a movement for national and cultural renaissance, which promoted Catalan language and culture, leading to demands for Catalan autonomy, in the first instance as a region, then as a federal state. Thereafter, its fortunes varied — autonomy under the administration of the Mancomunitat (1913–23), suppressed in 1923 after the coup d'état of Miguel Primo de Rivera, re-established during the Generalitat (1931–38) when Catalonia had a Statute of Autonomy but abolished by Franco's decree of 5 April 1938. Catalonia did not recover its autonomous government until 1977 after the demise of Francoism. A new Statute of Autonomy was passed by the Spanish Cortes in 1979. The president of the Catalan government, Josep Tarradellas, returned from exile in France. Jordi Pujol, leader of the Convergence and Union (Convergència i Unió or CiU) became the first president of the regional Catalan parliament after the first democratic election held in the region.

The Basque Country

The Basques are the only surviving pre-Aryan race in Europe, and their language (Euskera) is the only pre-Indoeuropean language in use in Europe. The Basques ruled themselves according to the Fueros (local statutes and charters) first established between the Basque regions North of the Pyrenees and the Foix of Occitany, and subsequently between the kingdom of Castile and Basque regions south of the Pyrenees. The

Fueros, mostly codified during the seventeenth and eighteenth centuries though some of them date back to the seventh century, exempted the local population from both military service and taxation, and gave provincial assemblies the right to veto royal edicts, a privilege they rarely employed. These institutions embodied the 'rights' of the people, rather than concessions granted to them. Throughout their history, the Basques have defended the Fueros, ensuring their autonomous status within the Spanish state.[2] Attempts by Madrid to abolish the Fueros were vigorously contested — Basque support for the Carlist movement was directly connected to their opposition to centralism — until their final abolition in 1876 after two long civil wars (Guerras Carlistas). Thereafter the Basque country was rapidly industrialised. Modernisation transformed every aspect of social life. The emergence of a Basque working class, the displacement of population from the rural areas to the countryside and the arrival of large numbers of immigrants from other parts of Spain — widely regarded as representing the oppressor — contributed to the emergence of Basque nationalism, initially as a cultural renaissance until Sabino Arana Goiri emerged as the ideologist of Basque nationalism, founding the Basque Nationalist Party in 1894.

A similar movement led by Arturo Campión and Juan Hurralde y Suit took place in Navarra although without the dramatic changes brought about by early industrialisation in the Basque provinces of Bizkaia and Guipúzkoa. Navarra remained a primarily rural area whose nationalists merely called for a recognition as a distinctive region. The difference was seen in 1932 when a referendum on political autonomy for the Basque country won overwhelming support in the provinces of Alava, Guipúzkoa and Bizkaia but was defeated in Navarra.

The end of Francoism brought change to this region too, but in a way that contrasts with the situation in Catalonia. Although the 1978 Spanish constitution was ratified by the majority of Spaniards, most Basque nationalists were opposed. The argument was that the new constitution was ambiguous about Basque rights. In the referendum on the constitution the abstention rate was 56% in Guipúzkoa and Bizkaia. The Basque Statute of Autonomy was, however, ratified by referendum in 1979, with 61% turnout and 89% voting in favour. The president — in exile — of the Basque government, Jesús María de Leizaola, returned from France and elections to the new Parliament took place in 1980. The leader of the Basque Nationalist Party, Carlos Garaikoetxea, became the first lehendakari (head of the Basque government) of the new democratic era.

National diversity within Francoist Spain

The meaning of both state and nation was contested during the Spanish Civil War. General Franco's supporters advocated a highly centralised, uniform image of Spain which rejected the progressive government of the Second Republic (1931–38), and its decentralisation tendencies. During the Republic, statutes of autonomy were sanctioned for Catalonia (1932), the Basque Country (1933) and Galicia (1936), although only the Catalan Statute had been implemented at the time of Franco's coup.

The impact of Franco's victory was marked in both Catalonia and the Basque Country, entailing not only the suppression of all autonomous political institutions and laws but the prohibition of the Catalan and Basque (Euskera) languages and cultures as well as all symbols of sub-state identity such as flags and anthems. The Francoists imposed a narrow 'image' of Spain emphasising national unity and condemned all forms of cultural or political diversity. This variant of state nationalism was a reaction to modern ideologies, especially socialism and anarchism, which were held to threaten traditional socio-political structures. As such, Francoism imposed a form of nationalism that was conservative, Catholic, centralist and Castilian as a brake on the modernisation begun in the early decades of the century by the Republic.

The Basque–Catalan contrast[3]

It can be argued that both communities, Catalonia and the Basque Country, were equally discriminated against by an authoritarian regime determined to crush intra-state differences, but the response in the respective communities differed. In Catalonia resistance was altogether less violent than in the Basque Country. The reasons why violence emerged in one community but not in the other can be explained by differences not only between Catalan and Basque nationalism but in the socio-political structures of these societies.

Catalan nationalism manifests a predominantly civic character with a tradition of participating in Spanish politics, whereas Basque culture is altogether more exclusive: there are, for instance, allusions to the uniqueness of the Basque race and blood in the very early formulations of the Basque nationalist doctrine. Sabino Arana promoted the idea of Euskadi (the Basque Country) as a country occupied by a foreign power. The Francoist regime, with its obsession to root out all symbols of Basque culture, merely gave plausibility to Arana's theory of alien occupation. Ideological preferences were also rooted in broader cultural differences. For example, though official language policy proscribed both Catalan and Basque, the number of people who could understand and speak Catalan greatly outnumbered those who could understand and speak Euskera.[4]

The profound social and economic transformations which affected the Basque Country in the 1950s brought an uncontrolled industrial expansion around the main Basque cities and a large inflow of Castilian-speaking immigrants from other parts of Spain. The Castilian language is often referred to as Spanish, a fact that reflects the dominance of Castile over the other peoples of Spain. Meanwhile, both the Basque language and its culture suffered erosion, being confined to ever-smaller circles of native Basques. In Jáuregui's view, this fact encouraged both the rejection of Castilian culture and hostility to immigrants; the presence of a strategic elite of Castilian origin, regarded as an agent of linguistic and cultural oppression, increased native hostility to Castilian-speaking migrants. Linked to this was an underlying fear of wholesale assimilation into mainstream Castilian culture. In short, there was a widespread sense of the Basque Country as a colonised country, and a conviction that all available means should be used to ensure freedom from foreign (Spanish) domination. It was in this context that ETA emerged as a paramilitary organisation embracing a radical nationalism with the clear aim of expelling colonial occupation by the use of force, and replacing it with self-government. ETA understood its role as waging a war of liberation akin to the revolutions in Cuba, Algeria or Angola. According to this rationale, armed struggle was the only available strategy since peaceful dialogue had failed.

The Francoist state responded to ETA's violence by increasing its repressive measures in the Basque Country. This served to enhance Basque national consciousness and to publicise ETA.

The Spanish transition to democracy

The transition to democracy after Franco's death was an attempt by the political class to synchronise Francoist institutions with the requirements of a modern society. A profound dislocation occurred during the 1970s between the social and the political spheres, highlighting the political system's incapacity for resolving the problems of Spanish society. Spain was now no longer a wholly rural country. There were zones of heavy industry in Catalonia and the Basque Country, and a demographic explosion occurred in the Sixties which, together with great internal migrations, led to the growth of urbanisation. Illiteracy substantially decreased from 50% in 1931 to 11% in 1981. Furthermore, the entrenched Catholicism which had been one of the principal pillars of the Francoist regime began an irreversible decline which led, in turn, to the onset of a new secular society. A new middle class emerged, and even some sectors of the bourgeois who had supported Franco demanded reforms. All these changes needed to be seen in the context of a new international political scenario within which Spain would only be fully accepted if it embraced democratic values. The isolation of the Spanish economy persuaded these new sectors to press for Spain's integration into the then European Community. In this context, reforming the political system along democratic lines became the antidote to the country's image as reactionary, underdeveloped and Conservative.

Though Francoism had endorsed significant changes in order to confront social change, it proved incapable of managing a society that had undergone far-reaching transformations since 1939. With unemployment standing at some one million and inflation reaching 30% by 1975, the sheer limitations of Francoist policies had become patently clear.

Dislocation or reform were the options facing Spain after Franco's death in 1975. The political establishment chose reform, but even this option meant a fundamental break with the past. The transition to democracy came from above, leading to an unusual situation: though the Francoist regime had disappeared, its public administration and most of its institutions remained intact. In this context, it has been argued that democratic transition could only succeed from a combination of three distinct factors.[5] First, from the institutional stability provided by the leadership of King Juan Carlos I who unequivocally backed the reforms. Second, a consensus reached between the various political factions over the terms of democratic transition, once the reform agenda had been sanctioned by the Spanish people in the first democratic elections (1977). And finally, the active mobilisation of large sectors of the population in favour of democratisation in stark contrast to the altogether more cautious attitude of significant parts of both the Catholic Church and the Army. A process of disentanglement of what, according to Franco's political last will, was 'tied up and well tied down', reached a turning point in the 1978 referendum when Spaniards ratified the new democratic constitution. It was at this moment that the need to replace a 'culture of resistance' with a 'culture of democracy' emerged.

The national question in the new democratic Spain

The most dangerous legacy of Francoism was the aggravation of the national minorities question, an issue that had been accentuated by the centralism of the regime. After almost forty years of mutual antagonism between the two sides of the Civil War — between outright winners and losers — there was growing pressure for what the Left and some progressive Catholic groups called 'national reconciliation'.

The 1978 Spanish constitution and the consensus between the main political parties emerged from the first democratic elections. The need to obtain support from both Francoist reformists and anti-Francoists generated endless discussions about the constitution and persisting ideological differences contributed to textual imprecision. Nevertheless, the outcome was a constitution that, for the first time in Spanish history, was not the consequence of the exclusive product of one dominant political tendency. Regardless of some limitations, the political model enshrined in the constitution was neither exclusive or divisive, but a model for integration. The extreme conservatism of the Francoist variant of Spanish nationalism was confronted in the 1978 constitution and it led to a double consensus: the transformation of Spain into a democratic state, and recognition of the existence of national minorities.

The Preamble acknowledges the 'will' of the 'Spanish nation to protect all Spaniards and all the peoples of Spain in the exercise of human rights, their cultures and traditions, languages and institutions (*Constitución Española: edición comentada*, Centro de estudios constitucionales, Madrid, 1979). Likewise Article 2, the most controversial in the entire text, reflects an abiding tension between national unity and the pressure to recognise the existence of historic nations such as Catalonia, Galicia and the Basque Country: thus, 'The constitution is founded upon the indissoluble unity of the Spanish nation, the common and indivisible *patria* of all Spaniards, and recognises and guarantees the right to autonomy of the nationalities and regions integrated in it and the solidarity among them.'

The autonomous system

During the Francoist regime, the demand for recognition of national identity and democracy had been central to Catalan and Basque calls for the political transformation of the state. The makers of the constitution devised a model of symmetric decentralisation widely referred to as 'café para todos' (coffee for everyone). Rather than directly responding to Catalan[6] and Basque demands to be recognised as nations within Spain, they preferred a system of seventeen autonomous communities some of which — Catalonia, the Basque Country and Galicia — are historically and culturally distinct, whereas others are artificially created, without any sense of territorial identity, for instance, La Rioja and Madrid. While the 'historical nationalities', Catalonia, the Basque Country and Galicia, were immediately allowed to practice a degree of 'full autonomy', the other regions had to undergo a five-year period of 'restricted autonomy' before doing so. But, once full autonomy has been achieved, the constitution makes no distinction between the communities.

Allowing substantial powers to the historical nationalities had two particular consequences. On the one hand, it fulfilled the nationalist aspirations of Catalans and Basques; on the other, it generated resentment amongst those communities with a restricted devolution.

Regardless of these variations, all communities are similarly structured: each has a regional legislative assembly consisting of a single chamber; deputies are elected on the basis of proportional representation, and the leader of the majority party or coalition usually assumes the Community presidency. The President heads a regional executive — ministers run administrative departments which, for the most part, though not in every case, follow the pattern of central government, depending on how much power is devolved to the respective autonomous community.

In many respects, the Autonomous Governments operate as states with regard to their devolved competencies. The Catalan and Basque governments, for example, provide wide-ranging public services —

education, health, culture, housing, local transport, agriculture. They even control their own autonomous police force which coexists with the Spanish National Police and Guardia Civil. The powers reserved to the central government are as follows: exclusive jurisdiction over defence, the administration of justice, international relations and general economic planning. A Compensation Fund administered by central government allocates special resources to poorer regions and is intended to promote equilibrium and solidarity among all autonomous communities.

Catalan nationalism

These novel arrangements raise some critical questions about the nature of democratic government in the post-Francoist state. How far does regional nationalism pose a threat to the governance of Spain? To what extent does decentralisation make for unstable central government? A brief review of the role of the main Catalan nationalist coalition (CiU), in government since 1980, sheds some light on these issues.

Tension between Catalonia's current place in the Spanish state and the aspiration for greater autonomy lies at the heart of the CiU's nationalist discourse. The coalition has been in power since 1980 with its leader, Jordi Pujol, consecutively re-elected as president on six occasions. The CiU defines Catalonia as a 'nation' in its own right but does not challenge the overarching idea of Spanish unity. The CiU supported the Socialist government (1993–95) in Madrid when it lost its overall parliamentary majority, and is currently backing the Conservative Popular Party which failed to obtain a majority at the 1996 general election, thereby illustrating Pujol's claim that it is quite feasible to be a Catalan nationalist as well as contributing to state governance. The rewards of this policy have helped to sustain the twin-track strategy: support for the PSOE (Spanish Socialist Workers Party), at a time of widespread political corruption, brought a substantial development of the Catalan Statute of Autonomy including the right to retain 15% of the taxes collected in Catalonia. Concessions have also followed the CiU's liaison with the Popular Party. After negotiations, the Catalan Government (Generalitat) managed to increase the percentage of taxes retained in Catalonia to 30%. Decentralisation in Catalonia, far from fostering uncompromising or extreme nationalism, has in fact opened channels for participation that have vastly improved both the Catalan economy and the quality of life in the region.

After twenty years of political decentralisation

The fact remains, however, that after some 20 years of political and administrative autonomy, the aspirations of Catalans and Basques for self-determination are not satisfied. They still desire fully to express their specificity, and to be recognised as nations within Spain. They demand yet more special treatment and show increasing reluctance to accept the 'coffee for everyone' option. A more asymmetrical arrangement, they argue, would better reflect the present Spanish reality. References are made to the recent decentralisation of power in Britain, where Scotland and Wales are being given substantially different degrees of political autonomy to reflect the intensity of their nationalist claims and the resurgence of national identity. This variant of devolution is now referred to as a model for Spain.

Both Catalans and Basques favour the asymmetrical decentralisation of Spain. They want to be recognised as nations within a 'multinational' Spain. This contradicts the 1978 constitution under which devolution to the nationalities and regions has been carried out at different speeds but with the intention that, at the end of the process, there will be no distinction between historical and newly created communities. It is in this sense that the Spanish decentralisation model is defined as symmetrical, and this is precisely what Catalans and Basques oppose. The 1998 Declaration of Barcelona raises this issue, as follows.

In July 1998, the main nationalist parties in Galicia, the Basque Country and Catalonia — the Galician Nationalist Bloc (Bloque Nacionalista Galego or BNG), the Basque Nationalist Party (EAJ-PNV) and the Convergence and Union Coalition (CiU) — signed a joined declaration demanding that Spain be defined as a multi-lingual, multi-cultural and multi-national state. After twenty years of democracy, Spain continues (as they see it) to retain its essentially unitary character and has not yet resolved the national question. In the words of the Declaration: 'During this period we have endured a lack of juridical and political recognition, and even social and cultural recognition of the specificity of our national realities within the Spanish state. This recognition, which if fair and democratic, is absolutely essential in the context of a Europe enmeshed in the process of political and economic re-structuration which in the medium term will involve the redistribution of political power amongst its different layers of government. A Europe whose union should be based upon respect for and the structuring of its different peoples and cultures.' (*Declaració de Barcelona*, BNG, EAJ-PNV, CiU, Barcelona, 1998.)

The principal demand of the nationalist parties which subscribed to the Declaration is for the recognition of Catalonia, Galicia and the Basque country as nations per se rather than merely as regions. We should recall here that, according to the 1978 constitution (Article 2) Spain consists of a single nation containing some 'nationalities and regions', though these entities are never substantively defined. The consequences of recognising the historical nationalities as free nations would be two-fold. It would imply a substantial revision of the constitution which presently acknowledges the existence of a unique Spanish nation. And it involves acceptance of the idea of Spain as a multinational state. The Declaration of Barcelona brought a negative response from the main Spanish political parties, the PP and the PSOE, a rejection which underlined the differences between elites at the centre and those in the regions.

Devolution to non-historical nationalities and regions

From the perspective of the mainstream Spanish political parties, one can quite understand the reluctance to concede too much autonomy from the centre to some regions to the detriment of others. The historical nationalities, however, see things altogether differently. How then should we evaluate the trend to political decentralisation from the perspective of the newly created autonomous communities, most of whom have a limited, even non-existent, sense of common regional identity? Three main aspects need to be considered here.

1. The creation of political autonomous institutions has added to the dynamism of civil society, generating a sense of common regional identity where it did not previously exist, and strengthening it where it was never more than a feeble idea. Devolution has contributed to the generation of regional identity amongst the people of various communities, with their own flags, anthems, and the promotion of folklore, cultural traditions and regional art. But while some of these elements originate in the local cultures now integrated within the boundaries of the autonomous community, others are the product of invention. Whether indigenous or invented, cultural distinctiveness both generates and strengthens the collective identities of each autonomous community. It is possible then to claim that the devolution of power — and with it, the creation of regional institutions corresponding to autonomous communities without previous historical or cultural identities — is likely to lead to the emergence and, thereafter, the strengthening of separate regional identities. Nowhere more so than for Spain's historical nationalities where there is a clear connection between past and present experiences of autonomous institutions, law and a separate political and cultural identity that accounts for the sheer force of nationalist feelings. Max Weber reminds us that shared political memories are elemental in the construction of a common national or ethnic identity, which are more than likely to persist for long periods after these communities have lost their political independence.[7]

2. Political decentralisation tends to strengthen democracy in as much as it brings decision-making closer to the people. Problems are identified, analysed and resolved where they emerge. Regional politicians usually have greater awareness of the needs and aspirations of their electorates, and the following table reflects the high percentage of Spanish people in favour of decentralisation. It also shows a greater number of people in Catalonia in favour of transferring further powers to the communities when compared

Opinion Poll: What political structure for the Spanish state do you favour?

	Spain (%)	Catalan (%)
Centralised state without autonomous communities	16	10.2
Autonomous communities (present arrangement)	44	35.5
Further devolved powers to autonomous communities	21	29.0
Right of secession to autonomous communities	8	20.9

Source: Centro de Investigaciones Sociológicas (CIS), La Vanguardia, 16 February 1997, p. 21.

with the rest of Spain. It is also striking that while over a fifth of Catalans favour granting the right to secession to Autonomous Communities, less than a tenth favour it in the rest of Spain (see Table).

3. The devolution of powers to regional institutions requires the re-allocation of resources to facilitate discrete policies and regional budget planning. These processes, in turn, contribute to revitalising civil society, encouraging local and regional initiatives including cultural, economic and social projects. Among other endeavours, autonomous communities are promoting regional businesses, restoring ancient buildings and creating regional cultural networks such as universities, museums and libraries. Some 20 years after the creation of the Autonomous Communities System, the particular national identities of Catalonia, Basque country and Galicia have been considerably reinforced through the promotion of their languages and culture together with the development of social and economic policies to improve the quality of regional life. None of this is necessarily inconsistent with sustaining an overall Spanish political identity. In Galicia, for instance, the conservative Popular Party has remained in government throughout the period of regional autonomy. Ironically, the new regionalism has been encouraged by Manuel Fraga Iribarne, president of Galicia but formerly a minister under Franco. Galician nationalism was virtually non-existent when the autonomous government was established, but it has registered a substantial increase in support, the Galician Nationalist Bloc (BNG) becoming the main opposition to the Popular Party. The nationalist parties which have ruled both Catalonia (CiU) and the Basque region (EAJ-PNV) since the onset of autonomous government, whilst defining themselves as nationalist, do not pursue secession from Spain but a greater autonomy within the current devolved framework.

After considering the likely impact of the Declaration of Barcelona on the shape of the Spanish state and the temper of nationalist politics, we may ask whether the nationalist discourse of these regional parties fully meets the aspirations of Catalans and Basques. We might include, too, Galicians in this political calculus. In short, are these newly assertive regional identities likely to settle for the status quo; or are they representatives of a transitional nationalism which will eventually seek full independence? The experience of Belgium and Canada might be

instructive in this regard: two federal and democratic states that have
been obliged to grant a substantial degree of autonomy to the provinces
of Flanders and Quebec, though this has not satisfied nationalist
demands for even greater self-determination. Does it mean that nationalist claims can only be satisfied by achieving independence? Once the
Statutes of Autonomy of Catalonia, the Basque country and Galicia are
fully developed, will their citizens be satisfied or will they regard
autonomy as a step towards independence?

Conclusions

Notwithstanding current criticism of the autonomous system, it has
permitted the peaceful accommodation of substate nationalism during
the Spanish transition to democracy. Even so, decentralisation has not
been without residual conflict and continuing tension between the
regional and central governments. The demand, for instance, that
additional resources and more powers should be allocated to the
autonomous institutions has characterised most of the relations between
the Generalitat — the Catalan government — and the central government
in Madrid. Conflict has arisen particularly over the nature of taxes to
be collected in Catalonia — whether these revenues should be retained
as own resources by the Generalitat rather than having them re-
allocated by Madrid.

Conflict has arisen, too, over the sensitive issue of language rights.
Laws concerning the use and promotion of the Catalan language issued
by the Generalitat were challenged by the central government and
examined by the Spanish Constitutional Court (Tribunal Constitutional) which subsequently ratified their constitutionality. Tension
arose, too, when some autonomous communities complained about
what they perceive to be better treatment by the state of the historical
communities.

A major consequence of Spanish decentralisation has been the redefinition of Spanish identity as a result of the strengthening not only of
Catalan, Basque and Galician identities but also of other emergent
regional identities in the so-called non historical communities. In the
new democracy, the state has played a creative role in mediating
between regional and Spanish identities. The process is by no means
completed. The definition of Spain will continue to be examined and
reformulated in the light of current and future experience.

The power structure of the Francoist state imposed its own constructed image of Spain, persuading local communities, if necessary by
force, to adjust to it, at least in their public life. This cultural hegemony
is now finally over and contemporary Spanish identity has to be
redefined in accordance with prevailing conditions; it has to reflect the
aspirations and new-found political confidence of its constituent
nations. At the same time, these nations are struggling to recover and
develop in accordance with their particular identities long suppressed

under the Franco regime. What is at stake here is the very definition of Spain as a nation and as a culture. By redefining themselves as nations per se, Catalonia, the Basque Country and Galicia have challenged the homogeneous image of Spain as this was expressed both by Francoism and, indeed, by an influential tendency within Spanish socialism, heavily influenced by the universalist, cosmopolitan variant of state nationalism championed by the French Jacobin tradition. As such, these radical elements share with their conservative opponents much the same antagonism to substate autonomy as conceded to Catalonia and the Basque country and they remain critical of further demands to expand its scope.

The new democratic regime allows for multi-level government located in central, regional and local institutions and devolution has contributed more than institutional variety to Spain's democratic culture. It has encouraged the emergence and strengthening of different layers of identity and, as such, has made it possible for many to hold multiple identities: to define themselves as both Spanish and as Catalan or Basque. This related outcome does not, of course, apply to those separatists who still seek Catalan or Basque independence.[8] The two layers of identity are further complemented by an extra layer of identity stemming from membership of the European Union.

In summary, decentralisation has indeed reinforced regional national identity but, so far, it has not encouraged the emergence of large pro-independence movements in Catalonia, the Basque country and Galicia. At the same time, the 'non historical' autonomous communities have benefitted from a decentralisation process which has generated a clear separate sense of regional identity. That too has contributed to the development of civil society and has brought decision making mechanisms closer to the people.

1 For an analysis of the process of industrialisation in Catalonia, see P. Vilar, *La Catalogne dans l'Espagne Moderne*, Flammarion, 1977. For an analysis of contemporary Catalonia see, S. Giner (ed), *La Societat Catalana*, Institut d'Estadística de Catalunya, 1998; and S. Giner, *The Social Structure of Catalonia*, Anglo Catalan Society, 1984.

2 According to Conversi, 'although the *Fueros* were slowly eroded, before their abolition the señorío ("seigniory") of Bizkaia was working as a state within the Spanish state, and was even expanding its powers (Agirreazkuenaga, 1987)'. D. Conversi,. *The Basques, the Catalans and Spain: Alternative Routes to Nationalist Mobilization*, Hurst & Company, 1997, p. 45.

3 For an analysis of nationalism in nations without state in the West which includes Catalonia and Basque Country among others, see M. Guibernau, *Nations Without States: Political Communities in the Global Age*, Polity Press, 1999.

4 See A. Gurrutxaga, *El Código Nacionalista vasco durante el Franquisom*, Anthropos, 1985 and A. Pérez-Agote, *El Nacionalismo vasco a la Salida del Franquismo*, C.I.S. Ediciones Siglo XXI, 1987.

5 J. Solé Tura, *Nacionalidades y Nacionalismos en España: Autonomía, Federalismo, Autodeterminación*, Alianza Editorial, 1985, p. 80.

6 For an analysis of Catalan nationalism during the Spanish transformation to democracy see, M. Guibernau, 'Images of Catalonia' in *Nations and Nationalism*, 3, 1, 1997, pp. 89–111. See also T. Lawlor and M. Rigby et al, *Contemporary Spain*, Longman, 1998.

7 M. Weber, *Economy and Society*, University of California Press, 1978 (1968), 1, p. 389.

8 In Catalonia, 11.5% of the population define themselves as more Spanish than Catalan; 36.5% as Spanish as Catalan; 25.7% more Catalan than Spanish. Those who define themselves as only Catalan

represent 11% and 12.9% define themselves as only Spanish. In the Basque country, 43.6% is in favour of independence and 32.2% against it. About 25% do not answer. In Catalonia, 33.6% are in favour of independence and 50% against it. See Centro de Investigaciones Sociológicas, *La Vanguardia*, 16 February 1997. See also ICPS, *Sondeig d'opinió Catalunya*, vols 1989–95.

Great Britain: From Dicey to Devolution

BY MICHAEL O'NEILL

> Should auld acquaintance be forgot,
> And never brought to mind?

Nation-building and democracy in Britain grew within a unitary state administratively and politically managed from the centre. The Union of the kingdoms of Scotland and England (1707), the formal annexation of Wales (in 1536) and the colonising of Ireland (a Union of Parliaments occurred in 1801) consolidated the union state. Political legitimacy was vested in institutions whose writ ran throughout the kingdom. Political power, fiscal control and legal supremacy remained with Parliament, underpinned by indivisible sovereignty, famously captured in Blackstone's pronouncement (1765) that 'what the parliament doth, no authority upon earth can undo'.[1] These arrangements were embedded in an all-embracing national identity, with regional elites assimilated into a metropolitan political culture.

The classical discourse on the British constitution reflects the political task of managing a plural polity — not by means of the federal architecture preferred by political elites in more fractured polities, but rather by acknowledging constituent nationalities within the fabric of the union state. Among the Victorian eminences who addressed this issue, Acton recommended moral equivalence between those 'different nations (residing) under the same sovereignty', precluding 'the servility which flourishes under the shadow of a single authority, by balancing interests (and) multiplying associations'. Rather than subjugation of minority cultures, the British genius for liberty 'provokes diversity, and diversity preserves liberty', so that 'the combination of different nations in one State is as necessary a condition of civilised life as the combination of men in society'.[2] This pluralist outlook did not, however, comply with the temper of the times. More influential by far was Dicey's summary dismissal of cultural diversity as a basis for efficient governance, because it undermined parliamentary sovereignty and deprived 'English' institutions 'of their strength, and their life; it weakens the Executive at home and lessens the power of the country to resist foreign attack'.[3] This Anglo-centric outlook, betraying a self-regarding account of history, and of governance as centralised authority, set the standard for succeeding generations.

© Oxford University Press

Managing territorial interests in a Union state

Some account was taken of historically rooted interests, though Gladstone's famous reference to 'local patriotism' reflects the preference of even a liberally inclined elite for a union state. Administrative adjustment to local identity was restrained, sufficient merely to subdue feelings of neglect or alienation on the margins. Public expenditure illustrates the point, being higher by some 20% per capita in Scotland than England. The minority nations were bound to the United Kingdom by a formula guaranteeing fiscal largesse greater than was justified merely by demography.

The electoral and party systems similarly reinforced British identity, ensuring that national politics was dominated by class-based parties. Each was committed, in some degree, to centralised macro-economic management and eventually to some redistribution of wealth through the mechanism of a welfare state organised on the principle of universal benefits. There was acknowledgement of territorial identity, too, in the arrangements of government. Scotland's history as an independent kingdom and the voluntary union of the crowns in 1603 ensured both a stronger residual identity and warranted greater political autonomy. There were distinct legal, local government and education systems, it had its own banknotes, a national press and an established Church. The distribution of parliamentary seats also favoured the territorial nations, Scotland being proportionately over-represented, seats to population share, by some 20%.

Administrative arrangements eventually followed suit with a Scottish Office and a Scottish Secretary instituted in 1885 (acquiring full Cabinet rank in 1926), though acting more as London's viceroy than Scotland's consul: exercising extensive competencies over health, police and judicial affairs, prisons, and regional development. Judicial autonomy required a separate passage of legislation when pertaining solely to Scotland, with a standing Scottish Grand Committee (1907) to steer it through Parliament. A Scottish Affairs Select Committee was added in 1979 as part of UK wide administrative reforms, rationalised by London, in response to nationalist stirrings, as proof positive of the special 'Scottish dimension' of British government.

These concessions to Scottish identity, such as they were, seemed to work, in as much as Scotland retained something of the illusion of a separate if constituent part of the union state. Popular support for a nascent nationalist movement was scant. Although two nationalist parties did emerge during the 1930s, merging as the Scottish National Party (SNP) in 1934, its appeal was largely confined to urban elites. In so far as the impression of a centre-periphery cleavage injected a radical temper into Scottish politics, it was mostly channelled into a narrative of class politics. Nationalism as a political movement capable of mass rather than marginal appeal took root only during the 1960s as a belated response to perceived neglect but revealing, too, of a pervasive uncertainty about relations with England. Equivocation was a reaction to a changing landscape by interests which had once embraced 'North British' status as a route to opportunity, in politics, commerce, the military and, not least, the Empire. Grafitto scratched into the covenanters' monument in Dreghorn bespeaks ambiguous relations with England:

> If Brother Bull complacently maintain
> Union secured us clear and wholesale gain
> Softly demurring we yet grudge him not
> Haply more gain by equal link with Scot.[4]

The sense of displacement that accompanied the loss of these prospects, together with cultural grievance over a displaced vernacular language and other discriminations by the centre, were increased by rising insecurities as the certainties of great power status, imperial grandeur, and economic security dissolved in a mutable postwar world. Change, and the apprehension it fostered, provided the catalyst for rethinking a Union barely questioned on its geographical margins for more than two centuries.

Affairs in Wales were a paler reflection of Scotland's experience of the Union. Longstanding English domination of affairs ensured an ambivalent identity. After its forced absorption into the English state, Wales did not enjoy civic institutions of its own. The use of English law precluded either special legislative or administrative status. The management of territorial affairs followed the union state model, balancing primary commitment to the integrity of the British state with special if limited territorial provisions: an advisory council (1948); a Welsh Grand Committee for debating Welsh concerns (1960) with full standing committee status (1969); a Welsh Office (1964); a Welsh Affairs Select Committee (1979); and territorial over-representation in Parliament by some 17% on the seats-population ratio.[5] Concessions to territorial integrity, notwithstanding, 'Welshness' was primarily expressed in cultural terms, through the demand for official recognition of an ancient language. As in Scotland, the dominant political narrative was rooted in class rather than territorial politics. A nationalist party, Plaid Cymru, was launched in 1924, to vent political grievances similar to those voiced by its Scottish equivalent. In spite of a reasonable showing at the 1970 general election (11.5% of the Welsh vote) Plaid failed to make significant headway and remains, regardless of recent successes in the Welsh Assembly elections, a more peripheral factor in Welsh politics than the SNP. Plaid has built only a modest support base in local government and in a handful of constituencies concentrated in Welsh-speaking counties.

Politicising territorial identity

Home rule was periodically championed by the Liberal and Labour parties, primarily as a solution to the crisis in Ireland, conferring self-government without breaking the Union. Constitutional reform became an issue in Britain for similar but not identical reasons. Political identity per se was less the root cause of territorial unrest than misgivings during the 1960s about the supposedly inequitable impact of national economic decline. The economic downturn was by no means confined to Scotland and Wales, but it did hit hard those heavy industries on which their economies had traditionally depended. Even so, the discourse on national decline was more readily expressed in the familiar narrative of class politics.

There were signs that nationalism was making inroads into Scottish and Welsh politics more as a protest than a serious challenge to the status quo: in 1966 Plaid won a famous by-election victory at Carmarthen, followed by the SNP at Hamilton in 1967. The discovery of large reserves of North Sea oil in 1971 utterly changed the terms of engagement between unionism and territorial nationalism, adding material incentive to the claim to independence that previously had seemed fanciful. In 1974, the SNP offered serious challenge to Labour dominance, taking almost a third of the Scottish vote in the October election and securing 11 Westminster seats. It was the best performance by an ethnic party since 1945. Plaid made rather less impact, but increased its vote sharply in 1974 to 11%, giving it three seats. Reflection on the state of the Union challenged complacency as the establishment confronted unprecedented difficulties. Concern to improve all-round national efficiency had already raised the issue of constitutional reform. The Kilbrandon Report (1973) on the Constitution, appointed by a reform-minded Labour government in 1968, was a signal event, proposing qualified devolution to directly elected Scottish and Welsh assemblies, though only recommending 'advisory' councils for the English regions. Kilbrandon's proposal for asymmetrical devolution set the pattern for future reform of the Kingdom.[6]

The Conservative government, preoccupied by a broader agenda that included negotiating European Community membership and facing down industrial militancy, discounted constitutional reform. It followed its unionist instincts by settling instead for reforming local government. A new Labour government (1974), also confronted by persistent industrial unrest and financial crisis, likewise reverted to ideological type, favouring its longstanding centralist project. Events however pressed hard, encouraging constitutional experimentation, not (it must be said) out of concern for shoring up the Union per se but from political self-interest. Electoral ground lost to the nationalist parties in its electoral heartlands persuaded Labour to embrace devolution, initially in the teeth of stiff opposition within its own ranks from assorted socialist centralists, resentful Scottish party loyalists, principled unionists and plain English xenophobes. And what was offered to Scotland could not reasonably be denied to the other historic British nation.

Separate devolution Bills for Scotland and Wales (1978), subsequently combined in a Scotland and Wales Bill (1979), proposed greater home rule for Scotland than Wales. There were to be directly elected assemblies in both countries by first-past-the-post (1978), some legislative competence and executive discretion for Scotland over devolved Scottish Office functions (local government, social policy and infrastructural matters), but only local government-style committees in Wales. Neither assembly was to have fiscal competence. The Secretaries of State, likewise, retained formidable powers. Westminster's sovereignty was underlined by retention of the prerogative to legislate on any devolved matter. The judicial committee of the Privy Council would arbitrate in any dispute between the centre and the territories. Moreover, a rider to the 1979 legislation, the Cunningham Amendment, required that the legislation pass a 40% threshold of *all* registered voters in the subsequent referenda. Neither bill cleared that hurdle. A bare majority was in favour in Scotland, but in Wales the margin was almost four to one against devolution.

The devolution episode, seen from the perspective of the early 1980s, seemed to be little more than a cursory footnote in the uninterrupted history of the union state. Events appeared to have moved on from the perplexed mood of the previous decade. Conviction politics was riding high, and with it an appetite for national hauteur, reflected in the Falklands war. The Thatcherite years seemingly put paid to constitutional experiment. Motivated by a blend of strident British nationalism and a neo-liberal agenda, Thatcherism set about harnessing the machinery of the state to a supply-side, business-led offensive against the postwar bipartisan settlement. As such, subnational identity was discounted as misplaced sentimentality, an obsolescent provincialism, and devolution was staunchly resisted as another tier added to already overblown bureaucracy.

Reaction to rising nationalism saw a reversion to the tried and tested strategy of national assimilation. The Conservative government sought to reconcile economically self-excluded regions of the Union with a mainstream enterprise culture. For its part, Labour too abandoned its commitment to constitutional reform. Its 1979 defeat relaxed some of the political pressure for change. Whereas the party's lurch to the left — an instinctive reaction both to defeat and to Thatcherism — saw a reversion instead to a convenient ideological prescription which explained territorial nationalism as a class reflex by the economically deprived, socially disadvantaged periphery against the beneficiaries of the core economy. Even heavier defeat in 1983 changed the terms of ideological engagement. As Thatcherism moved sharply rightwards, Labour opted for a pragmatic leadership, revisiting constitutional reform as the nationalist vote rose sharply in Scotland in response to Labour's failure to keep the new right at bay. Nationalism's challenge was now less a protest vote against a governing party than an attempt to displace Labour as the focus of territorial opposition to the Conservatives' drastic cutbacks in social policy expenditure and retrenchment of public sector investment. The decision to impose the new community charge or 'poll tax' in Scotland, a year ahead of England, was seen as a mark, not merely of Conservative indifference to Scotland, but of Labour's inability to defend Scottish interests at Westminster. Another defeat in 1987 confirmed Labour's apparent impotence in the face of continued endorsement of Thatcherism by a majority of English constituencies. Support for nationalist parties increased thereafter, and more sharply in Scotland than in Wales.

The 1980s watershed

By 1987 Labour, unable to restore a substantial electoral presence in middle-England, became more dependent than at any time since 1945 on its Scottish and Welsh seats. It was therefore increasingly sensitive to political forces threatening its tenure therein. Meanwhile, the Conservatives, reduced to only 24% and ten seats in Scotland and seven seats in Wales, were losing their once sure foothold in Celtic Britain. It was now in danger of becoming an English more than a British party.

A territorial axis had acquired salience in mainstream British politics. The dynamics of the party systems of Scotland and Wales had been diverging from that in England over more than two decades. Thereafter, the principal cleavage of party competition was to revolve around a territorial axis, with nationalist parties seeking to mobilise support for a distinctive provincial agenda against traditional British parties. Devolution has been Labour's response to this unprecedented challenge, with much prompting from opinion favourable to home rule in preference to the blind bargain of outright independence demanded by resurgent nationalists.

The Campaign for a Scottish Assembly (CSA) — a coalition of interests drawn from civil society, churches, trades unions, environmentalists, academia, business, and so on — set up a committee of 'prominent' Scots, whose Claim of Right for Scotland (a latter-day Declaration of Arbroath) demanded a parliament with real powers.[7]

The response from the centre was indifference. Regionalism figured in official policy as little more than a strategy for improving macroeconomic management and had nothing whatsoever to do with acknowledging ethnic identity. Objectives such as enhanced indicative planning, increased inward investment, better land use, improved economic development, reorganised transport, efficient resource allocation and scale economies, were the primary foci of Conservative policy, and all were entirely consistent with the Thatcherite project of national regeneration. The only concession to subnational governance was again local government reform. Rather than increasing bureaucracy, rolling back the state was official policy. It meant divesting cumbrous public bodies of traditional functions and reallocating them amongst stream-lined non-democratic agencies such as government regional offices and quangos. It was reform of sorts, but by no means inconsistent with concentrating power at the centre and, as such, an ill-judged response to fast-changing politics.

A mellowing in tone, if not a change of style, replaced unalloyed centrism in the shape of the Major government's strategy of a 'compensating unionism'.[8] Acknowledgement that territorial dissatisfaction, if left unchecked, could damage the constitutional fabric saw belated initiatives to stem the nationalist tide. Government emphasised the positive benefits of the Union, a guaranteed territorial voice at the centre of national affairs and in the management of public policy through the medium of the Scottish Office and parliamentary representation. There was to be representation in wider European Union councils, Scottish ministers attending Council meetings, and local government representatives sitting in the new Committee of the Regions.

A concerted effort to turn the tide now running for home rule saw a Secretary of State, cast in the Thatcherite mould but of Scottish progeny, tackle the Scottish question on two fronts: on the one hand, ploughing on with privatisation and deregulation measures that confronted, head-on, Scotland's deep-seated collectivist instincts and public sector preferences; on the other hand, addressing with similar ideological zeal Scotland's apparent shortcomings in the global market place, by setting up non-elected quangos, notably the Scottish Economic Council to review training, infrastructure and competitiveness.

There was a limited constitutional dimension to this strategy which included changes in the conduct of Scottish business in the Whitehall–Westminster nexus expressly designed to answer, short of home rule, territorial grievances over putative neglect. Local government acquired increased discretion. The Scottish Office gained additional administrative competencies: in industrial support, further and higher education, care in the community, the Scottish Arts Council, and responsibility for supervising European Social Fund expenditure. The Scottish Grand Committee was likewise empowered to hold debates on third as well as second readings. Cabinet ministers, including the Prime Minister rather than just the Scottish Secretary, were permitted, indeed encouraged, to attend its meetings, to put motions and reply to questions, though not to vote. Its powers and the frequency of its sittings were increased, thereby extending parliamentary scrutiny of Scottish bills, with more opportunity for informed debate. Enhanced opportunities for questioning the Secretary of State in the Committee amounted, in effect, to 'the creation of a mini House of Commons for Scotland within the orbit of the UK Parliament'.[9] Arrangements were made to hold special standing committees of Scottish bills in Scotland, and to make a concerted effort to bring the Scottish Office closer to the people by holding its meetings throughout the country and setting up information points in key urban centres.

These reforms did increase the time available for, and enhanced the representation of Scottish interests both in the conduct of parliamentary affairs and the management of government business. But events north of the border moved faster than the government's ability, let alone its readiness, to keep up with them. After years of apparent indifference by London, territorial identity had acquired political momentum. The mindset of Scotland, and to a lesser degree in Wales, had irrevocably shifted. There was now resistance to gesture politics and to cosmetic attempts to flatter but not assuage territorial sensibilities. The return of Scotland's ancient coronation stone, along with more substantial administrative changes, were too little and too late. The SNP polled a remarkable 21.4% of the Scottish vote in the 1992 general election, a mere four points behind the Conservatives, and came a close second to Labour in the 1994 local government elections.

The debate on home rule in Wales mirrored that in Scotland, but moved at its own pace and had its own flavour. There was less support for devolution, reflecting deep ambivalence about political identity. There was more success, too, in view of the closer integration of Wales with England, for the Conservatives' assimilation strategy. Circumstances helped to abate the appeal of home rule, with successive Welsh Secretaries moderating the worst excesses of Thatcherite modernisation by securing symbolic concessions for cultural distinctiveness: notably, a Welsh Language Board and a Welsh Development Agency.

These achievements notwithstanding, friction between those imbued with collectivist values, and a government driven by unalloyed faith in the market, invariably raised the tempo of territorial politics.[10] The arrival of John Redwood, a Thatcher zealot, at the Welsh Office served only to emphasise the deep lacuna in empathy, the lack of common ground, between central government and the provincial establishment. Gratuitous insults, studied indifference to local sensibilities — most notably a refusal to sign any official documents written in Welsh or to implement reform of the Welsh Grand Committee agreed by his predecessor — were all compounded by a vice-regal demeanour. Nationalist sensibilities were offended to the point where even the solicitous attentions and civility of his successor, William Hague, failed to allay them.

By the beginning of the 1990s the Labour parties of both Scotland and Wales were ready to embrace home rule, not as was the case in the 1970s as merely a strategy for outflanking a nationalism threatening separatism, but as a response to political realities closer to home.[11] The realisation dawned on party managers that anything less than a spectacularly good election result would leave Labour heavily dependent on its Celtic support base. How then were they to diminish the appeal of out-and-out territorial nationalism amongst this important constituency? And how, too, could they reconfigure the constitution so that even in the dog days of extended opposition Labour politicians might still exert some influence over public policy?

A start was made by launching a cross-party Scottish Constitutional Convention on devolution. Ideological movement also confirmed the reform trajectory. By 1992 Labour was prepared to jettison excess ideological baggage and rethink its radical mission. It was now more favourable to post-modern notions of community politics, cultural pluralism and democratic empowerment. 'New Labour' broke with its own centralist past and embraced devolution for principled as well as for pragmatic reasons. When Labour returned to office with a record majority in 1997, constitutional reform became a legislative priority.

External factors, too, have facilitated political change. Reorganisation of the EU's structural funds (1988 and 1992) to ensure some compensation for peripheral regions outwith the mainstream of Single Market expansion, favours member states with a concerted regional strategy. The European Union offers a fiscal inducement, and provides an increasingly important institutional arena, for regional interests. Multi-level governance encourages regions to operate on their own initiative, above as much as within member states, with inducements to participate in trans-European networks, to liaise directly in the Committee of the Regions, and to work directly with the Commission.

The formal acknowledgement of the subsidiarity principle in the Maastricht treaty—that power should be exercised at the lowest possible level compatible with effective use of resources—has confirmed a political trend away from centralised power in Britain as elsewhere in the Continent. Awareness of the enhanced opportunities for prosecuting regional interests beyond the nation state has done much to increase the credibility of Britain's nationalist movements. The SNP's adoption of the slogan 'Scotland—independent in Europe' is a testament to new-found confidence in separatism as a viable option. Britain's political leaders have been obliged to respond to this challenge.

Reforming the British state: the Scotland and Wales Acts 1997

Reform of an outmoded constitution was central to the New Labour project, but the party was careful to reaffirm the integrity of the union state. The Prime Minister, concerned not to alienate new-found voters in middle England with a too radical prospectus, and just as wary of devolving tax-raising powers that might alienate Labour voters in Scotland, added a second referendum question on this matter. The latest devolution reforms proposed in the Scotland and Wales Acts (1997) reiterate most of the elements of the 1979 proposals, extending them to reflect significantly increased support for change.

Legitimating reform. Both Acts were approved in referendums in September 1998, but only by the barest of margins in Wales (50.3 to 49.7%) on a low turnout of 51.3% — in effect, by fewer than seven thousand votes in 1,112,117. It was hardly a ringing endorsement and revealed doubts about the value of even limited home rule. It brought evidence, too, of a problematic Welsh identity. The figures confirmed the differential appeal of a Welsh polity. The long-held assumption that home rule was more appealing to the Welsh-speaking north than the English-speaking south was evident from the referendum returns, but in fact the picture was altogether mixed. Despite the distorting effect of low turnout, there is a positive correlation between strong cultural identity and support for home rule, more reticence about devolution in areas with a higher proportion of English-born voters, and clear division between east and west Wales, reflecting correspondence between resistance to constitutional change and cultural-cum-geographical proximity to England.

With their embedded sense of ethnic nationality, regardless of ideology, social class, religious affiliation, or geographical location, Scottish voters exhibited less circumspection. They endorsed devolution by a three to one majority (74.3 to 25.7% in favour, with 63.5 to 36.5% in favour of the new parliament's tax raising powers) from a much higher turnout (63.5%), far exceeding the slender 33/32% margin in favour in 1979. All 32 voting regions endorsed the parliament with only two, Dumfries and Galloway and Orkney, voting marginally against tax-raising powers.

The principal features of the current devolution arrangements are as follows.

Asymmetry. Devolution is variable, an untidy, asymmetrical constitutional architecture, reflecting differences of both history and political aspirations between the constituent polities that make up the UK. Scotland, and for that matter Northern Ireland under the terms of the Stormont Agreement, enjoy greater self-government (similar as to Bavaria's semi-autonomous status within Germany's cooperative federalism) than Wales (which enjoys rather more self-government than a French regional council, though less than for any Spanish comunidade autonomas). The English regions are presently denied devolved status.

Political rhetoric in Scotland refers to home rule as restoring an 'ancient right', a claim now embodied in a full-fledged parliament with wider powers than those of the Welsh Assembly. An altogether more ambivalent political identity in Wales has been satisfied so far with enhanced regional status: in the words of a *Financial Times* commentary in July 1999, 'bringing Whitehall to Wales and making it more accessible'. The former Welsh Secretary referred to an 'all but inseparable' status in relation to England, betokening the lack of sure identity and political self-confidence which has sustained Scottish or Irish national-ism. Home Rule is less about maximisng territorial autonomy than ensuring Welsh interests are heard on their own terms after years of unremitting centralisation by the Welsh Office and a plethora of non-elected 'quangos', estimated by 1997 at some 120 in number. Neverthe-less, this is not the end of the matter. For asymmetrical arrangements do invite less autonomous polities to catch-up the pace-setters as circumstances and aspirations change. Scotland's wider devolution is invidious to committed Welsh nationalists. It offers an incentive to emulate its neighbour, as and when public opinion feels ready to close the gap.

Asymmetrical architecture is difficult to manage in a polity used to a single uniform regime, but it is by no means as weak as critics aver. There is strength in flexibility as much as there is jeopardy in clinging to an unduly rigid formula in any state embarked on reform. Any constitutional arrangement where there is power-sharing between dis-crete levels of governance depends both on constant vigilance by the central authorities and mutual goodwill to sustain the bargain.

Cooperative inter-governmentalism. British devolution does not con-form to the neat separation of powers usually found in formal federal-ism. Rather than ceding outright authority, central government accommodates territorial interests, agreeing to share its competencies in a restricted list of legislative and administrative matters. Boundary disputes are certain to arise in these areas of concurrent or overlapping power. Again, there is nothing untoward in this, though a culture of common sense inter-governmental cooperation is indispensable if these conflicts of interpretation are to be contained, let alone resolved.

There is scope for contested jurisdiction: in Scotland, because of the very extent of legislative autonomy and even quite modest fiscal com-petence, and in Wales, paradoxically, because of closer fusion of the Assembly's authority with that of Westminster underpinned by a com-mon legal base. The 1997 Act shares responsibility for all legislation between Westminster and the Welsh Assembly: Westminster passing primary legislation, the Assembly providing the secondary legislation. A less febrile nationalism and the more remote prospect of a nationalist administration in Cardiff suggests rather better prospects for resolving such disputes.

The balance of power between the centre and the territorial authori-ties depends as much on events as constitutional formalities, on how these arrangements actually work out in practice. Westminster retains an interest, not only in those policy areas devolved to the territorial governments, but also continues to exercise de jure power, subject to the usual exigencies of practical politics. Public policy decided at Westminster for England in devolved matters is bound to impact on the arrangements in these same areas in Scotland and Wales. This is a usual outcome of inter-governmental relations in other devolved, and even quasi or fully fledged federal systems. The legal requirement for central government to implement European Union policy directives and regulations, as well as similar obligations under international treaties, also makes for awkward relations. The territorial governments' limited fiscal autonomy means that even their devolved policies cannot significantly vary from those devised by central government for England. The fact that Scottish and Welsh civil servants remain ultimately answerable to the UK civil service further confirms the central government's dominant role in national policy.

Bold predictions about the eventual balance of power, or the temper of relations between central and territorial governments, are bound to be wide of the mark. Politics is contingent, driven by events. What is clear so far is that the UK is embarking on the volatile politics familiar in every polity with some devolution. Outcomes will depend on the capacity of elites at every level to construct procedures and adopt habits that make cooperation rather than conflict the prevailing standard of inter-governmental relations. There is a new political culture to be learned by all sides.

Institutions. The principal institutions are as follows. A four-year fixed-term Parliament for Scotland with 129 seats — 73 members to be elected in single-member constituencies (first-past-the-post) for constituencies based on the present Westminster boundaries, with a further 56 'top up' members elected by the additional member system: seven each from eight regional lists based on the current Euro-constituencies to ensure that representation is as proportional as possible to the total share of the vote for each party. In Wales a 60-member Assembly is elected by the same hybrid system: 40 directly from existing Westminster constituencies, with 20 from regional lists controlled by the parties. Executives are appointed by the First Ministers (the leaders of the predominant parties) of each legislature. Proportionality in elections means that power-sharing is the most likely outcome. The inaugural elections of both bodies produced a formal coalition in Scotland and an informal inter-party arrangement in Wales. In both cases there was an exclusion of the nationalist parties.

Constitutional limits to self-determination are built into both systems. Responsibility for framing the rules and procedures of elections remains with Westminster, a markedly different arrangement to the degree of autonomy enjoyed on these same matters by constituent polities in federalism.

Legislative competencies. The territorial legislatures exercise jurisdiction over some aspects of public policy previously reserved to Westminster. The Scotland Act seeks to limit the potential for future disputation on contested jurisdictions by avoiding a definitive list of devolved powers that might tempt nationalists, looking for a symbolic fight with London, to challenge rigid boundaries. The preferred approach is to emphasise continuity of governance, underlining the primacy of the union state in the crucial aspects of 'high politics' by reiterating Westminster's reserve powers in the following matters: constitutional issues and defence and foreign affairs, albeit with Scottish ministers accompanying their UK counterparts to European councils when matters relating to devolved competencies are to be discussed, with an a priori bargaining position agreed, as it is between the German *Laender* and the Belgian regions and their national ministries. Although, under British devolution, this is not a right formally entrenched in statute.

The centre likewise decides taxation (though Scotland's Parliament has the right to levy an additional 'top up' income tax of up to three pence in the pound), company regulation (with the express aim of avoiding undue distortion of Britain's internal market in goods, services and manpower), macro-economic management, fiscal policy, and social security policy. All other matters — including health, education (schools and universities), local government, housing, social policy, law and order/criminal justice matters, transport, fisheries, food standards, trade and exports, sport and the arts, forestry — are devolved, with a budget of some £14 billions per annum available for the parliament/ executive to spend on them as it sees fit.

A more limited devolution to the Welsh Assembly, and a smaller annual budget allocation of £7 billions, makes for less problematical relations between centre and periphery. The devolved areas include economic development, agriculture, fisheries and food, industry and training, transportation and roads, the arts, culture and the Welsh language, recreation and sport, and forestry. Westminster retains control of primary legislation in *all* aspects of public policy, as well as responsibility for the same designated areas of 'high policy' as in Scotland.

Executive styles. Devolution establishes Cabinet-style government, directed by 'First Ministers'. Differences in both scope and functions mark this asymmetrical devolution. As with legislative competencies, the Welsh Executive is the weaker arrangement. Scotland provides the benchmark for devolution, how much, or how little, power has actually shifted from central government. Scotland's First Minister is invested with the constitutional trappings of power: a territorial Prime Minister in all but name. As keeper of the Scottish seal, the symbol of legitimate power in the realm, he embodies the supreme executive authority previously vested in the office of the Scottish Secretary. Less authority by far is vested in the Welsh chief executive, though both offices are formally appointed by the monarch after 'election' by an absolute majority of the Parliament/Assembly.

The First Minister has considerable formal power and informal prestige, and enjoys extensive patronage, including appointment of executive members. Unlike the British Prime Minister, however, this elective prerogative is circumscribed by the requirement to consult on legislative proposals with the parliament's presiding officer, should elections result in hung parliaments, and by the political imperative to bargain with other party leader(s).

The prospect of coalition government, increased by proportional representation, enhances the role of presiding officers in an office that combines the familiar functions of Speaker vis à vis internal parliamentary procedures with those of a non-party political interlocutor or arbitrator between the parties, or between the territorial and central governments in the event of a breakdown in relations. Presiding officers embody the parliaments' legitimacy, officially overseeing the appointment of a First Minister, either after an election, or by designating a substitute to act in his/her stead should the incumbent resign or be otherwise proved incapable of carrying out their duties. They also take the chair at plenary sessions, or when the parliaments exercise their prerogative to hear expert evidence on matters within their jurisdiction. Another formal prerogative is to propose a suitable date for elections, notifying the monarch of this fact, although only if the elected members support this course of action. They have responsibility, too, for facilitating smooth inter-governmental relations, ensuring that legislation does not incur central government's wrath.

Real power and effective authority reside with the executive, subject to constitutional checks and political balances. Coalition governments will make for a more mutable politics than those at Westminster, perhaps even facilitating some legislative independence.

Centre-periphery relations. Though their functions are not specified in either Act, Secretaries of State with British Cabinet rank will continue for the time being to operate as the principal link between London and the territorial executives, constraining the latter's discretion, ensuring direct intervention by the centre in territorial affairs, and embodying the Union's duty to promote an overarching British national interest. By working closely with the First Ministers and presiding officers, they will coordinate inter-governmental relations, facilitating a cooperative rather than tense association, and foster effective two-way communications to avoid policy impasse. Concordats will specify, in principle at least, the respective competencies of central and territorial government, though how these will work out in practice is less clear-cut.

Though the Secretaries of State exercise no overt veto power, sovereignty clearly does reside at Westminster. The definitive statement here is Clause 33 (Scotland Act), which allows the Secretary of State to rescind any proposed legislation deemed to be constitutionally improper. Furthermore, Clause 27 (Scotland Act) leaves no doubt about the locus of legitimate authority: though the parliament is empowered to 'make laws, to be known as acts of the Scottish parliament', this is in no way intended to abrogate Westminster's ultimate right to make Scotland's laws, even in devolved matters. Central government interventions are anticipated, especially in the constitutionally grey areas of shared or overlapping jurisdiction. These intrusions will be subject to challenges by territorial governments in the courts, for the legislation specifies (in the 'spirit' of devolution) that the centre must show 'reasonable grounds' for incursions into devolved areas. The tenor of the new politics promises to be lively.

Welsh arrangements mirror those for Scotland, though with rather less uncertainty, as things currently stand, as to the constitutional outcome. The Welsh Secretary, too, remains in the Cabinet for the time being, representing the Principality's interests at the centre and Westminster's preferences in Wales. In effect, this office remains in both countries a palpable symbol of London's intentions, embodying the Union's constitutional supremacy. An anticipated change in the official title (as the influential Constitutional Unit predicts), by merging both offices into a combined Secretaryship of a new Department of Constitutional Affairs, points to a far from settled arrangement.[12]

Contested jurisdiction and conciliation procedures. Devolution is bound to test the inchoate boundaries between the respective jurisdictions and even, perhaps, induce friction over some matters where authority explicitly resides at the centre. Energy policy, for instance, remains a UK prerogative that uncomfortably touches on the symbolic matter of 'Scottish' oil. Nuclear energy, not least its perceived risks and environmental impact, may also lead to a fall-out between central and territorial governments.

The 1997 Acts seek to deter any regional political interest minded to push the boundaries of its legislative/executive discretion beyond what is consistent with the putative national interest. This much implies a veto power, though if such an interdict is exercised it will almost certainly be as a last resort, and with due regard to regional sensibilities. Otherwise crisis beckons. The possibility does exist for ultra-nationalists, dissatisfied by constrained devolution, to challenge what are still nebulous constitutional boundaries — especially in Scotland where separatism holds greater appeal. Those bent on mayhem will only be marginalised if public opinion is content with present arrangements. A situation that depends, in turn, less on formal vetoes exercised by the centre — stringent fiscal control or bringing official censure to bear on recalcitrant legislatures — and more on instilling common sense into inter-governmental relations. The need is for, on the one hand, satisfying demands for meaningful self-government and, on the other, sustaining an abiding sense of a shared endeavour. The equivalent is what is widely understood elsewhere as a 'federalist culture' — those habits of mutual tolerance and cooperation between levels of government indispensable to stable power-sharing arrangements.

Goodwill is a necessary but by no means a sufficient resource for carrying this off. Experience elsewhere suggests that durable power-sharing arrangements depend on embodying effective conciliation procedures in specific institutions. There is rather less guidance on this matter in the legislation than there ought to be for ensuring stable inter-governmental relations.

Residual tension is the usual by-product of all power-sharing arrangements, as the history of federalism shows. Boundary disputes between territorial parliaments and Westminster remain a distinct possibility. The legislation by no means settles the demarcation between respective jurisdictions. Provision for the Judicial Committee of the Privy Council to resolve disputes might be seen as recourse to a procedure too readily identified with the established constitutional order. If inter-governmental friction does become a regular feature of the new politics, it might require a conciliation mechanism seen by those affected as altogether more detached from the centre. The arbitration issue is likely to be confronted in the early stages of devolution as the boundaries between jurisdictions are tested and precedents set. Undue challenge might strain this procedure. The common law tradition, with its faith in ad hoc judicial review, is altogether less appropriate for formally adjudicating relations where power-sharing between multi-level governance is the way of things. Not surprisingly, demarcation disputes are widely anticipated, and 'cases will inevitably arise in which there are a range of issues, with devolution matters intermingled with other areas of law. The proposed bifurcation at the apex of the UK court system may lead to a division and a lack of coherence in the case law'.[13] Clearly, further constitutional reform beckons, as precedents indicate the shortcomings of present arrangements to manage uncertain governance.

The experience of conflict management in other devolved or federalist systems suggests some likely procedures. They include inter-governmental conferences, heads of government, ministerial and senior officials' meeting as regular channels for communication to facilitate cooperation, or as summits called to resolve particular crises. Devolution does present a real challenge to the British art of fitful constitutional reform, but the prospects are by no means bleak. Nor does the likelihood of inter-governmental friction imply the break-up of the United Kingdom. Political tension can be a creative as much as a subversive force, encouraging the search for positive solutions to what may seem a crisis.

Financial arrangements. Fiscal matters are another problem of devolution. Experience elsewhere suggests that transparency in fiscal affairs is the key to stable inter-governmental relations, whether as direct fiscal transfers from the centre (as in Germany) or fully fledged tax-raising powers (Canada and the USA). These are all, of course, fully federal systems which embed power-sharing norms not yet realised in Britain.

The legislation is explicit about territorial competence over tax-raising. Prohibited in Wales, it is confined in Scotland to a 'top up', though it is far from clear how Westminster might react should this power be used. The Secretaries of State remain as the principal paymasters to the devolved administrations. The perception of London holding the purse strings, thereby exerting an implicit, even an overt, veto over spending, could easily become another source of friction since the fiscal arrangements of the union state remain largely intact. According to the Goschen/Barnett formula that provides the fiscal cement of the Union, public expenditure levels (both increases and reductions, depending on national economic circumstances) for Scotland, Wales and England alike takes account of needs, and are calculated as territorial bloc allocations according to an agreed ratio. Scotland, for instance, receives a fixed proportion — originally 11.65% of any increase/decrease in public expenditure, reduced in 1992 to 10.66% to reflect declining population.

Change here is modest. Lobbying by both Secretaries during the cabinet's annual fiscal round looks set to continue as standard practice, alongside scope for negotiation by the territorial executives/parliaments. Regardless of the Scottish Parliament's modest tax-raising powers (denied to its Welsh equivalent), the current Prime Minister, Tony Blair, has explicitly ruled out its use by any Labour controlled administration in Edinburgh. It is reasonable, nevertheless, to assume that, sooner or later, the Scottish Parliament will use this power. This will be a defining moment in devolution, critical not only for the status of inter-governmental relations but for its likely impact on British politics. The House of Commons Select Committee on the Treasury will almost certainly be provoked into responding, perhaps even to review the balance of overall public expenditure presently favourable to Scotland and Wales. Compensatory financial provisions for socially disadvantaged or economically marginalised regions are a feature of centre-periphery relations in every developed state.

But there is a political agenda behind such formal provisions. Devolution has undoubtedly unsettled territorial relations. Implicit in this favourable allocation was an incentive for these regions to remain committed to the union state. Devolution has undermined that bond, weakening loyalties on both sides. English MPs from every party, including some senior ministers, are critical of a ratio of public expenditure to population that gives Scotland and Wales a 20% advantage over England. A policy for equalising social provision for disproportionately disadvantaged regions, with dispersed population, far-flung communications and greater welfare dependency, is now under serious challenge as the dynamics of devolution confront a residual London hegemony.

The demand from English interests for a more equitable public expenditure ratio may worsen the climate of relations. Separatists will choose to see such an adjustment as malice, using it as a lever against the union state. Nationalist opinion rejects as 'patronising' the very suggestion of England furnishing a net subsidy, citing a suitably selective version of official Treasury figures to make the counter claim that

Scotland more than pays its way. An alternative fiscal strategy — a variant of fiscal federalism — might be that Scotland would purchase central services, making a pro rata payment for the armed services, diplomatic representation and so on.

Friction generated by money and related matters is likely to spread to other fronts where the boundary between central and territorial jurisdiction is less than clear-cut. Inward investment, for example, remains a central government prerogative, though economic and industrial development is a devolved matter. The Board of Trade has already challenged the privileged status of Development Agencies in Wales and Scotland in attracting a disproportionate share of inward investment compared to English regions with similar levels of unemployment and social deprivation. The potential for confusion, and thence conflict, over this issue is discernible, with calls from England for a more 'level playing field' preventing Scotland and Wales from making bids outside the Treasury guidelines that apply to the English regions.

Futures. The critical question is not *whether* tension is inherent in inter-governmental relations but how it might be best *managed* to avoid outright crisis. Devolution raises more questions than it settles on this score — notably, how sensitively the centre will deal with the outstanding matter of territorial representation at Westminster. The question is not only one of numerical strength but its competence to discuss English matters and whether English impatience might not lead to testiness. These issues must be addressed, and sooner rather than later if constructive relations are to be embedded in a new political culture. The future remains uncertain on these matters but with some reason for optimism once a culture of devolution is implanted in the expectations and habits of the political elites which must, after all, manage affairs. A constructive and pluralist politics might then flourish. The devolution legislation is merely the beginning of a process, but as one seasoned observer sees it, editorialising in *The Scotsman* (19 December 1997), 'such constitutional plans cannot take any regard for the intangible at the heart of government: politics itself'. Constitutional engineering is more a contingent and continuous process than a conclusive bargain, and requires periodic fine-tuning.

Northern Ireland: resolving an ancient quarrel?

The Irish Question dominated Anglo-Irish relations after the formal union of the British and Irish Parliaments in 1801, and remained so throughout the period of direct rule from Westminster. Catholic Ireland resisted assimilation into British political culture. Native nationalism was reinforced, because of the influx of Scots Presbyterians into the Ulster plantation and by English colonial rule, both events that institutionalised sectarian discrimination against the native Irish. After successive Home Rule bills (1886, 1893 and 1912) failed to pass into law, Ireland's political status was only partly resolved by an agreement between London and a provisional government in Dublin in 1921 to implement a truncated independence for the 26 southern counties. After partition, the six northern counties, containing a clear Protestant majority, exercised devolved powers within the Union. A parliament at Stormont was able to gerrymander local constituency boundaries to suit its sectarian interests in defiance of Westminster.

This parody of democracy fuelled nationalist resentment against partition on both sides of the 1921 border. Moreover, the practice of sectarian discrimination by Ulster's Protestant majority in disbursing public goods — notably employment and housing — poisoned territorial politics, a situation that was largely ignored by London until resentment provoked a mass Catholic civil rights movement. A Protestant backlash, and increasing paramilitary activity in both communities led in 1972 to a British military presence, first to help the Catholic minority, then to keep the peace, and to the imposition of direct rule.

Such spectacular mismanagement was hardly a viable model for Home Rule when the demand for devolution eventually surfaced in other parts of the union state. Initiatives by representatives from both communities, and by governments in both countries, to resolve this problem have contributed much to the climate of change in the UK. The changing context both of Anglo-Irish and North-South relations in the 'ever closer' European Union has softened once intractable mindsets. Whether there is a lasting change or not will depend on instilling a non-sectarian disposition. At the outset there was some cause for optimism; latterly, an impasse over the decommissioning of paramilitary arms has rekindled doubts on this score.

The Stormont Agreement sealed on Good Friday, April 1998, was an attempt at an historic breakthrough in this ancient quarrel. Arrangements for devolved non-sectarian government in Northern Ireland, and cross-border bodies that introduce a novel all-Ireland dimension into public policy, are the essence of reforms that seek to tackle the intransigence of loyalist and republican communities. The terms of the 1998 accord are as follows: a Northern Ireland Assembly (108 members) is established, elected by Single Transferable Vote from six constituencies, and exercising both legislative and executive authority for wide-ranging competencies devolved from the Northern Ireland Office to six Northern Ireland government departments. There is provision, too, for increasing its jurisdiction should local opinion concur, subject to formal agreement with London. Government is to be located in a multi-party, inter-community power-sharing executive of 12 ministers, so constituted as to be 'inclusive' of interests on both sides. It will be led by joint First and Deputy First Ministers, one from each community, with commensurate status and equal powers.

The executive — briefly instituted in 1999 — will be reconvened, should agreement be reached on the outstanding issue of decommissioning paramilitary weapons. In effect, the principle of parity of esteem now replaces institutionalised sectarianism as the basis of self-government — a remarkable shift in the foundations of governance, measured against the normal yardstick here. Decisional procedures likewise embrace a consociational logic previously unheard of in this divided society, by employing qualified majority voting so that critical decisions (for instance, election of both chief ministers, and the Assembly Chair, as well as budget allocations, and setting up Standing Orders) are to be inclusive of both communities. There is provision, too, for operating similarly 'weighted' votes on other matters, should Assembly members petition for them.

The special majorities precept is a classic 'proportz' mechanism similar to those used in other culturally divided or socially 'pillarised' societies: a requirement for passing measures, either by *parallel consent*, by an Assembly majority including *both* sides, or by *weighted* majority — 60% of the Assembly, with 40% of *both* camps supporting a proposal.

The 'new politics', if it is consolidated, will represent a far-reaching change in both behaviour and expectations — not so much by resolving visceral differences over political identity, but by displaying at least sufficient commitment from moderates in both communities to bring to an end a mutually reinforcing cycle of sectarianism and political violence. Indicative of this is a civic forum, drawn from business, labour, churches and social groups, and intended to embed non-sectarian practices in the very interstices of civil society. The long-term impact of such changes on Irish identity are not easy to predict, with any number of outcomes possible. The next stage of the process of communal reconciliation, setting up an executive, is, at the time of writing, stalled over the issue of decommissioning terrorist weapons.

The most that can be said is that the 1998 Agreement has the potential for institutionalising, if not yet for reconciling, competing political identities that once threatened to tear the Province apart. Some Unionists may now be reconciled to power-sharing, assured by the positive experience of power-sharing and cross-border cooperation. The demons of republicanism may finally be exorcised by experiencing positive benefits from closer regional collaboration at the European Union level. Enough Protestants might be encouraged to rethink an insular mindset forged in more perilous times; to reimagine blind allegiance to a Union that is itself embarked on an analogous process of reconfiguring itself at every level. And they might be encouraged, too, by unprecedented developments in the Republic. The rise of secularism there may ameliorate Unionist intransigence about dealing with Dublin. Even more salutary, perhaps, is the Unionists' experience of British reticence about unconditionally maintaining London's commitment to 'loyalist' Ulster.

Nationalists, no longer excluded from power and reassured by the all-Irish dimension to Ulster's governance, may also become reconciled to citizenship of a democratic Ulster, less attracted in turn to relocating in a Republic where mainstream public opinion has distanced itself from the excesses of Northern republicanism. One outcome of these reciprocal shifts might be a dual Anglo-Irish identity, an abandoning of both exclusive British or Republican/nationalist identities. Reconciliation, education, prosperity, secularism and, of course, generation change can all play a part in remaking perceptions of what it is to 'belong' to a responsive, representative body politic.

These devolved arrangements were the subject of historic twin referenda, held concurrently in both parts of Ireland. Ulster's voters were asked whether they favoured power-sharing, and the Republic's electorate whether they would authorise changes to the 1947 Constitution (Articles 2 and 3) relinquishing Dublin's territorial claims to sovereignty over the six counties. Partition persists, as do abiding communal differences within the Province, but these events do at least indicate a willingness all round to settle an ancient quarrel. Both sides now recognise the right of Ulster's people to determine its own political future by the democratic principle of consent. Institutionalised sectarianism in Ulster is set aside in favour of power-sharing and non-discriminatory access to public goods, though the present impasse underlines the scale of the challenge to be faced if peace is be permanent.[14]

Just as remarkable as this bold attempt to manage the residual political consequences of historic communalism are the provisions in the Agreement for reconciling competing political identities enshrined in the 1921 Treaty. The provision for cross-border bodies will give unprecedented relevance to the 'Irish dimension' of public policy-making on both sides of the border. A North South Ministerial Council will cement cooperation between authorities in 'both' Irelands that are already encouraged by European integration. A British Irish Council (or Council of the Isles) will, likewise, encourage mutuality as an antidote to separatist tendencies. Participation in this 'islands forum' by every territorial component of the union state — Ulster, Wales, Scotland, the UK and Irish governments, and eventually, too, the English regions and lesser islands (the Channel Islands and Isle of Man) — confirms a climate of territorial cooperation, and possibly too a willingness to look for a sense of common regional purpose in a fast-changing Continent. There is historic irony here: unprecedented cooperation in this most divided part of the UK will establish a forum whose practical outcomes may help to put into perspective the centrifugal tendencies of home rule elsewhere in these islands.

English regionalism: will this dog ever bark?

All is change in the state of the Union except in its dominant English heartland. Public opinion here remains, for the most part, broadly supportive of the tried and tested union state formula.[15] English nationalism appears to be stirring, but is largely confined to sporting venues or is purloined by far-right zealots who confuse, for their own sinister

purposes, nationality and malignant notions of racial purity. Englishness has not taken off as a political idea in a country where the
prevailing temperament, following perceived advantage, has seen fit to
fuse — or confuse — English and British identity. At its most benign,
Englishness remains a notional idea, a subdued, self-conscious, even
embarrassed sense of an ancient nation that is much misunderstood and
is now besieged. At its most militant, it manifests surly xenophobic
defiance against the 'demons' of Europe, ungrateful Celts, or other
imaginary enemies.

There seems to be, on the face of it, rather more political mileage in
the idea of administrative regionalism developed as a corrective to
excessive centralisation. The constitutional debate since the 1960s
raised interest in the idea of English regional councils as a political
counterweight to devolution to Scottish and Welsh assemblies, though
it was appended as only a minority recommendation in the Kilbrandon
Report. The Blair government has revisited regionalism for much the
same reasons. Yet it still has little appeal in England on its democratic
merits: that is, as an intermediate tier of governance standing between
the municipal and state levels. Social geography complicates the politics
of subnational governance. One persistent stumbling block to setting
up regional authorities is the absence in England of either a distinct
cultural identity or obvious geographical boundaries demarcating distinctive regional entities, in marked contrast to the well-defined historic
nations.

A regional tier of governance cannot be ruled out, though it will be
more of an afterthought to devolution elsewhere in the UK than a
cogent strategy for balanced governance. The Labour government has
instituted Regional Development Agencies, but these organisations — as
with the Conservatives' Government Offices for the Regions, which
amalgamated and streamlined regional bureaux of the Whitehall
departments — are primarily concerned to maximise economic efficiency, improve competitiveness and secure more of the expanded
European Union structural funds for the regions, than with empowering
regional communities. Regional Chambers are also floated as a possible
development, albeit subject to local demand communicated in referendums. But thus far there is little enthusiasm from the main British
parties to reform English government to match devolution to the UK's
constituent nations. An assembly for London is rather more a solution
to the challenge of coordinating services in the capital city than a model
for regional government as such. Imbalance between the present
devolved polities with considerable capacity for self-government and
the populous but centralised governance of England remains a source
of disquiet. This issue is certain to be revisited, not least because of
resentment in some English quarters at perceived privileged treatment
for Scotland and Wales. A campaign for a Northern Assembly has
already been launched.

Recrudescent reaction to devolution is as much of a challenge to the integrity of the UK as Celtic nationalism. The 'solution' offered by the Conservative opposition, to divest members of the UK Parliament from Scotland and Wales of any role in English law-making, implies petulance, or at least short-sightedness, instead of mature reflection on a sensitive subject. The party leader recently adopted G.K. Chesterton's die-hard provincialism as his motto, summoning up 'the people of England, that have not spoken yet'. Appealing to 'little England' sentiments is no answer, however, to the quandary of how best to accommodate England, so long used to hegemony over these islands, to the new realities of British, or indeed, European governance. Retreat into autarchy will merely exacerbate the problem of reaching an amicable constitutional settlement appropriate to changing times.

Beyond devolution: a federal future?

Constitutional reform is a risky business, though unavoidable as social change requires new constitutional arrangements. Victorian complacency about the body politic, as exhibited by Dicey, has long since been overtaken by events. The challenge confronting Britain's political leaders is precisely that of striking a balance between a growing sense of subnational identity, giving rise to demands for more self-government, and the avoidance of mistrust between the constituent parts of the Union. The vitality of the constitutional order is now a central issue on the national agenda and is likely to remain so. The critical issue now is how to accommodate cultural diversity without weakening the bonds that bind together constituent territories within a mutually beneficial, efficient and, in policy terms, an optimum polity. There is, clearly, a new politics with its own esoteric rules to be learned.

These are the questions at the heart of the debate on British devolution. So far, the solutions to the dilemma of managing diversity, whilst maintaining unity of national purpose, has centred on asymmetrical variants of territorial home rule. It is unlikely, however, that this solution will be the end of the matter. No one can predict with certainty where the process of adaptation will end. It is reasonable to assume, however, that the recently acquired taste for home rule will flourish as new habits replace former dispositions and territorial elites become adept at operating the bargaining strategies calculated to maximise independence from, or leverage with, central government.

Elections fought on provincial agendas are likely to impact on the political parties in ways not yet anticipated by them. Territorial elites may demand expanded competencies in their affairs, whereas Westminster is just as likely to resist them—a war of nerves that will test the effectiveness of existing conciliation procedures, as well as the resolve of those so engaged. The very asymmetry of present arrangements, too, might encourage a leapfrog effect, with less empowered polities, Wales and the putative English regions, pushing to catch up the pace-setters of

Scotland and Northern Ireland. A contested balance of power between the central and territorial tiers of governance is an occupational hazard of power-sharing arrangements, as the history of federalism well illustrates. Separatists will need little excuse for provoking crisis politics, demanding a final reckoning with the Union. Moreover, the momentum for further redrawing boundaries is more likely to accelerate in response to a comparable governance problematic elsewhere in the continent.

All around is change . . . and yet! Devolution is undoubtedly a radical project in relation to the historic British experience. But it is bounded reform, a pragmatic response to managing political expectations; sharing a degree of power, but far short of undermining the common authority, diluting the mutual endeavour, or weakening the cement of shared history that has long sustained the British project. To say this is not to be complacent, let alone to gainsay the constitutional significance of the recent changes. Nor is it by any means to discount the significance of the reform of the state, either for the conduct or culture of British government and politics.

Devolution is the beginning of what will almost certainly be a cumulate process of constitutional change, with the boundaries and functions of a classic nation state being redefined in response to ubiquitous forces reshaping governance everywhere. An interim verdict here might well be 'so far so good'. Westminster and Whitehall have begun to address growing dissatisfaction with outmoded 'top down' notions of governance. The mainstream national parties, albeit with variable enthusiasm, have assimilated the fact of subnational identities. This phenomenon is likely to flourish as the experience of elections fought on separate territorial agendas, the spectacle of provincial politics fought out within devolved assemblies, of interests and preferences quite distinct from those of Westminster government, potential clashes between the centre and territorial governments, and distinctive subnational identities nurtured within the European Union's multi-level political architecture, all conspire to sharpen and refine the sense of a singular territorial politics.

These are changing times, but it would be fatuous to forecast the break up of the Union. On the contrary, constitutional change does represent both a timely and an imaginative response to an unprecedented challenge to British identity. Devolution is an attempt to loosen the rigidities of a union state that once privileged national interests as narrowly defined by political elites at the centre who showed scant regard for those operating on the perimeter of national politics.

How, then, might the reimagined and reconfigured union state develop in future? Politics is, of course, contingent. It may well be that the current trend to deconcentrate power from the centre will be reversed; that, after a flexing of territorial muscle, the novelty will simply wear off, with old habits restored, leading in turn to a restoration of the centrist model of the union state. This outcome is possible but unlikely. The sheer political momentum driving the current changes suggests otherwise. And not only in Britain. The classic Westphalian state system is under stress across the Continent and beyond. These trends reflect a global phenomenon, a structural shift in governance in response to unparalleled changes in the international political economy.[16] Yet, even these prodigious forces must be put in proper perspective. For while the idea of the nation state is severely challenged by forces beyond its limited resources to cope with, it continues to draw deeply from a reservoir of public loyalty, identification and expectation. As it does, too, on elite preferences for exercising the appetite for leadership within manageable political bounds. Nor is this a case of vainly clinging to the wreckage, misplaced nostalgia. A residual sense of political identity, cultural belonging, sheer force of habit by its stakeholders, makes reform of the nation state rather than its improvident dismemberment or casual obsolescence the first instinct of those charged with conducting its affairs.

In short, the nation state is everywhere in the process of being reimagined and reformed, rather than becoming obsolete. A remarkable endeavour for all that, offering a practical challenge to politicians, as well as testing the theoretical acumen of social scientists to explain prospective trajectories. The reform of the British state is, in part, a response to insidious global forces. The unitary state proved to be an ineffective, because unduly rigid, model for the governance of subnational territories that had rediscovered differences both of interest and identity alongside their shared concerns with the metropolitan centre. Political boundaries today are altogether more fluid. A new politics beckons. In the circumstances, Dicey's classic prescription for a centralised Union is simply out of fashion. The nation state will almost certainly survive, but in a much changed format. A territorial dimension is now as crucial to democratic management of affairs in these islands as it is in most other European states.

To say this is to identify the problematic rather than offer solutions. The political management of a vibrant territorial diversity is a daunting challenge that faces future British governments, one that is bound to reconfigure national politics at every level. The devolution so far experienced is a cautious compromise between the centrifugal pull of reinvigorated territorial identities and the centripetal pull of market logic and other economies of scale. Whether it is an adequate response, or merely an interim stage in an altogether more radical constitutional settlement, is impossible to predict with any certitude this early in developments. However, if the strains between centre and perimeter accumulate without effective redress, then the sort of reimagination of the United Kingdom that is under way in the ethnically diverse polities of Canada, Spain, Belgium, and even prospectively in Italy, might well be the next stage in the retreat from the union state.

One possible solution for managing such pressures — a positive alternative to sundering the British state — is to embrace a variant of federalism, an outcome that is now by no means as far fetched as it appeared to Dicey and his contemporaries, who summarily dismissed the prospect as unBritish.[17] The trend to regionalism, territorial politics and devolved governance across the Continent is, after all, accelerating, encouraged by an European Union polity rooted in notions of subsidiarity, variable geometry and other metaphors that reflect new ways of thinking about governance. Divested of the ideological connotations placed on it by xenophobes and ultra-nationalists on the political right, federalism is one way — perhaps the logical corollary — of divesting power from unitary states created in an era when central functions and collective goals were more salient in politics than current post-materialist preferences for local empowerment, alternative identities and regional integration.

In effect, federalism is a model of government whose time may have arrived in a Continent that gave rise to centralised authority and hierarchical polities. Conceived by the Enlightenment project as a rational formula accommodating respect for the pluralism of emergent status civitatis with civilised governance, federalism has, finally, come into its own at the conclusion of a century where unitary states failed to strike a judicious balance between order and representation. The essence of federalism is the reallocation of power between territorial and central authorities to close democratic deficits. Devolution is consistent with this logic. Yet a clear difference of degree remains, for devolved governance is about sharing power rather than a separation of powers. Devolution is not quite the unravelling of the unitary state that equates with historic federalism: the implicit sense of urgency about renegotiating the implied bargain between political elites and the people at large, whether to avert impending national crisis or to celebrate political reconciliation between freely consenting territorial constituencies. Or at least, not yet.

Times do change, and with it the need to rethink the very fundamentals of social and political organisation. Reallocating to territorial polities some of those functions once vested in central government would seem to be in keeping with the current preoccupation with postmodern governance.[18]

As presently constituted, the UK is some way removed from the sort of imbroglio that requires the dramatic accommodation between its constituent nations represented by a federal compact. It may be that this historic Rubicon will never be crossed. Recent events, however, suggest that unparalleled change is in train. There is serious cultural slippage in the once secure idea of the historic British bargain. In the circumstances, a novel constitutional outcome is less fanciful now than it appeared to be to those foundational thinkers whose ideas became the prevailing myths of the British Constitution. An altogether less certain future beckons.

1   W. Blackstone, *Commentaries on the Laws of England*, 1870, Book 1, p. 160.
2   Lord Acton, 'Nationality' in *The History of Freedom and Other Essays*, 1909.
3   A.V. Dicey, 'Home Rule From an English Point of View', *Contemporary Review*, July 1882.
4   V. Kiernan, 'The British Isles: Celt and Saxon' in M. Teich and R. Porter (eds), *The National Question in Europe in Historical Context*, 1993.
5   I. McLean, 'Are Scotland and Wales Over-Represented in the House of Commons?', *Political Quarterly*, 66, 1995.
6   *Report of the Royal Commission on the Constitution* (Kilbrandon), 1972. Though a minority report (Crowther Hunt and Peacock) did propose to give English regional councils parity with those in Scotland and Wales.
7   O.D. Edward, *A Claim of Right for Scotland*, 1988.
8   J. Bradbury, 'Conservative Governments, Scotland and Wales. A Perspective on Territorial Management' in J. Bradbury and J. Mawson (eds), *British Regionalism and Devolution: The Challenge of State Reform and European Integration*, 1997.
9   J. Bradbury, ibid, p. 83.
10 D. Griffiths, *Thatcherism and Territorial Politics, a Welsh Case Study*, 1996.
11 J.G. Kellas, 'The Scottish Constitutional Convention' in L. Paterson and D. McCrone (eds), *The Scottish Government Yearbook*, 1992.
12 R. Hazell and B. Morris, 'Machinery of Government: Whitehall' in R. Hazell (ed), *Constitutional Futures. A History of the Next Ten Years*, 1999, p. 137.
13 R. Cornes, 'Inter-governmental Relations in the Devolved United Kingdom: Making Devolution Work', ibid, 1999.
14 *The Belfast Agreement*, Command 3883, paras 1(ii), 1(v) and 1(vi).
15 C. Harvie, 'English Regionalism: The Dog That Never Barked' in B. Crick (ed), *National Identities. The Constitution of the United Kingdom, Political Quarterly*, 1991.
16 W. Muller and V. Wright, 'Reshaping the State in Western Europe', *West European Politics* 17, 1994.
17 J. Kendle, *Federal Britain. A History*, 1997, ch. 2.
18 J. Hesse and N. Johnson (eds), *Constitutional Policy and Change in Europe*, 1995.

Switzerland: A Paradigm in Evolution

BY CLIVE H. CHURCH

FOR many years Switzerland has been seen as the paradigm of successful integration of diverse language and ethnic groups. It was hailed as
such by Karl Deutsch back in 1976. And in 1998 the country was
invited to the Frankfurt Book Fair as guest of honour because of its
multi-culturalism. So, when the writers of the television comedy programme *Drop the Dead Donkey* wanted a totally unlikely scenario for
a book to celebrate the millennium, they invented a civil war between
the language groups of Switzerland. This reflects a conventional view
that not merely has Switzerland solved all such problems but, because
of its success, the country offers a model for the emerging new Europe.

While it is true that, until recently at least, Switzerland has 'worked',
the conventional wisdom is not a wholly accurate guide to the paradigm, for three reasons. First, Switzerland's cultural diversity is neither
as clear-cut nor as simple as is often assumed. Nor has it been managed
by a few simple consociational or federal mechanisms. Formal institutions have been only part of the Swiss solution while its federalism and
general success owe much to wider patterns of culture and governance.
So the Swiss story is more one of finessing latent divisions by purpose-
fully agreeing to work together than of containing rancid and open
conflicts.

Secondly, the paradigm has not been as unchanging as often thought.
In recent years these broader underpinnings have come under considerable pressure. Indeed, over the last 20 years or so the country has been
subject to new, often externally derived, developments and challenges.
These trends are complicating the underlying problems of diversity and
making them harder to deal with. Not merely is the nature of Swiss
multi-culturalism changing but the foundations of the way the country
works have come under pressure. Globalisation, new socio-economic
tensions and the operation of the political system have all become
problematic. As a result the country can no longer rely wholly on its
territorial arrangements, its prosperity and the smooth running of its
power-sharing style to resolve its differences. Hence the talk of crisis,
notably in the wake of the narrow, but very divisive, referendum defeat
on proposals for entry to the European Economic Area on 6 December
1992.

Finally, because of this new malaise, the country has sought to
address the problems of language through an active programme of
research and a more limited amount of policy development, targeted on

developing new attitudes amongst the population. To some extent this seemed to have succeeded since, aided by helpful trends in the wider environment, tension seemed to have diminished. Unfortunately, in June 1999 the problem flared up again following a very clear division between the main language groups — German and French — on a maternity assurance referendum. For many, this revealed an even deeper divide than that of 1992 and sent politicians back to the drawing board in a search for means of healing the breach.

So while it would be wrong to suggest that Switzerland has not managed to avoid conflict far more successfully than most countries, or is heading for a stormy Belgian style future, the paradigm is going through a difficult period. Internal divisions are changing and ways of addressing them successfully have yet to be found. This emerges clearly from looking at the three assumptions about the paradigm, beginning with the nature of Swiss cleavage problems and their traditional solutions.

The problem identified

Switzerland has always been a diverse country but the nature and salience of its diversities have changed more over time than the conventional wisdom suggests. In the late middle ages the most dangerous and sometimes violent conflict was that between the pastoral mountain cantons and the urban manufacturing centres. This division was then overlaid by the religious divide between Catholic and Protestant which almost split the country in two and made it impossible for the Confederacy to play an active external role. Religious conflict remained a key factor up to the beginning of the present century, contributing to social and political conflicts, notably in the run up to the 'Sonderbund' civil war in 1847.

By the end of the last century, however, language had become an increasingly important divide. This dated back to the addition of non-German-speaking cantons to the Confederacy in the Napoleonic era. It played a part in the 1874 constitutional reform and almost split the country during the First World War when there was a huge gulf between the German and Latin communities. At the same time, new class divisions were emerging, as the 1918 General Strike showed. Nonetheless, for much of the present century, the country was to succeed in managing these changing divisions better than most. This was especially so after 1945 when Switzerland emerged as an exceptionally successful, independent and harmonious democracy. There was growing ecumenism, virtually no strikes, and the one example of language strife was accommodated by the creation of the new canton of the Jura. All this facilitated Switzerland's phenomenal postwar economic expansion. So it is not surprising that the Swiss came to think of themselves as a 'Sonderfall', or special case.

When political scientists came to look at the reasons for this Sonderfall they tended to favour structural explanations such as consociation-alism.[1] As defined by Lijphart this argues that deeply divided societies can live in harmony if the individual segments are given autonomy, are proportionally represented in government, enjoy a mutual veto and provide representatives to an overarching elite cartel who run their national affairs for them.

There are three problems about this. The first is that though the idea has been much invoked in the case of Switzerland it has rarely been specified, and very often is used as a short hand description of something else, usually consensus democracy. Secondly, and more importantly, the picture adduced by Lijphart does not work for Switzerland. Essentially there are no simple pillars in Swiss society. Religious, social and language groups are all divided up inside or among cantons so that cross cutting cleavages are the norm. Nor are the cleavage groups always at each other's throats as the theory supposes. Swiss society has been stable, harmonious and in little need of a wise elite to save it from itself. In any case, proportionality and mutual veto neither exist nor work in the consociational way. Equally, far from taking decisions for their constituents, elites are often suspected and rebuffed. The third problem is that by concentrating on mechanisms, the idea overlooks the combination of more complicated behavioural and contextual considerations which actually underlie Swiss cultural stability.

The actual underpinnings

The historical facts are — firstly — that the various cleavage problems did not all come to a head at the same time. That allowed the country to resolve one set of conflicts before others really became salient. The past also contributed both a slow and unthreatening pace of state building which introduced the democratic devices which are now used to support linguistic harmony and the socio-economic foundations of stability.

Secondly, economic prosperity and social balance have been crucial foundations for stability. The fact that since 1945 Switzerland has been an exceptionally wealthy country has removed one of the most common grounds for ethnic conflict. Katzenstein and others would also argue that external pressures helped this by forcing economic flexibility and political consensus on the Swiss.[2] Equally, the fact that the country has had a more balanced society with no overweening cities and no desperately deprived regions also helped. So have traditions of good labour relations, social inclusion and tolerance.

Thirdly, neutrality has also been cited as a stabilising factor thanks to the way it has controlled internal arguments over foreign policy issues. Indeed, it has been said that Switzerland has had no real foreign policy, only an internal policy which sought to prevent external difficulties and divisions from disturbing domestic stability. The armed neutrality this produced means that the army serves as an essential focus for national cohesion. All this provided a shield behind which the

Swiss could develop a political system both federal and based on direct democracy. The latter meant that the Swiss have unparalleled opportunities for participation and so are willing to accept public decisions, even when these go against them. At the same time it interacts with federalism and proportional representation to make power sharing an essential element of Swiss politics.

So, fourthly, while much debate on cultural diversity in Switzerland assumes that the problem, as in Belgium, is how to keep the lid on the pressure cooker of incipient conflict, the reality is rather different. It is the desire to avoid conflict that stands out most strongly. Many believe the country did not so much resolve such questions as avoid posing them by allowing communities to live their own lives undisturbed, thanks to the emphasis on national harmony and unity in contemporary Swiss political culture. This shows itself in the way Swiss politics goes beyond federalism and direct democracy to a bottom up system of governance, with extensive consultation, negotiation and participation. Indeed, civil society can be seen as having the upper hand over the state. So, even though the Swiss are a quietly but intensely national people, this does not disturb national harmony.

The Swiss believe the country is the product of their own continuing efforts, or what Germans call a 'Willensnation'. Indeed, some see themselves as something of a chosen people, thanks to their scenery, their myths and their economic success.[3] Certainly they are strongly committed not merely to national independence but also to the maintenance of those things which hold the country together, its pluralism and its political system.

On the one hand the Swiss are supportive, and not merely tolerant of, multiple identities and are concerned not to see Switzerland as mono-cultural. Hence there is a strong and positive desire for understanding and agreement amongst the various groups. Power sharing is a sine qua non while solidarity rather than competition marks their vision of federalism. There is, thus, no need for the kind of alarm bells built into the Belgian system. On the other hand, these things focus on a political system which does much to hold the country together. The Swiss show a high degree of interest in political institutions and see these as defining Swiss identity. Thanks to direct democracy the people are seen as sovereign in a very real way. They form the official opposition.[4] Left and right are, thus, equally devoted to grass roots self government and direct democracy. The latter may seem to be divisive and majoritarian, but such is its legitimacy that it can act as a unifying force.

These consensual attitudes are not vague ideas but are built into the way the Swiss politics works. In fact Swiss politics has long been a matter of governance resting on civil society and steered rather than directed by government. The constitution makes it clear that the state is a limited one and its operation owes much to the 'militia' system of part-time service in parliament and elsewhere. Equally the norm is that government adjusts to the popular will, so resignation after a policy reversal is rejected. Political parties also play a different role from that found in other majoritarian countries, centring on training and selecting for people in the militia system, rather than shaping government policy. And the flexible system of PR allows new parties relatively easy access to representation.

Swiss governance is greatly marked by the extensive processes of consultation, or Vernehmlassungsverfahren, which precedes all Swiss legislation. The government goes out of its way to seek the opinion of cantons, economic interests and professionals both before and during parliamentary consideration of its proposals. The aim is not a minimum winning coalition but rallying as many people as possible behind the proposals, thanks to referendumsdrohung or the fear of referendum challenges. The so-called Economic Articles of 1947 gave employers and unions a constitutional right to be involved in deciding economic policy, thus making Switzerland something of a corporate state. All this means that policy making can be very slow, especially if a proposal is initially defeated. However, once taken, decisions carry extra legitimacy.

At the same time the implementation of federal legislation often involves parastatal and voluntary bodies. The central administration is relatively small and relies mainly on local government and NGOs to carry out its tasks, notably in health and welfare provision. Indeed, the country pullulates with voluntary bodies like Pro Juventute and Pro Senutucte, not to mention the Red Cross, all of which encourage cooperation and social participation in governance and policy networks beyond the state. Direct democracy is also very influential in developing cooperation. It calls for wide coalitional committees to support or oppose referendum proposals. In other words, Swiss political culture works with its formal and informal institutions to encourage power sharing and consensus. So, while there are latent implicit conflicts within Swiss society, the system makes it hard for them to boil over, especially as such underpinnings have always been mutually reinforcing.

These structures alone would not have guaranteed linguistic harmony. Policy and processual provisions are also needed. Formal rules on language equality, representation and federal autonomy are very important. All full languages, though not schwyzertütsch — 'Swiss German' — have equal constitutional rights, with the partial exception of Rheto-Romansch. Federal assistance can also help although it is limited to encouraging dialogue through the obligatory teaching of a second language, financial help for economically disadvantaged language groups and arrangements for contact across the language divides. This is because the practice of territoriality reserves most decisions on language to local authorities, reflecting the general principles of Swiss federalism which empower both communes and cantons, the latter remaining quasi-sovereign, especially in matters of culture, education and religion. Equally, the federal approach permeates the party system, so that parties are essentially congeries of cantonal associations. All this has made systematic oppression of minorities virtually impossible. It has also contributed to the complex of factors which have allowed the Swiss to live harmoniously together for so long.

Recent changes

Seen from the outside they may still seem to be doing this. However, the reality is changing. Over the last twenty years or so the country has been affected by three linked developments: globalisation; unusual domestic economic and social change; and blockages in the way Swiss political institutions work. These have questioned the Sonderfall and the underpinnings of successful ethnic relations. Partly because of this, there has been a growing malaise in ethnic and federal relations.

To begin with, global economic and political changes have undermined the country's international position. On the one hand the Swiss have been exposed to intense international business competition as well as to outside pressure, notably from the European Union, on domestic policies and politics. This has faced the country with increasingly divisive issues, such as European relations and Alpine Transit. On the other, the end of the Cold War has made neutrality much less helpful, especially with the new questioning of the uses to which it was put during the war. There have been controversial new military initiatives and the admission that the 1940s were not so glorious a period as many Swiss had assumed, notably where Nazi relations were concerned. All this has had a marked effect on Swiss standing and self confidence, as the failure of its bid to host the 2006 Winter Olympics in Sion showed.

At the same time, the country ran into the deepest and longest economic depression since 1945 thanks to the high level of the Swiss franc. As a result exports and the trade balance fell, while at home domestic consumption was flat and there was a real crisis in the construction industry. Hence, for the first time the country experienced negative GDP growth and growing unemployment caused by enforced restructuring and contraction. The number of jobless shot up to a peak of 200,000 (over 6%) in 1996 compared to only 17,450 in 1989. Although this was well below the European average it was a real jolt and brought most Swiss, especially French speakers, into personal contact with unemployment. The resulting calls on the social security budget had a negative impact on government finance, inflation and taxation.

Social changes have reinforced this. The country has now passed the seven million mark and it is less dynamic and balanced than it was. Demographically the country has become increasingly elderly and dependent on its 19% of foreigners. Ironically the Swiss have remained uncertain about this and have been reluctant to provide their foreign population with stable and equal social rights. Traditional forms of cultural management have really had little to say about this new problem, something which many assessments of Swiss success in achieving cultural harmony overlook.

At the same time, the population has increasingly moved into the towns. A third now live in the five big cities. As a result the country has experienced a growth in previously low levels of crime as well as of AIDs, drugs, divorce and suicide, not to mention the ravages of the 'new poverty'.[5] At the same time, two fifths of Communes now have less than 500 residents which makes it hard to sustain rural life. All this has impacted on cleavage structures since such social unease, especially when accompanied by a rising secularisation, is not guaranteed to assist understanding across the language frontiers.

Finally, while the external environment was changing, the success of the Swiss system made internal political adaption increasingly difficult. Whereas institutions like neutrality, federalism and direct democracy were originally tools to allow the Swiss to solve their problems, their postwar role turned them into values in themselves. Hence, for many, the system has helped to prevent necessary changes. Attempts to reform such institutions, when they failed to respond to external challenges, caused new political divisions to emerge, encouraged by the way that since 1977 foreign policy questions were increasingly brought within the remit of direct democracy.

Questions of foreign relations have become a source of increasingly bitter division and neutrality is no longer the shield it once was. To begin with, the Nazi Gold affair has triggered renewed criticism of what is seen as the immorality and self interested nature of Swiss neutrality in the Second World War. Swiss rejection of both UN membership and the provision of Blue Helmets has developed such criticisms. More importantly, the ending of the Cold War and the expansion of the EU has changed the geopolitical situation which had made neutrality necessary in the first place. All Switzerland's neighbours are now peaceful and democratic as well as engaged in creating an over-arching security structure in Europe. The absence of Switzerland almost makes the country a potential source of instability in Europe rather than one offering the certainty claimed in the Cold War era. Equally there have been fewer calls for Swiss good offices and more demands that Switzerland join in common ventures such as the Gulf crisis and Yugoslavia. This reflects the way that other European neutrals have reconciled their neutrality with active EU membership.

Whereas neutrality had previously worked by limiting engagement in outside politics, it was precisely this lack of engagement which annoyed many in Switzerland, notably but far from exclusively in the Suisse Romande. Neutrality began to seem a source of controversy rather than a shield against division. It can be seen as a barrier both to the European aspirations of many Swiss and to the wider defence of Swiss interests needed in a changing world. Much opinion is willing to accept the more flexible interpretation being practised by government, but because neutrality has moved from being a simple policy instrument to an untouchable characteristic of Swissness, not to say an ideology, attempts to downplay it can be fiercely resisted. Armed neutrality is also problematic and can limit its contribution to national integration. And not merely are neutrality and foreign policy divisive in themselves, they also interact with other forces threatening the foundations of Swiss cultural harmony.

Internally, the Swiss political system no longer works as smoothly and successfully as it did. But, because its institutions have become so deeply rooted, adaptation has become increasingly difficult. Swiss political structures are becoming less an arena in an increasingly polarised political debate deriving from contested views of Swiss identity. So trust in the system has declined, the tone of politics has become much harsher and conflictual, and this at a time when increasingly difficult issues have to be faced.

One of the major trends in Swiss politics in recent years has been declining confidence in government and the political system. This began in the 1980s with the Kopp affair and the revelation that the 'snooper state' had been keeping secret files on virtually a sixth of the entire population. It showed itself very clearly in the 1992 vote on the EEA where lack of trust in government was the major determinant of negative voting. Since then it has been encouraged by the economic crisis and by the revelations of the Nazi Gold affair. None of this has helped declining electoral turn out or support for orthodox parties but it has assisted unconventional political activities which can be difficult to reconcile with the Swiss system.

At the same time the tone of Swiss political life has greatly changed. Encouraged by the new media it has become much more shrill, more concerned with personalities and more wide ranging in its coverage, spreading across traditional cantonal boundaries, encouraging people to see themselves as being in an unfair minority position rather than as participants in a process of negotiation. Political culture has thus become less tolerant of the views of others and less willing to bargain and compromise, not to mention less respectful of traditional institutions. Reacting against this, some on the right are increasingly inclined to accuse the establishment of treason. All this makes cross language consensus harder to maintain, especially as many orthodox politicians — chosen for their collegial appeal and administrative capacity — are not always effective in this new environment. Meanwhile attempts to modernise the governmental system have been blocked.

The lack of confidence in governing elites and the new strident political style have meant that Swiss politics have become much more competitive, not to say combative. Recent elections have therefore seen an increasing polarisation between the Social Democrats and the Zurich wing of the increasingly populist Swiss People's Party (SVP). The rise of the latter at the expense of the Christian Democrats and other smaller far right parties has intensified pressure on the system and on the Suisses Romande, where the SVP is poorly represented. It also threatens a major realignment on the right which would call the Magic Formula of party representation in government into question and exacerbate French speakers' fears. Already the latter are more inclined to see themselves in regional terms than are German speakers.

What makes things even more fraught is that the system is having to face up to zero sum issues like drugs, environmental protection and, especially, Europe. For many the problem of Europe is that it threatens the institutions which make Switzerland, notably national independence and direct democracy. Since the present federal structure tends (as already noted) to over weight the small conservative cantons of central Switzerland, such supporters of 'Swissness' have a built in veto, and one which now extends to foreign policy issues. Hence, since the 1970s there have been an increasing number of votes in which the failure to gain a cantonal majority has blocked the popular will. This has increased the Swiss-French sense of alienation. It has also meant that direct democracy has become increasingly divisive. In the past, perhaps paradoxically, it had become a means of unity since all Swiss accepted the legitimacy and value of popular endorsement of controversial laws, even if they regretted the precise decision. These new integration deficits have tended to block policy making, thereby increasing feelings of frustration, and while none of this is any worse than the situation in many other countries it has all been very unsettling for the Swiss who increasingly feel that things have changed — and for the worse.

A French and federal malaise

Given these challenges to the underpinnings of stability it is hardly surprising that Swiss multi-culturalism is encountering difficulties. Language divisions have become more salient, more complex and dangerously marked by a deterioration in relations between French and German speakers, at a time when the media and other cultural institutions are decreasingly supportive.

Despite the resolution of the Jura question, language has replaced religion as the key cleavage, so that from the late 1970s there has been increasing talk of a 'rosti graben'. In May 1991 Ribeaud claimed that: 'Never has the unit of the country been so threatened.'[6] Language divisions have increasingly taken on social characteristics as well so that cross cutting seems to be partially giving way to the emergence of language blocs. A 1995 Military Department report concluded that linguistic threats to national cohesion were the greatest danger facing Switzerland.

Language problems are, moreover, not restricted to the French/ German divide. A first complication is the parallel pressures on minority languages. The highly fragmented Romansch dialects are increasingly hard to sustain and most Romansch speakers have to become bilingual, causing real doubts about its survival. And while Italian is unlikely to disappear, it is being edged out of national life because the Italian-speaking communities are somewhat marginal in size and location. So many Swiss Germans, with no knowledge of or interest in Italian, have moved into the Ticino (and the Bregaglia and Poschiavo valleys in the Graubunden) in search of retirement sunshine, that some villages have become almost wholly Germanophone.

A second complication is that while outsiders talk loosely of German, much of the problem comes not from the conventional 'High German' taught as the obligatory second national language in the schools of the Suisse Romande, but from the growing domination of schywyzertütsch in German-speaking Switzerland, the so-called 'mundartwelle' or dialect revolution.[7] As a result schwyzertütsch is becoming more homogenous and mutually comprehensible across north-eastern Switzerland. While many German Swiss deprecatingly refer to it as a 'dialect' it is really a separate language, and one which is not easily accessible, even through standard German. It has become a barrier to communication across the language line, especially as its development makes standard German harder for Swiss Germans. This, in turn, reduces the willingness of French speakers (who generally speaking are weaker linguistically than their fellow citizens) to learn German. Hence, there has been a real deterioration of relations across the Sarine between French and German speakers.

This is not simply a matter of language as such although demands for industrial transplantees for German language facilities in what are nominally French-speaking villages like Marly in Friburg, encourage French fears that their language and culture are coming under attack. The division is deeply rooted in Swiss society and politics, because the economic heart of Switzerland — the 'golden triangle' of Basle, Berne and Zurich — is German speaking. Not merely is this more prosperous than the Suisse Romande but it is the seat of most big firms. Hence, there is much talk of the economic colonisation of the Suisse Romande whose businessmen take the early morning flight from Geneva to Zurich to get their orders. Decisions by Swissair to withdraw flights to the US from Geneva and operate them from Zurich, and opposition to rebuilding the Lotschberg as part of the new St Gotthard base rail tunnel project, are seen as confirming this. Some Zurich interests believe the nation would be better served by building on its golden triangle strengths rather than by trying to support everything.

Equally, the French can feel themselves marginalised politically. This derives essentially from Swiss German opposition to the country's participation in external ventures like the European integration and Francophone Summits. German speakers are seen as preventing Switzerland from drawing close to Europe. It is not just a matter of foreign policy in the abstract because Union membership would strengthen Swiss ties with a mainly French-speaking institution, allowing Brussels to balance the power of Zurich. Similarly, the French see Chrotoph Blocher's ultra-right wing SVP becoming increasingly the vehicle for a narrow, inward looking German-Swiss nationalism which excludes them. They feel that German speakers dominate the civil service, government and parliament, perhaps even trade unions too. There can also be quite distinct views on economic policy where the German-speaking areas take a more Anglo-Saxon view than the traditional Continental approaches to economic management preferred by the French. There are divisions too on the environment and on social policies such as drugs and maternity assurance. Because this makes the French feel an oppressed minority they can become somewhat aggressive.

What makes things worse is that cultural institutions which might have smoothed away such conflicts no longer seem to be doing so. Language policy is not always as fully committed to encouraging national comprehension in face of the rise of English as a lingua franca. This is claimed to be prevalent in army, business and the scientific community. Hence some cantons like Zurich have refocused their language teaching on German and English, downgrading French. This caused bitter criticism, from the President down, even though opinion polls show preferences for English over the native language, and the Bernese cantonal government is now asking for federal funds to strengthen English teaching. Secondly, encouraging bilingualism favours German speakers rather than French. Hence attempts to strengthen language rights by a revision of what was Article 116 of the Constitution were thwarted by conflicting desires and a fear of opening Pandora's box.

Changes in the media have also contributed to the problem. Local and party based newspapers have increasingly come under the control of larger unattached combines interested mainly in selling papers. This encourages coverage of the broader language area, a development even more marked in radio and TV. The effect not merely limits contact, especially when not all language programmes can be heard throughout the country, but helps to constitute language group identity. At the same time the federal system of managing linguistic divisions has been called into question. It was an issue in 1998 during the 150th anniversary celebrations of the founding of the Federal State (though it was not in 1991 when the 700th anniversary of the presumed foundation of the country was celebrated). The federation has not been working as well, therefore, as in the past and its basic structures are now being queried.

Attempts to redefine the complicated division of responsibilities between cantons and confederation have not been wholly successful; since both levels are running large deficits they are anxious to transfer costly duties to the others. There is also concern about differential levels of taxation with rich cantons like Zug and Zurich levying up to a half less than the average, and poor ones like the Valais a third more, encouraging entrepreneurs to exploit the system by switching head-quarters, reflecting continuing barriers to a genuine internal market. Nonetheless attempts have been made to try and overcome costly divisions through moves to share hospitals, link up universities and coordinate waste disposal provision.

Politically, federal fragmentation has been attacked for its conserva-tive effects, notably where modernising legislation is concerned. It can reflect defensive cantonal sovereignty or the way conservative populism exploits the system to block innovation. Social and external changes have also brought the present cantonal structure into question. Some believe it prevents recognition of the new demographic realities of urban Switzerland. More significantly, there have been a growing number of suggestions for encouraging subregional cooperation by merging existing cantons to produce more rational and viable units. Proposals have been tabled both for merging Vaud and Geneva and for creating a new grouping round Basle, while there is large support for enhanced cooperation amongst the cantons of central Switzerland.

More revolutionary proposals are now being considered because of feelings that the present system is inappropriate for statistical and economic needs, making international comparisons difficult. Moreover, the present pattern would be hard to fit into the EU's regional policy and representational frameworks. At present the Union would probably classify the whole country as a single (NUTS1) region which would be unacceptable. Hence, Lausanne University's Centre for the Built Environment was commissioned to advise the National Statistical Ser-vice and its 1998 report proposed seven new statistical regions: the Lemanique, the Mittelland, Central Switzerland, the NW and Basle, Zurich, Eastern Switzerland and the Ticino. The proposal caused considerable debate, both technical and political, since some think the new scheme should be the basis of a major territorial remodelling given that many Swiss cantons are much weaker than regions in neighbouring countries with which they compete.

The Green Party and some left wing Social Democrats are pushing for a move to fewer cantons. They believe that between six and twelve would be cheaper, simpler and less likely to create boundary effects or block progressive legislation. It might also help poorer regions by levelling out differences in growth, thanks in part to opening up public procurement. Similarly, it might allow cantons more input into the processes of EU-based legal harmonisation as well as more say in Swiss foreign relations in Europe. Conversely others see these proposals as a real threat to national identity and as a step to language based blocs. Hence, there has been a real malaise within the paradigm.

State responses to the crisis

The malaise was symbolised by the explosion of ill feeling which followed the 6 December vote against joining the EEA, and the erection of barricades on the French side amidst violent polemics. The political elite was gravely worried and sought to explore ways of bringing the country back together. Their efforts made relatively little use of structural mechanisms, partly because of the blockages in the system. Instead they relied on research and policy adjustment in the hope of changing conflictual attitudes. However, not a great deal of concrete legislation ensued and, as general conditions improved, interest in the problem faded, prior to flaring up again in the summer of 1999.

Post-1992 discussions of language questions derived from the Interior Ministry's 1989 Expert Report from the Interior Ministry which argued that the quadrilingual model was under threat from a lack of tolerant comprehension, the rise of English and the problems of the lesser languages. It resulted in the suggestion of a more expansive constitutional article to safeguard language diversity and liberty. In the event Parliament whittled this down to a limited revision in 1996 stressing linguistic liberty rather than protection and comprehension.

In any case the debate was overtaken by the authorities' rush to bridge the post-EU gulf through new research into the problem. Thus, the two Chambers of Parliament created Commissions on Comprehension which produced a Joint Report in October 1993. Reflecting the deep shock engendered by the 1992 referendum, the Report argued that the crisis had made clear what many had suspected was the case. Hence, while noting that there were other language problems, it concentrated on the French/German divide. The reasons for this gulf went deep into history and culture and reflected four factors, beginning with economic divergence. Secondly, came the rise of schwyzertütsch, which meant that three quarters of German speakers hardly used standard German, a fact which annoyed the Suisse Romandes and led them to undervalue the tremendous contribution the language makes to Swiss German individuality and identity. Thirdly, stress was placed on the fact that most French-speaking cantons were frontier zones contrary to most German-speaking cantons. Lastly, the Report discerned problems in the media and education. The former were felt to have moved too far towards schwyzertütsch and did not reflect the variety of cultures in Switzerland. Equally, more needed to be done in education and training, including reviving the habit of student exchanges between the two main parts of the country.

The remedy was seen as requiring a new spirit which saw cultural diversity as an opportunity and an enrichment, rather than a problem. The Swiss needed to work together in stressing the things which united the country, as well as remembering minorities and enhancing national identity. A series of moves to assist this change of heart was proposed, including encouraging a national debate on national identity through constitution reform, the 1998 anniversary and the national exhibition of 2001. The report also urged taking the minorities into account in any reform of the central government, especially by increasing subsidiarity as part of a strengthening of the federal system.

At the same time the Federal Office of Culture commissioned an analysis of the extent to which the Suisse Romande has been in a minority at Federal level from the Politics Department in Geneva.[8] This reported in September 1995 making the point that for many Swiss the linguistic problem was not a priority compared to other problems. Moreover, all regions shared the same basic values and, as a result, differences in voting patterns had actually diminished over time. However, the growing number of referendums meant that French and Italian regions found themselves in a minority on more occasions, notably on transport matters. Hence, 'mutual ignorance' no longer worked, and French speakers felt their inferiority more keenly. Again, the solution was felt to lie in developing a new overall consensus, increasing the level of general and linguistic knowledge of other regions, and providing more infra structural and general economic aid to peripheral regions.

The academic world took the country's language problems on board, notably through a debate in the new *Swiss Political Science Review* in 1996–97.[9] This derived initially from the arguments over the new constitutional article but was carried on by the controversy over Zurich's proposed change to its schools' language policy. While some contributors believed that for the first time there might be a real language policy, and analysed the changes made by the government, others were more inclined to see growing tensions rather than happy plurilingualism which, for some, was a myth. Grin's conclusion was that language was indeed becoming increasingly important and, despite its legal provisions, Switzerland was in some ways surprisingly poorly equipped to deal with it. However, there was the potential for a solution.

Parallel to this research, the government took the problem very seriously and sought to develop policy accordingly. Thus, the Federal Council — when reporting its priorities for the period 1995–99 to the new Parliament in March 1996 — made reinforcing national cohesion its 'idée force'. It stressed that the peaceful coexistence of its cultural communities was a great strength for the country and sought to encourage it as a means of maintaining competitiveness, despite the shrill arguments both about Europe and resident foreigners. It declared that it would seek to support national cohesion through social policy, regional development aid and cultural exchange arrangements. In 1997 it promised to give concrete form to its key idea by encouraging cooperation among and between the cantons and regions via changes in the division of duties and resources to the benefit of the cantons. Equally, it stressed its new regional policy and the way that it was enhancing its 'amenagement du territoire' provision, including setting up an advisory committee. It also supported bilingual education, exchanges and assistance to regional broadcasting. Pointing to the interest in the problem shown in debates on constitutional reform and forthcoming national celebrations, it also urged Parliament to ratify the Council of Europe's Minority Languages Charter.

The Federal Council clearly believed that it had met its objectives. This meant that the issue declined in prominence and implementing linguistic legislation slowed down. In fact, the new Constitution, narrowly approved in 1999, does enshrine clearer commitments to mutual respect and comprehension. However, none of this did enough to change popular attitudes and thus prevent the problem resurfacing before the reforms had a chance to work through.

Changing circumstances and the future

The concerns which had given rise to the reform programme began to wane in the middle 1990s. This was especially so at the level of civil society. Declining public alarm probably reflected a general improvement in the Swiss situation. However, events were to show that underlying differences and tensions had not gone away. So there was a new round of breast beating in 1999 and the future of the paradigm remains uncertain.

The media reflected the way the language question went off the public agenda. While there was a good deal of coverage in 1992–93, thereafter interest died away until, in 1996, French Swiss TV mounted a controversial programme between the two language communities. This did not mean that there were no conflict between the language groups. In fact Suisse Romande sensibilities were further offended by the February 1994 Alpine Transit Initiative which was seen as a diktat by German-speaking environmental extremists. There was also a sharp division over a 1995 vote on foreign purchase of land. The next year French-speaking MPs complained that the use of the term 'Landi' for the 2001 exhibition was a further example of Germanisation. But although German speakers showed little resentment of such attacks, reservations about change did emerge in Parliament where further motions on bilingualism were postponed until the constitutional article on languages and implementing bills were completed. The former went through Parliament in October 1995 and was carried by referendum the following February.

The decreasing level of angst reflected a distinct improvement in the country's international and domestic situation. By late 1998 the Swiss seemed to be putting the Nazi Gold crisis behind them and were starting to develop a new style foreign policy. Thus, the Brunner Commission reported that the real threats to the country at the end of the decade came from societal problems like crime, migration and terrorism and not from military challenges.[10] Such threats could only be met by cooperation with European institutions, and this in turn demanded more solidarity and engagement on the ground. So neutrality needed to be applied pragmatically since it could constrain this. And they advised against any formal renunciation of neutrality because of its place in the Swiss psyche. This line was opposed by Blocher and the populist right, but it seems to have carried general conviction. Hence, the Swiss are slowly moving to a more engaged position and may even send troops abroad. Equally, on the European front, the bilateral negotiations have finally concluded and seem likely to gain domestic acceptance judging by the reception of the voluminous report on Integration published at the turn of the year. Thereafter, the question of EU entry will be faced squarely and indications are that this will have more chance of success than it has had in the past, although entry is not certain. So external policy may be becoming less divisive.

One other positive political sign is that the incessant outside attacks on Switzerland during the Nazi Gold affair, which were sensibly handled by the Federal Council, have done something to restore domestic confidence in government. This is likely to be accentuated by the gradual ending of the depression. There have been steps towards both policy liberalisation and restructuring. Thus, employers' organisations are thinking of working together to facilitate the modernisation of corporatism, although differential unemployment rates are still fairly evident. On the other hand, blockages to social adjustment have not been removed, despite the defeat of hard line initiatives on drugs, and the country has been slow to comes to terms with the Kosovo refugee problem.

Just as the economy is coming round so federalism has been painfully adjusting in several ways. To begin with, there has been some progress on redefining duties and financial responsibilities. Furthermore, there have been moves to modernise and expand cantonal representation in national politics. The conference of cantonal governments has become more prominent and the cantons now have their own representative in the Integration Bureau as suggested in 1994. So they have been more involved in foreign policy in line with the revised constitution. Equally there has been growing support for Swiss participation in the EU's Intereg II programme. So while there are still questions about cantonal cooperation and fusion, such changes have helped to dedramatise the language problem in recent years, pushing it down the agenda. This was not because the Swiss changed their attitudes. In fact the evidence of recent referenda suggests that conservative attitude to Swiss identity has persisted. It was because of new problems such as the linguistic divide over the 14 June 1999 notation on maternity assurance. This revealed an even deeper cleavage than in 1992 and led to yet new questioning of national unity.

However, the language question played only a marginal part in the recent election campaign. Though the election did lead to the ultraconservative SVP emerging as almost the largest party at the expense of the Christian Democrats, there was no real crisis. In fact the SVP proved to have strength across the country and language played no part in the bitter political rows over the Magic Formula and its composition. Nevertheless, if the bilateral accords with the EU were to be defeated, or if controversial changes to direct democracy urged by the SVP were successful or if domestic policy proposals were to be decided in ways which were felt unfair to the Suisse Romande, then the gap could become increasingly acute. Further economic pressures from global pressures, or new attacks over the country's behaviour in the last war, could also affect things. So could attempts to remodel the cantonal structure in line with new social and demographic realities. As it is, French activists in Moutiers have pushed on with divisive demands for rejoining the Jura, setting at naught the fence building attempts in the Jurassian Assembly under a 1994 agreement.

In other words, the Swiss paradigm has its problems, mild though they may be in comparative terms. The post-1992 malaise showed that the problem was not well understood, but while subsequent efforts identified the need to change attitudes they have yet to do this. Nor is it clear that today's renewed concerns will prove more than merely a therapeutic exercise for the elite, specially when the media remain unhelpful. Concentrating on the Latin/German split, as the media does, can mean that the country's other language problems may get over-looked, notably the need to adapt multi-culturalism to accommodate new arrivals in the country. There are no simple answers but the complex of factors engrained in Swiss political culture and its long and successful record of avoiding language conflict are likely to see them through. It may be, as Grin suggests, that they need to look outside for ideas but, in one way or the other, the evolution of the Swiss paradigm seems likely to continue.

1   A. Lijphart, *The Politics of Accommodation*, 2nd edn, University of California Press, 1974. For contrary views see C.H. Church, 'Beyond the Consociational Screen', *West European Politics*, XII(2), 1989; H.P. Kriesi, 'Federalism and Pillarization', *Acta Politica*, XXV/4, 1990; Y. Paddadopolous, 'La Suisse: Un Sonderfall pour la Science Politique', *Université de Lausanne Travaux en Science Politique*, 2, 1991; D.L. Seiler, 'La Suisse comme Democratie Consociationalle' in B. Prongue et al (eds), *Passé Pluriel*, Fribourg: Editions Universitaires, 1992, 341–59; and J. Hottinger, 'La Suisse, une Democratie Consoiatif or de Concordance?', *Revue Internationale de Politique Comparée*, IV(3), 1997.
2   P. Katzenstein, *Corporatism and Change*, Cornell University Press, 1984.
3   E. Kaufman and O. Zimmer, 'In Search of the Authentic Nation', *Nations and Nationalism*, IV(4), 1998. Cf also R. Bernhard (ed), *Die Schweiz alls Wille und Vorstellung*, Aarau: Saulerlander/NHG, 1994.
4   K. Kobach, *The Referendum: Direct Democracy in Switzerland*, Dartmouth, 1993.
5   R. Levy et al, *Tous Égaux?*, Zurich, Seismo, 1997. See also S. Hug and P. Sciarini, 'Switzerland — Still a Paradigmatic Case?' in G. Schneider et al, *Towards a New Europe*, Westport, 1995, 55–74.
6   J. Ribeaud, 'Essai sur la Mésentente Confédérale', *L. Hebdo*, 8 May 1991. Cf A. Treschel, 'Clivages en Suisse', *Diplome d'études Supérieurs*, Université de Genève, 1994.
7   C.H. Church, 'German-Speaking Switzerland since 1937', *Contemporary German Studies Occasional Papers*, University of Strathclyde: Department of Modern Languages, 1989.

8   H.P. Kriesi et al, *Le Clivage Linguistique*, Bern: Bundesamt fur Statistik, 1996.
9   The debate, edited by F. Grin, can be found in volumes 11(2), 1996, III(1), 2 and 4, 1997 with the last having his review of it.
10 Report of the Study Commission on *Strategy Studies*, Berne: Department of Defence, 26 February 1998.

Belgium: Language, Ethnicity and Nationality

BY MICHAEL O'NEILL

Nam tua res agitur, paries cum proximus ardet.
(For it *is* your business, when the wall next door
catches fire. Horace.)

The issue of political identity based on language has become so entrenched in Belgian politics that it threatens the break-up of the state. Linguistic communalism is the principal, though not the exclusive, cleavage in contemporary Belgian politics. The critical problem is how to accommodate two language communities, each dominant in its own region, to the shared endeavour of a nation state. The problématique belge is a residuum of history, though it was not always as politically potent as it has become during recent decades. The fusion of the south Netherlands peoples into a single state in 1830 represented a triumph of common purpose over much less palatable options for the two cultural groups inhabiting a territory that bestrides the ancient fault lines between Romance and Germanic culture. Friction over language and cultural differences eventually crystallised into a full-blown ethnic conflict and what was once merely an irritant in national politics has assumed crisis proportions.

Considerable political energy has been expended in an attempt to resolve this issue. Whether this endeavour succeeds or not will depend on settling outstanding issues during the forthcoming stage of constitutional reform. Prospects for success depend on maintaining the spirit of compromise that has prevailed during the four previous stages. History offers some cause for optimism, though there are no certain outcomes in a country where intercommunity cooperation is under unprecedented pressure from both sides of a growing divide. Political elites in both communities have so far approached the matter of a problematic identity with both imagination and commitment. Regardless of mutual hostility from entrenched factions on both sides, those engaged in the reform of the state have reached much the same conclusions as the founders of Belgium: that however unpalatable the prospect of sharing a common homeland with people of different aspirations and political identity, the vagaries of outright separation threaten even greater uncertainty in an unpredictable world.

Survival of the state is far from being a foregone conclusion. On the surface at least, it seems a less likely prospect with each cycle of constitutional change. The pragmatic option of enduring an ever more tense marriage of political convenience, instead of negotiating a messy divorce, has rather less appeal now than it did even a decade ago, an unravelling of a common purpose due, in part, to a shifting geopolitical landscape. At the outset, the unitary state was the normal model for European state-building. It guaranteed security of sorts, fostered a sense of belonging in a changing world, facilitated industrialisation and market-making, guaranteed an effective fiscal base and sound money, and ensured political self-determination. At this stage of political development, alternative forms of governance were generally regarded as eccentric at best, and at worst contrived. Federalism, for instance, was one such exotic model, though there was a brief acquaintance with federal government in the republic of Les États Belgiques Unies/United Netherlands States, established after the rebellion of the Netherlands provinces in 1790 against Austrian rule. Otherwise, multinational government meant either the despotism of imperial governance, or imposed incorporation in 1815 of the southern and predominantly Catholic provinces of Brabant, Hainaut and Liège into the Netherlands. The result was civil war and rebellion in 1830.

The Belgian state that emerged drew, initially, on a manufactured sense of national identity, manipulated to its own advantage by a francophone elite which adopted a strategy of assimilation. Shared historic experience, and what passed for mutual interests, supposedly overlaid residual cultural differences, reinforced by an invented territorial 'past' rooted in a medieval 'Belgian' heartland with its own 'national' icons, such as the lion of Brabant. For a time this elite-led bargain held.

From 'founding identities' to fighting over tongues

Linguistic divisions were accommodated within this founding bargain, but latent cultural tensions were only 'resolved' by being discounted. Flemish identity was simply overlaid by a dominant francophone culture using the convenient alibi of universal values to disguise its narrow intentions. The strategy worked well enough, and francophone culture was embraced by Flemish aspirants in public life and civil society alike. The predominant goal of 'Belgian-ness', a common national endeavour, was maintained by superimposing the culturally 'superior' French tongue on both primordial Flemish and Walloon dialects.

Tensions were evident, nevertheless, from the outset. There was particular opposition to the law (1831) that established French as the sole official language of politics, administration, the law and commerce. Flemish cultural interests resisted assimilation with a campaign (launched in 1840) for recognition, if not yet parity, of their language. The issue was temporarily marginalised by the growth of democratic politics whose predominant cleavages, as with mass politics in Europe's other industrial states, were those of class rather than territorial or cultural awareness. However, the identity issue was now at least in the public domain, where it has remained ever since. Government responded with caution, establishing a Commission for Grievances (1856) which recommended bilingualism in Flanders and unilingualism in Wallonia, but then fuelled a rising sense of exclusion in the former community by failing to legislate these modest reforms. Even after language laws did reach the statute book they merely permitted bilingualism for non-francophone speakers in the judicial process (1873), public administration (1878) and secondary education (1883). There was some success for an inclusive Belgian identity when both languages were used on bank notes and postage stamps. Agitation continued, eventually ensuring parity of the languages (1898), but it was at most a symbolic victory, as discrimination continued against non-francophone citizens in employment, education, and the public services. Obstacles to personal advancement persisted, regardless of formal linguistic parity, and increased tensions encouraged a marked shift in the direction of the campaign when the Flemish movement widened its ambitions to demand complete cultural parity. The political stakes were raised, from merely the demand for language recognition to a claim to identity rooted in ethnicity as such, leading to 'the emergence of a new Flemish ethnic identity, which for the first time could be separated from Belgian identity, although to a certain extent still forming a part of it'.[1] The problématique belge has been the abiding legacy of this shift.

The consequences of politicising ethnic identity

Ideological prominence in matters of ethnicity and racial origin during the present century has consolidated a sense of Flemish ethnie as the basis of a distinct political identity, calling into question the very meaning of Belgian nationality and by degrees destabilising the state to the point of threatening the country's existence. German occupation in the two world wars encouraged Flemish separatism; Germany's defeat in 1945, and the recriminations in Belgium that followed the inquest on the occupation, brought to the surface deep-seated antagonisms, fuelling a bitter debate over patriotism throughout the postwar decade. Anti-Flemish feelings and francophone triumphalism were rekindled as the country tried to exorcise the ghosts of collaboration. A dispute over the wartime role of the King, leading eventually to his abdication, exacerbated Flemish/Walloon divisions. Meanwhile, another issue, a dispute over state subsidies for denominational education, distracted attention, until it was resolved in 1958. Thereafter, however, cultural and language rights, and ethnic identity, grew in significance. By the 1960s the language issue was the focus of simmering communal friction. What would have been an acceptable compromise in a previous era was now upstaged by accelerating demands. Flanders finally secured unilingual status in 1962 and the cultural autonomy that went with it. The country was divided into two unilingual zones, but Brussels and some of its environs — located in historic Flanders but long the symbol of francophone ascendancy—became a bilingual region, and as such a new cultural battleground. Economic change served to intensify the issue of linguistic/cultural parity. Agricultural decline, initially costly to Flanders, brought economic restructuring which encouraged a new regional prosperity; and with it the political self-confidence to assert a renewed sense of ethnic identity. Wallonia's experience was the reverse of this trend. A steady decline in heavy industry saw unparalleled uncertainty, reactivating a long dormant sense of Wallonian nationalism. Both sides of a widening cultural divide mobilised, either in pursuit or in defence of their own advantage, adding to a climate of opinion that downgraded the idea of 'Belgian-ness'.

The politics of identity became the principal modus vivendi of national politics, which by degrees precipitated nothing less than a crisis of state. Prior to the 1960s, language rights were a Flemish grievance: Wallonian concerns were primarily economic. Thereafter, economic and cultural issues became fused in both communities. Anti-Flemish feeling in Wallonia (and to a lesser extent in Brussels) confronted an increasingly assertive identity within Flanders. Ethnic parties mobilised, some of extremist disposition. Even the established 'national' parties, once ranged along the traditional left-right ideological spectrum, divided into their linguistic components, adding to the difficulty of negotiating stable coalition governments. The once routine consociational procedures that had kept political crisis at bay were harder to sustain, though to date political elites—and a majority of the people—have still preferred to negotiate a national bargain than move towards outright separation. The most significant outcome of this accommodation has been to remake the unitary state, obliging the political class to restructure the architecture of government. The critical question remains whether, after four stages in the reform of the state, and with another stage imminent, the federal experiment has accommodated distinct cultural identities, thus preventing the disintegration of Belgium, or merely postponed (and perhaps accelerated) the demise of an artificial state.

Unravelling the unitary state: accommodation or demise?

By 1970 it was apparent that ethnic identity was sufficiently entrenched amongst the dominant linguistic communities. What was equally clear was that the unitary state, established for the very purpose of nation-building under francophone domination, was now anathema to Flemish identity and self-interest. Reform at this stage was, however, more reactive than considered, an ad hoc rather than a priori project. Incremental adjustments were made as socio-economic change fundamentally altered the balance of advantage between the communities, and reform of the state followed this piecemeal pattern over more than two decades.[2] Its central concern was how best to satisfy increasingly divergent communal interests without tearing asunder the state.

As events have accelerated, the rise of separatist tendencies means that reconciling both communities to the idea of a unitary state is now simply out of the question. The challenge is how to accommodate competing territorial interests within a loose-structured federal polity as an alternative to outright partition. Extremist parties have tested the nerve of moderate politicians in both communities, as well as raising the stakes of constitutional politics. After 1991, the extremist and separatist party Vlaams Blok (VB), became committed to a state restricted to a Flemish ethnie (and campaigning on the slogan 'own people first'). Its sanitised version spoke of a language 'test' for citizenship to curb francophone immigration, but it was also wedded to explicit racist notions by proposing to restore jus sanguinis to Belgian nationality law, so excluding non-whites.[3] Meanwhile, Wallonian counterparts, such as the Mouvement Wallon pour le Retour à la France, demanded secession from Belgium. The Front National (FN) is a racist party that celebrates Belgian patriotism on its own narrow ethnic terms. The far right-wing faction, Agir stands as the 'defender' of the Wallonian people.

Even the mainstream parties have contrived, in this febrile climate, to prise loose the cement of a common nationhood. Under growing pressure within its own electoral heartland, from a constituency facing multiple socio-economic disadvantages, the Wallonian Parti Socialiste (PS) has begun to play the cultural card alongside more familiar class politics, though not entirely to the exclusion of an inclusive sense of 'Belgitude' rooted in the left's commitment to universal political values.[4] Elements, too, amongst both the Flemish Christian Democrats and Liberal parties have responded favourably to the idea of a semi-autonomous Flanders, independent in all but name albeit within a loose Belgian confederation.

Centrifugal tensions are apparent on all sides, but the more insistent threat to a Belgium state comes from Flanders where cultural identity has been transformed into a politicised ethnicity bolstered in recent years by economic well-being and demographic supremacy. Important differences of historical conditioning and sociological experience account for the relative absence in Wallonia of an *ethnic* as opposed to a merely an abiding sense of *cultural* identity. It can be argued that Wallonia clings more stubbornly to the idea of Belgium because it needs Flanders to prop up its ailing regional economy, but this is only a part of a more complex reality. The legacy of an assimilationist Belgian culture is deeply etched into the Wallonian psyche. The region's industrial base always attracted immigrants from Flanders who were readily absorbed into its class-based culture. The francophone culture has always been more reflective of universalism than of exclusive, particularistic values.

The significance of this tense battleground should not be underestimated. Federalism is certainly the heart of the matter: how to remake, indeed reimagine, a once unitary state in order to accommodate rising ethnic-communal tensions within an inclusive and democratic political architecture, and thus avoid break-up. One critical question is whether federalism is more the problem than the solution. Some observers have argued that federalising Belgium has had the very opposite effect to that intended. Institutionalising — and expanding in regular cycles of constitutional reform — the differences between distinct cultural identities has, as some see it, progressively denuded the state of either meaning or common purpose. More than that, increasing the autonomy of territorial governance has accelerated ethnic tensions, obliging the political class to contemplate the previously unthinkable, outright separation. According to this scenario, federalising the state can be construed as an institutionalised response to a fast disappearing resolution to live together in an agreed national partnership.[5]

The obverse of this pessimistic narrative is to see federalism as a testament to the commitment of most of the political class to calm communal tensions. The pace of recent developments has made it difficult to balance communal interests, though this is precisely the objective of federalism. What is clear is that the unitary state has been federalised by stages. Unilingual zones became the basis for francophone and Flemish cultural communities, permitting a degree of autonomy in language matters, though not initially in the politically sensitive area of education. Three economic regions were also instituted, in Flanders, Wallonia and Brussels, each with authority over some aspects of economic policy. Both principal ethnies enjoyed parity in the arrangements of national government. But these initial arrangements amounted to little more than devolution as an attempt to facilitate self-government. Limits were placed on the discretion of community councils, while the supremacy of the national parliament, the embodiment of sovereignty in the unitary state, was ensured by the requirement that all laws passed under the new jurisdictions needed to be endorsed by a *constituant* (two-thirds) parliamentary majority.

The unitary state then began to unravel, with the politicians in uncharted territory and lacking any consensus about the next stage. The Brussels question became the main bone of contention. Linguistically mixed communes in the capital's suburbs defied a neat territorial solution. Located geographically in Flanders, but a 'francophied city' since 1830, Brussels was on the front line of rising ethnic tension. Demography ensured tense politics: Fleming moderates demanded linguistic parity and power-sharing, more militant voices preferred inclusion in Flanders, while the francophone majority demanded full regional status. As such, the capital issue has become the principal gauge of success of the projected reforms, though far from being resolved and certain to re-emerge in the forthcoming constitutional round.

The reform project was launched in 1970. A familiar pattern emerged: incremental adjustment by concentrating on issues where compromise was feasible, leaving aside more difficult matters until a period of reflection restored the will to tackle them. The normal exigencies of politics reinforce this cyclical pattern. The politics of identity is, after all, a critical but not the exclusive concern of government. Other issues — redistributive policy, ecological matters, civil rights and so on — retain political purchase and periodically relegate the constitutional question to a low ranking on the national agenda. The reform project has also been waylaid at various critical junctures by mounting economic crisis. After 1970, for instance, the upheaval in the management of the international political economy raised critical issues for every modern state.

It was only in the 1980s that Belgium's political class was able to return to the unresolved matters of constitutional reform. Intensive negotiations ensured a consensus to take reform a stage further. Two language communities were instituted, as well as recognition of the small German speaking enclave in the south east, although economic development was reserved to the Wallonian region in which the German community was located. Brussels remained the principal outstanding issue. The tenor of these latest changes was devolutionary, in as much as legislation by subnational authorities was accorded the full status of law, though parliament retained its status as the supreme sovereign body. Moreover, regardless of modest prerogatives over public expenditure in devolved matters, the principal source of revenue remained grant aid from the centre, with the central revenue department continuing to collect taxes and direct the national finances. Nevertheless, these latest changes represented a clear stage in deconcentrating power from the centre, and there was a growing consensus in favour of more far-reaching reform. An agenda was agreed that amounted to nothing less than federalising the state: the transfer of social and related policy matters to the subnational authorities which were to be directly elected, an agreement that regional legislation had parity of status with national law, and was so regarded by national agencies and citizens alike; with provision, too, for 'own fiscal resources' — an elaborate formula for allocating revenue from death duties, registration and radio/television licence fees, a proportion of VAT returns and other national taxes, as well as the right to levy a supplement to national income tax and to exercise independent borrowing rights. A proportion of a national solidarity fund would then replace bloc grants from the centre. Effective arbitration procedures — a sine qua non of federalism — are intended to settle demarcation disputes between complementary or overlapping jurisdictions. This ambitious agenda was been the basis of subsequent reform.

A programme along these lines was implemented between 1980 and 1993. It included an arbitration court, extra fiscal powers for communities and regions, additional devolution from central government in education, culture and language policy, in transport, public works, energy policy, the environment, supervision of local authorities, town and country planning and scientific research.⁶ Settling the status of Brussels was postponed until, with most of the straightforward issues out of the way, energies could be concentrated on resolving this impasse. The eventual settlement was a familiar positive-sum bargain that fits the Belgian consociational temper. On one side, francophones secured regional status for the city, but only after agreeing to reserve to central government some responsibility for managing affairs in a city that is both the national capital and the seat of the European Union. The minority Flemish community, on the other hand, secured a guaranteed role in the governance of the new region in proportion to its demographic size, giving it, in effect, a virtual veto over affairs.

The resolution of the Brussels question has confirmed an asymmetrical federalism. The coexistence of ethnic communities in Brussels and its far-flung suburbs in the Flanders region has prevented a more symmetrical territorial arrangement. Instead, the less than clear-cut demography requires a novel federal architecture to ensure that the city is governable. The council of the Brussels capital-region divides into its linguistic constituencies when dealing with community matters but sits as a composite body when common or regional issues are discussed. In order to ensure maximum consensus, as well as to reassure the Flemish minority, some responsibility for the city's affairs remains with central government, and the city-region's legislation has less formal authority than that of the other two regions. The arbitration court retains the right to overrule Brussels' legislation if it is deemed to be contrary to an acceptable national standard of communal equity and non-discrimination. The executive, too, must be communally balanced.

The federal end game

The most recent, but certainly not the final stage in the reform project occurred with the formal acknowledgement in 1993 that Belgium is a fully fledged federal state.⁷ The Accord de la St Michel completed the gradual federalising of the state, formally demarcating the respective powers of the federal and constituent governments. The regions now manage most aspects of economic and employment policy, trade, urban planning, housing and environment policy and some aspects of scientific policy, supervision of local government, agriculture—except pricing policy (which has implications both for a single national market and Belgium's obligations to the European Union's Common Agricultural Policy) and external trade. The communities deal with cultural matters (including the broadcast media and sport), education, social matters (including health and family policy). Substate authorities are now 'federal authorities', directly elected from 1999 and with increased powers; their executives have the status of governments in their own right, able to engage in foreign relations: for instance, signing treaties with foreign governments or international organisations, albeit only in those matters for which they have competence and after consulting with the centre, but a prerogative which nevertheless enhances their authority and political profile. The imperative of adopting a coherent position in the increasingly important international arena, where so much of what is eventually legislated as domestic policy is determined, helps modulate out-and-out separatism. The federal state and the subnational authorities have adopted a cooperation accord (1994) that enjoins each side to act in concert in external relations.[8] There is rather more evidence of a truly federalist tenor in setting constitutional norms; revision of procedures is no longer at the sole discretion of the centre. The constituent authorities have, albeit modest, constitutional prerogatives. Subject to a two-thirds majority of elected members, they may, without reference to the centre, alter their own size, electoral boundaries and procedures.

Fiscal federalism is less extensive than it might be. The centre manages the national budget, though it now raises revenue for policy matters over which it has little direct control. The critical boundaries of fiscal federalism are yet to be determined. There is a residual tension between central and regional governments over the management of macro-economic policy, maintaining an equitable internal market, responsibility for the national debt and social expenditure. Other sources of friction familiar to federal arrangements promise a febrile politics. The centre, as in any federal polity, retains considerable reserve powers in the devolved areas and manages the usual common services — defence and security, foreign policy, citizenship, some legal matters and judicial review, monetary policy, social security (family allowance, pensions, unemployment benefit) and public health. Some concurrent or reserve powers exist, too, in devolved matters where an overarching national interest is deemed likely to collide with narrower communal interests: inter alia, setting environmental and professional standards, basic social security norms, energy pricing, broadcasting regulations, national cultural and scientific policy, infra-structure and national transport networks. The administration of justice is also subject to central oversight.

The parliamentary system — once the fount of national sovereignty — has been substantially revised to accommodate the shift to a fully federal state. The lower house (Chamber) has gained some powers, reflecting its critical role as the sole democratic institution that embodies whatever remains of national solidarity. The Senate, meanwhile, has been substantially reduced, both in size and powers, and is now merely a place for discussion and deliberation on the great issues of the moment — another indication of the increased authority of the regional tier of governance.

Reform of the state remains an incremental rather than a conclusive project, with occasional bursts of energy followed by a period of adjustment to unprecedented change on the ground. As such, it was agreed to revisit the constitutional issue after the 1999 elections, when all authorities are directly elected. Meanwhile, Belgium has continued to experience a period of political pressure, excessive even by its own frenetic standards, which intensified the demand for further reform and emphasised widespread resentment in both communities at political pelf and administrative incompetence. Corruption at the very highest level, and loss of faith in the effectiveness of the policing and criminal justice systems after the Dutroux paedophile case, provoked the so-called 'White March' and brought 300,000 protesters to Brussels in 1996. A protracted crisis of national governance has led to multiple ministerial resignations and criminal prosecution, most notably the Agusta-Dassault trial (1998) in the wake of revelations about bribes paid into the coffers of both regional Socialist Parties in exchange for defence contracts, and whose defendants included four former ministers, two of them deputy premiers. More than half the cabinet have been forced from office between 1995–99. A scare over public health management, with dioxin poisoning of food supplies, broke during the recent election campaign — a débâcle that saw supermarkets emptied of chicken, eggs and meat. It provoked two further ministerial resignations and, above all, confirmed the broad perception of government incompetence that touched politicians of all mainstream parties in both communities.

Changes further afield also served to increase public ambivalence about the meaning and expediency of the state. The government's decision to join the European Monetary Union in the first wave, despite a budget deficit double the target set in the Maastricht treaty of 3% of GDP and a massive public debt burden, required prolonged and painful fiscal retrenchment. The deficit did fall to 1.3%, and the debt subsided by 1999 from 135 to 118% of GDP, with the economy back to surplus growth, but this has been achieved at heavy political cost. A notable consequence of EMU membership, for instance, has been a sea-change in national economic management, including the much publicised take over by foreign (principally French and Dutch) companies of many flagship Belgian companies. The Société Générale de Belgique which formerly controlled a third of the economy, underlines this trend of losing national control of some of the key levers of economic management, an outcome whose irony is not lost on Belgians aware of their own history. Belgium once again faces, albeit in circumstances altogether different from those that confronted the state's founders, a squeeze by more powerful neighbours.

This shift in global power puts into perspective more narrowly focused tribal quarrels about the locus of constitutional authority. What this will mean over the longer term for a residual national psyche is less than clear. The circumstances of such changes do not quite add up to an impression of a state without an abiding sense of its own national interest, since external forces tend to give a sense of perspective absent when the principal focus of affairs is shaped by abiding domestic rivalries. Besieged it may be, but Belgium (on this reading of events) is not yet a state wholly lacking a common purpose. To this extent, Belgium is not facing terminal decline. But there is a mood of perplexity which may have any number of outcomes. On the one hand, it may deepen already implacable communal identities, as the impact of globalising forces has elsewhere, by persuading culturally coherent fragments that their best option for surviving a relentlessly competitive international economy is to play to its ethnic strengths and to cut adrift from the drag of a larger polity that submerges and discounts their particular interests. On the other hand, it may enjoin them to realise a common fate and give them an awareness that the sheer task of economic survival requires a pooling of efforts in order to survive. The reform project is a response, in part, to this predicament. It is unclear what its outcome will be — whether federalism will be underpinned or outright separation — but the scale of the task is apparent from the outstanding issues yet to be settled in the forthcoming reform round.

Facing up to divorce or contemplating a shared future?

The 1999 elections were a minor earthquake in Belgian politics, confirming the steady decline in support for the Flemish Christian Democrats (Christelijke Volkspartij — CVP), the longstanding national powerbrokers; a modest rise in the vote of the Flemish Liberals (Vlaams Liberale Democraten — VLD), though not of their Wallonian sister party (Parti Réformateur Liberal PRL); and a surge for both Green parties (Agalev and Ecolo) helped by the dioxin débâcle, but rewarded too for their steadfast endorsement of communal cooperation. Support for the extremist VB was less than anticipated on the basis of pre-campaign opinion polls, thereby preventing an impasse in the Brussels assembly that would certainly have complicated the 1999 reform round. These elections have added, nevertheless, to the difficulty of finding sufficient consensus for the next reform stage. The national power balance has shifted from a centre-left to a right-left axis under parties diametrically opposed over both ideological and constitutional preferences. It remains to be seen, with Flemish Liberal and Wallonian Socialists as the principal coalition partners, whether a *constituant* majority exists in the Chamber for dealing with what are, after all, unresolved and immensely perplexing constitutional issues. The return to national government of the VLD, a party hardly noted for its benign outlook on the present federal arrangements, and the exclusion of the centrist CVP and Parti Social Chrétien (PSC), the most consistent architects of communal accommodation, promises difficult negotiations.

These events have put at the epicentre of affairs a party whose leading lights are, at best, lukewarm about the federalist trajectory, together with a party widely perceived as the very embodiment of venality. In the circumstances, the 1999 reform round promises to be the most contested so far. Even the CVP, painfully aware of electoral ground lost to its more extreme regional rivals, is now more inclined to intransigence, challenging much in a federal formula that it was instrumental in negotiating. One particularly unhelpful contribution to the present debate illustrates precisely the degree of consociational slippage in a movement once noted for common sense on communal matters. The Minister President of Flanders, Luc Van den Brande, has taken up populist Wallonia-bashing, criticising that region's 'sick man' status and jibing at its 'Marxist economic policies'. The stakes have been raised, too, by the growing support in both the Chamber and regional assemblies for extremist parties in both communities (most notably VB) which support a separatist agenda or worse, an unalloyed xenophobic celebration of what they deem ethnic/racial 'virtues'.

Evidence of a rising temperature can be seen in the re-emergence of the bilingual quarrel in the mixed communes around Brussels. Six communes, formally part of Flanders region but with substantial francophone minorities or majorities, and each providing both public services and documents in both languages, were ordered (1998) on the instructions of the Flemish regional Interior Minister to rescind this provision. The six mayors resisted the instruction, arguing that it challenged their legal status as 'communes facilité': that is, communes where official use of both languages is permitted under the 1962 law. The Flemish region has ruled that hereafter no commune shall issue official documents in French unless a resident specifically requests it; and that no such documentation will be valid unless first issued in Flemish. It insisted that the 'original arrangement was only intended as temporary until francophone residents acquired Flemish. This dispute, marginal as to its demographic impact, has far-reaching political implications for the approaching constitution round, mirroring the equally significant tribalism of the Fourons/Voeren dispute in 1995 — a Flemish enclave in Wallonia. The same issue has reappeared in Brussels where Flemish politicians have resisted an EU directive that permits non-nationals voting rights in local elections, arguing that as these immigrants speak French rather than Dutch, they are more likely to vote for francophone candidates. The Minister for Brussels in the Flemish regional government, a leading CVP member, refused to allow the change, unless the federal government guaranteed automatic representation for the Flemish community in the Brussels assembly.

This issue is as potent now as when it first surfaced. Cultural exclusivism continues to simmer on the surface of politics, a stark reminder of what is at stake for the negotiators who must address this still raw issue. The Flemish *Laatste Nieuws* in August 1999 summarised the elemental, still unresolved question of political identity reflected in these quarrels as follows: 'What are we doing together? What should we ask the federal government to do? Such questions on the ultimate meaning of Belgium have to be answered in the end. If we avoid them the volcano will explode.'

The principal contentious issues for the next constitution reform round are as follows.

Federal taxation arrangements. The 1989 financial agreement, whereby the federal government continues to collect the bulk of taxation but distributes these revenues to regional governments to meet their expenditure, was always an interim arrangement. The logic of rising disparities of opportunity in a country where one cultural community is disproportionately more prosperous than another, raises the stakes of fiscal federalism. The negotiators will have to return to this issue, precisely because of the growing gulf in the perceived self-interest of the respective communities. There was only interim settlement of this thorny issue in 1993, with further reform postponed, following the usual practice of piecemeal adjustments which use up the political capital required for more far-reaching reform, but with the issues at least clarified for a future constitutional round.

As with redistributive politics in any fragmented society, this issue has the potential for exacerbating intercommunal relations. In short, Flanders has more to gain, Wallonia most to lose from separating out the public finances so as to ensure a closer link between the regional contributions to national revenue and the regional expenditure levels. So far, the impact of devolving fiscal functions to the regions has been weakened by central government's retention of the taxation prerogative and the allocation of revenue share by bloc grants. In addition, the differential service provision that would result from public spending based on purely demographic calculations is adjusted by use of a compensation mechanism—a 'national solidarity fund'—to ensure a degree of equity in public goods across the communal divide. Flemish interests regard the present arrangement as a direct subsidy to Wallonia, preferring a fiscal formula that more closely balances the ratio of public expenditure in the regions with their contribution to GNP. It was felt to be inopportune to tackle this sensitive issue in 1993. Instead, the Flemish centre-right settled for a review of finance procedures within the decade. In view of the growing regional disparity, both in the levels of prosperity and employment opportunities, compounded by the severe economic downturn that has disproportionately affected Wallonia, this issue promises to be a real test of what remains of a residual national solidarity between the communities.

Federalising social security. Much the same can be said about the parallel demand by some Flemish politicians to federalise the national social security system. Economic interests and ethnic identity are unavoidably linked. Flemish assertiveness is, in no small measure, a direct reflection of shifts in the balance of material and demographic advantage between the communities. Profiting from population growth, inward investment, and the relocation of the tertiary and new technology sectors to a region at the very heart of the new European market, Flanders has seen economic regeneration and falling unemployment.

The Language Valley, once a battlefield of the Great War, has become a European 'Silicon Valley'. Prosperity, likewise, has consolidated the position of centre/right parties in a predominantly conservative political culture. Wallonia's economic fortunes, on the other hand, have declined: deindustrialisation and unemployment have increased the region's dependence on social welfare transfers

The Socialists, meanwhile, have maintained their electoral pre-eminence, regardless of recent scandals. Regular participation by the Parti Socialiste in national coalitions has helped maintain one of the most generous social security systems in the Continent, though costly to business, with average wage costs at some 15% higher than in Belgium's principal EU competitors. This burden has provoked resistance from centre-right liberals, demanding reform of inflexible, non-competitive wage-bargaining and social security arrangements. The incoming VLD-led government will be rather less squeamish about tackling this issue head on.

The close connection between ideological preference and political identity affects constitutional discourse. Flemish opinion sees, by and large, only advantage from federalising social welfare provision. It is amenable now to the arguments of those preferring, at the very least, a region as hermetically sealed as possible from the exogenous drain on its enterprise by profligate Wallonians. In a country now confronted by some unpalatable economic choices, as it strives to meet the demanding fiscal criteria for participation in EMU, this issue, too, is bound to loom larger still.

Some of the tension from the debate is attributable to the relative deprivation that accrues when one self-identified community perceives lack of interest by another. This is a familiar feature of territorial politics that only widespread prosperity and employment opportunities can settle. The recent efforts by the Wallonian region to attract inward investment and employment will be crucial to resolving this grievance, though success is by no means assured, or may not come soon enough. The prognosis is, at best, mixed: transforming an archaic industrial base, reskilling a traditional workforce, promoting more flexible work practices and coping with massive environmental clean-up costs present a formidable challenge. On the positive side, Hainaut, the most populous province, has acquired formal status as an EU Objective 1 area, and Liège is classified as an Objective 2 area. As such, both are eligible for development aid. Moreover, Wallonia's workforce has a residuum of skills and is mostly multilingual, and there is abundant land for development (including surplus office space) and an excellent transport infrastructure in a region at the very core of the EU market. The Office for Foreign Investors (1991) had already attracted some $6 billions worth of inward investment in the decade up to 1997. Economic regeneration takes time and patience as well as resources: meanwhile, communal relations will not be well served by calls from clear economic

winners across the language divide to force the less advantaged region
to take full responsibility for its own welfare.

Federalising the public debt. The improvement in the state of the
national finances has not removed indebtedness or abated the Flemish
preference to apportion its burdens 'equitably' so as not to penalise its
own 'thrift' by carrying the welfare burden of prodigal neighbours.
Reducing the debt level to 118% of GDP is only a relative achievement.
It remains twice the Maastricht criterion of 60%, though debt reduction
is a central objective of fiscal policy and there is a 6% surplus in the
annual budget put by to cover retrenchment.

Whether this strategy will satisfy the demand from Flanders for
wholesale reallocation, indeed a repatriation, of the public debt remains
to be seen. As with the parallel debate on federalising social security,
such compromises seem unlikely to appease a population convinced
that its own enterprise is subsidising wasteful outsiders. Restricting
growth in public expenditure (to 1.3% against projected economic
growth of 2.4% for the current financial year), and a reduction in the
proportion of GDP allocated to public expenditure (from 38 to 37.7%),
is regarded by critics of current arrangements as no more than trifling
measures. Flemish opinion regards the federal government's reluctance
to curb public spending as clear evidence of a regime whose political
will is paralysed by archaic fiscal notions; the counter view regards the
demand for reallocating the debt burden as sheer malice.

Policing and legal reform. The spectacle of local police services and
the national gendarmerie refusing to share information in the hunt for
a child rapist, each force preferring to win plaudits for solving the case
on its own, merely adds to public disquiet over cumulate ineptitude.
The Dutroux débâcle, and other instances of police incompetence, have
facilitated consensus — the so-called 'Octopus' eight-party initiative — to
reform the criminal justice system. Legislation is already going through
parliament to replace three existing police forces by a single federal
force; communal forces and gendarmerie brigades are to be fused into
'zonal' units at local level, and a federal prosecutor's office is to be
instituted to coordinate national investigations. Judges will cease to be
political appointments linked to local authorities, but will be appointed
by a Supreme Council of Justice elected by judges and senators. This
initiative should reinforce the cement of national self-interest, enhancing
in some degree the perception of a national endeavour long associated
with nation statehood — the reasonable expectation that citizens should
enjoy public order and safety.

Federal asymmetry and the Brussels question. As a predominantly
francophone island within Flanders, Brussels reflects the very tensions
that are the root of the problématique belge. Capital-region status and
the presence of the European Commission have brought the city unparalleled advantages. But the city's prominence has, if anything, raised the
political stakes. Its febrile politics reflect every type of identity in play

in Belgium. Unitarists, for instance, see Brussels as a model European city, a fount of modern enterprise and multiculturalism, a testament to what could be achieved in communal cooperation in the country at large when politicians dwell on what unites rather than divides the communities. This reconciliation model has prevailed in the administration of the city during its first decade as a region in its own right. The Minister President, Charles Picque, argued for more 'own resources' — a greater return from the federal exchequer for the 35% of Belgium's corporate taxes that the city's businesses contribute to the federal exchequer — in the form of an annual bloc grant. That would acknowledge the capital's special contribution to national affairs, but it is a viewpoint vigorously resisted by the other two regions.

There is resistance amongst cosmopolitan interests well represented in the capital, which are anxious to defend a residual Belgian identity, to moves in the regions to drag Brussels deeper into the mire of communalism. Elements in both linguistic groups regard Brussels as the natural locale of 'Belgitude' — a city with a federal status akin to Washington DC, Ottawa or Canberra. Louis Tobback, the president of the Flemish Socialistischa Partij, has taken this idea further, proposing a self-governing, self-financing city state, designated as Brussels DC, in whose governance the EU would play a significant part. This project is rejected by moderate opinion on all sides of city politics which prefers to see Brussels as proof extant that communal cohabitation in the national capital is a template for cooperation in the country at large. Charles Picque, for instance, has spoken of a 'residual belgitude', with the city remaining as 'a *fédérateur*, or unionist, part of Belgium'. He argues that: 'It would be a tragedy if the capital of Europe became a symbol of cultural division. It would be a real paradox . . . an unimaginable paradox, though the risk is there.' According to this benign view, Brussels represents a bridge of communal understanding between two entrenched communities which 'have not always realised Brussels' importance to their own development . . . Belgium is undergoing a test at the moment, and Brussels is part of that test. It is a bilingual region and we have shown the capacity of Flemings and francophones to work together, against the background of a cosmopolitan and multicultural city'.[9]

Other views reflect mindsets more exercised by communalism. The Wallonian Socialists have one eye on a dwindling regional power base, another on an already coherent Flemish polity. They are mindful, too, of less ideologically reliable francophones in the cosmopolitan capital who prefer to keep their distance from traditional Wallonian roots. They have advocated instead a fusion of regional and community authorities within its own geographical area. The current trajectory of state reform does favour tidying up an asymmetrical federal architecture. The St Michel Accord did acknowledge the right of the francophone community to transfer powers to the Wallonian regional council, and in the Brussels region to the francophone community commission. Yet resistance remains, amongst some of the capital's francophones, to weakening the city's regional status. The Front Démocratique des Francophones are staunch defenders of capital-region status under francophone hegemony.

Flemish opinion, on the other hand, resists any proposal for strengthening francophone dominance, preferring instead to retain parity of status in Brussels' governance. Evidence that the city's delicate linguistic balance is under severe pressure from accelerating communalism came with a dispute (1998) which saw Flemish politicians call for—and the francophone majority duly resist—a formal language ratio in the city's fire service of 70% francophone and 30% Flemish, though the actual demographic ratio is 85:15% francophone. Political opinion, too, reflects increased intercommunal tensions. In the 1995 regional elections the Front National took four of the 65 seats reserved for francophone parties, and VB two from the ten reserved Flemish seats. In spite of dire predictions, however, the 1999 elections have not significantly increased the base of extremist parties, though VB went into these elections with the intention of securing enough seats to obstruct assembly business.

The Brussels 2000 project, which aims to launch the capital as one of nine European Cities of Culture and is directed by a committee which brings together language and political groups on all sides, captures the enduring paradox of a city that bestrides an historic fault-line. Yet all is far from straightforward, even in a city with some enlightened community leaders. The British project director, quoted in the *Financial Times*, detects deep-seated tensions simmering beneath surface civility: 'a ritual dance around the fire but no one has actually jumped into it yet . . . though if one (faction) pushes too hard it forces the others to push hard too (and) that's how the construction could end in chaos' (31 March 1999). As such, this project for civic renewal reflects in miniature the country's persistent crisis of identity.

Futures: will the Belgian bargain stand?

Federalism is a political strategy as much as a constitutional formula, and its success depends on the sociological conditions that underpin political arrangements. As a response to declining national solidarity, federalism can be as much a risk as a remedy. The endeavour of the Belgian political class to accommodate pronounced cultural diversity has added momentum to these centrifugal tendencies as much as it has ameliorated them. In short, federalising the Belgian state has confirmed the everyday experiences of citizens inhabiting two distinct communities: it has not enhanced a common national interest, and without countervailing forces the affective solidarity that sustains federal states elsewhere may become so diminished as to threaten the very continuance of the body politic.

Several aspects of social life confirm this predicament. Federalisation of the broadcasting media, for instance, has meant that broadcasters concentrate on 'domestic' events, discounting or portraying negatively those in the 'other' community. The same can be said about the adoption of separate curricula in education and the abolition of conscription — removing what has long served in fractured societies as a unifying experience. Meanwhile, the federal division of large areas of socio-economic experience into distinct cultural/linguistic zones has tended to inhibit demographic migration between them. And though Brussels does remain as a cosmopolitan magnet, rising communalism there does not bode well for a continuing sense of national purpose.

Constitutional change has primarily been a response to rising communal frictions, but events in Belgium have also been influenced by developments further afield. Imitation is a natural instinct and particular events, for example the peaceful 'divorce' of the Czech and Slovakian republics, have encouraged separatists on both sides to believe that even small polities breaking free from larger entities are now a viable prospect. The very success of the EU in fostering regional identity has boosted the appeal of micro-states, independent but integrated into wider regional political arrangements, monetary systems and markets. Other examples exert a contrary pressure. The ethnic barbarism that accompanied the dismemberment of the former Yugoslavian federation is a persuasive object lesson of what can follow the break-up of any state into its communal constituents. Any number of less malignant solutions are possible short of break-up.

The Belgian problematic is by no means a singular predicament, even if its particular circumstances bespeak a singular history. And a comparative perspective adds a sanguine tenor to the debate. The politics of territorial and cultural identity are indeed a universal phenomenon; one that is influenced by wider structural changes rewriting the rules of politics, encouraging a fundamental re-evaluation of the architecture of government. Changing expectations, new aspirations and revised notions of identity are all forces actively challenging the classic nation state everywhere, even in culturally coherent societies used to stable politics. Change continues apace in the wake of unprecedented structural shifts in contemporary political economy. The prospect of 'ever closer' European integration, the porosity of national boundaries, the exponential growth of transnational interests and accelerating globalisation are insidious forces 'hollowing out' existing nation states, encouraging novel prospects for multi-level governance above the state, as well as influencing subnational interests to pursue self-government as a more manageable option within a highly regulated international order. Socio-economic shifts are, of course, ambiguous: both a conservative influence and a force for progress, fostering insecurity as well as encouraging experimentation. On the one hand, an increasingly competitive, far from stable international environment does encourage exclusive ideas of belonging, the craving for past certainties in a mutable world, in turn causing ethnic groups to follow atavistic instincts.[10] But unremitting change opens up prospects for radically rethinking the architecture of politics, reimagining political identity. Belgium is far from being unique in confronting this challenge, even if its particular history suggests an especially daunting predicament.

Pessimists have seen in these developments the obsolescence of the nation state, an unravelling of national purpose. On this reading of events, Belgium might seem to be a prime candidate for partition. Certainly, separation is openly discussed nowadays and is eagerly anticipated in some quarters. An intermediate position, between outright separatism and the more usual variants of top-down or even cooperative federalism, continues to prefer a confederal arrangement to secession. The principal power-brokers had already begun to reassess the present federal arrangements before a combination of political mismanagement and deeper shifts in both public and elite loyalty to the historic national project undermined their customary power base. Even as his national party leaders were constructing the federal edifice in 1993, the then CVP head of the Flemish government, Luc Van den Brande, was arguing volubly for a confederation of two sovereign but cooperating states, and laying claim to Brussels as the capital of the putative Flemish state.[11]

There is, however, a more constructive, indeed optimistic, interpretation of current events. As a unitary state, the Belgian project was bound to experience centrifugal tensions once Flemish identity began to assert itself over language rights when the region discovered the political self-confidence that usually accompanies prosperity. The one-sided founding bargain that was the unitary state could hardly be expected to survive a persistent, determined demand for cultural parity. Wallonia's steady decline was also bound to provoke negative reactions across the communal divide. As Louis Vos sees these contending forces working on the political imagination of the respective communities: 'From a long perspective of time, it can be said that the Belgian nation had to make room gradually for the birth of a Walloon and Flemish ethnic identity which in recent years have grown into almost fully fledged nationalities. Today the waning of Belgian identity is almost complete . . . distinct Flemish and Walloon national identities have by and large superceded it.'[12]

There may be life yet in the idea of Belgium as a single if no longer a unitary state. The coexistence of what are now politicised ethnies within a still evolving federal architecture does suggest that, for many of the political class, and even for a 'silent majority' of citizens, including those in the minority German speaking community and in bilingual Brussels, a residual Belgian patriotism continues to exist alongside assertive national identities. Several groups, including the Mouvement Pour une Belgique Rénovee dans une Union Fédérale, recently issued 'An Appeal by Supporters of Reconciliation' to whoever became the next government *formateur* to reject the 'attitude of considering the partitioning of Belgium as inevitable', and to speak for 'the silent majority that wants to see Belgium continue to exist as a federal state and wants solidarity to be maintained beyond language frontiers'.

Political elites are central actors in the continuance of any intercommunal bargain, and the balance of political probabilities remains, for the time being, with these forces. As M. Martiniello views current prospects, Belgium remains 'sufficiently concerned with its potentiality for internal conflicts and with its intrinsic risk of self-demolition, to establish and maintain permanent pacts between the various actors about social issues considered to be critical'.[13] The reform of political institutions, the imaginative use of political procedures and the remaking of the state itself, are elemental to this project of continuing the national bargain. The public, too, though more equivocal is not entirely disengaged. The recent public outrage against official corruption and incompetence summoned as much indignation on behalf of a nation 'betrayed' as it provided an easy target for separatists seeking vindication of their cause.

Belgium's pivotal role in the European Union is also more likely than not to sustain the fragile national bargain. There is considerable prosperity and prestige to be had from being host to the principal EU institutions. There is formidable pressure, both from within these institutions and by the member states, for Belgium's communal elites to settle their differences some way short of outright separation. The very logic of EU governance — the encouragement of subsidiarity, but not at the expense of administrative coherence and efficiency — is another positive influence binding the communal parties to mutual endeavour, here as elsewhere on a shrinking Continent. Leaders of large-scale business also endorse this cooperative logic in the face of competitive global forces that reward large, coherent markets and penalise autarchy. The president of the Federation of Belgium Enterprise, Georges Jacobs, for instance, warned after the last constitutional round that 'we need to keep our tribal wars to ourselves. Outside Belgium, people do not know about the regions, they only understand Belgium as one country' (*Financial Times*, 28 June 1995).

For the time being then, Belgium continues to operate, especially on the practical level if less convincingly at the affective level, as a more durable political bargain than two exclusive ethnies which just happen, by the accident of history and the exigencies of Great Power diplomacy two centuries ago, to share an international football team, a national airline, a flag and a king. The problématique belge remains an enigma, continuing to defy those who predict national collapse. This political paradox survives the negative rhetoric of its assailants. So far, at least, fractious neighbours continue to make common cause, using parliamentary institutions calibrated now to take full account of persistent ethnic identities, to douse any sign of combustion in the flimsy wall that separates their respective habitations.

1   L. Vos, 'Shifting Nationalism: Belgians, Flemings and Walloons' in M. Teich and R. Porter (eds), *The National Question in Europe in Historical Context*, 1993, p. 136.
2   P. Peeters, 'Federalism: A Comparative Perspective — Belgium Transforms from a Unitary to a Federal State' in B. de Villiers (ed), *Evaluating Federal Systems*, 1994.
3   H. Gijsels, *Le Vlaams Blok*, 1993.
4   This concept was coined by H. Dumont in 'Belgitude et Crise de l'État Belge, *La Revue Nouvelle*, 44, 1988.
5   M. Martiniello, 'The Dilemma of Separation Versus Union: The New Dynamics of Nationalist Politics in Belgium' in H.R. Wicker (ed), *Rethinking Nationalism and Ethnicity: The Struggle for Meaning and Order in Europe*, 1997, p. 290.
6   A. Alen, B. Tilleman and F. Meersschaut, 'The State and its Subdivisions' in A. Alen (ed), *Treatise on Belgian Constitutional Law*, 1992.
7   M. O'Neill, 'Re-imagining Belgium: New Federalism and the Political Management of Cultural Diversity', *Parliamentary Affairs*, 1998.
8   B. Kerremans and J. Beyers, 'Belgium: The Dilemma Between Cohesion and Autonomy' in K. Hanf and B. Soetendorp (eds), *Adapting to European Integration, Small States and the European Union*, 1998.
9   *Financial Times*, 31.3.99.
10 H.R. Wicker, 'Introduction: Theorizing Ethnicity and Nationalism' in Wicker (ed), op. cit.
11 *Le Soir*, 2.3.93.
12 L. Vos in M. Teich and R. Porter, op. cit.
13 M. Martiniello, 'Ethnic Leadership, Ethnic Communities', Political Powerlessness and the State in Belgium', *Ethnic and Racial Studies*, 16, 1993, p. 251.

Slovakia: Language and National Unity

BY DESMOND THOMAS

WITHIN the mosaic of states, nations and societies of eastern Europe, language is a powerful index of nationality. The essence or soul of nationality, said Joshua Fishman in his study of *Language and Nationalism* in 1972, 'is not only reflected and protected by the mother tongue, but in a sense the mother tongue is itself . . . the soul made manifest'. So, too, Dr Johnson who told Boswell that he was always sorry when any language is lost 'for languages are the pedigree of nations'. Why should we mourn, therefore, the collapse of the Tower at Babel? Instead of a single monotony of language we have a worldwide diversity of languages as a positive force, clarifying national divides and contributing to the independence of nations. Such a view, however, assumes a one-to-one relationship between languages and nations, a misleading assumption in view of the linguistic plurality of most nation states, and a gross illusion in the overlapping societies of central and eastern Europe. The illusion in fact is quickly dispelled by recognition of two simple facts: the spread of powerful external languages such as English, and the existence of internal languages which have a claim to be the mother tongue of at least a portion of a nation's population. Both can be seen as a threat; both are typically dealt with by some form of 'language planning' — as we shall see.

In 1996 the writer was approached by a complete stranger while talking with a group of friends in the Slovak town of Banska Bystrica. His words of greeting, 'na Slovensku po slovensky!' translate as 'in Slovakia you should speak Slovak'. It was perhaps an isolated incident but it indicated the extent to which ordinary citizens in post-communist Slovakia can feel apprehensive about linguistic change. From primary school onwards, the education system ensures an awareness of how the Slovak language itself, at various points in its country's history, has been under threat, sometimes as a result of the deliberate intervention of governments — as for most of the nineteenth century. Slovakia is a new country, and also a small country of only 5.5 million people who rely on their language — spoken by some 86% as a first language — as a means of asserting a perceived national identity and culture. In the uncertain post-communist world there are fears that the language may once again be threatened with radical change and even ultimate extinction because of the influence of more widespread languages such as Hungarian, Czech or English. And with the threat to the language, threat to national identity and culture is feared.

Since the country became independent, Slovak governments have actively encouraged this association in people's minds between language and national unity. In 1995, a year before that encounter with the stranger, a debate concerning the status of the Slovak language had already resulted in the passing of a set of language laws, aiming to establish Slovak as 'the national language' with precedence over all others in certain clearly-defined contexts. The Slovak Nationalist government party led by Prime Minister Vladimir Meciar justified the need for language legislation with the following argument:

(1) The Slovak language, although ranked 'among the oldest civilised languages of Europe' was only codified in 1843. 'With the codification of Slovak literacy, Slovak national unity was established.' However, from the end of the eighteenth century a programme of Magyarisation was imposed on Slovakia, then part of the Austro-Hungarian Empire, and Hungarian rather than Slovak was awarded the status of 'language of the homeland'. In addition, Hungarian occupation of much of southern Slovakia during the Second World War 'inflicted wounds that remain open to this day'. (2) Following the creation of Czechoslovakia in 1918, 'the myth of a twin-pillared, unified Czechoslovak nation was conceived'. In this spirit, only one 'non-existent' state language, 'Czechoslovak' was recognised, implying that Czech and Slovak were to be given equal status. In practice, the Czech language was considered to be the state language, and its use was never restricted in any way in Slovakia. An earlier Czechoslovak language law (passed in 1990) is seen as being inconsistent, since it considered Slovak only 'an official language' and Czech as a 'secondary official language'. This contradicts the present Constitution of the Slovak Republic, which provides that: 'On the territory of the Slovak Republic, Slovak is the state language.'

The new language law was thus seen not only as a means of promoting Slovak as 'the state language', but also of reducing the influential status of Hungarian and Czech as alternatives. Whether by accident or by design it also had the effect of deliberately restricting the spread of 'outside' languages, in particular English. Some implications of the new law can be seen from the following quotations from the Slovak State Language Law of 1995:

Article 3: State agencies and entities, organs of the territorial self-governments and public institutions . . . are obliged to use the state language in exercising their competencies on the entire territory of the Slovak Republic . . . In the state language appear all laws, government decrees . . . all official documents such as birth certificates, the names of communities, street names etc.

Article 4: Instruction of the state language is compulsory. Textbooks are to be issued in the state language.

Article 5: Radio and television are to be broadcast in the state language, with the exception of foreign language programmes and original-language musicals.

Article 8: All signs, advertisements and notices designed to inform the public, primarily in stores, at sports facilities, in restaurants, on streets, in airports ... must be written in the state language. Translations must always follow the state-language text and must be of the same size.

Other articles prescribe the state language for use in the armed forces, court and public administration proceedings, in service industries and healthcare.

The consequences of such legislation are wide-ranging and immediately produced anomalies such as the requirement for Czech-language films (perfectly comprehensible to a Slovak audience) to be subtitled in Slovak. In fact, it was pointed out (in the *Times Higher Education Supplement*, January 1996) that 'university lectures, concert halls and opera stage' were virtually the only places where the Czech language would be allowed in public. But while the law appeared to be primarily seeking to curb the use of Czech, it was the Hungarian minorities within Slovakia (and to a lesser extent the Romany minorities) which reacted most strongly, regarding the new legislation as a clear violation of linguistic rights. During the 15 November 1995 debate in the Slovak parliament several opposition MPs condemned the law with one remarking: 'For you, Sirs, who formulated this law ... the mother tongue is only an object for cool political calculation', while another added that: 'The proposed form of the law ... is not only unconstitutional, but also against the interests of the Slovaks themselves.' In reply a government representative, argued that: 'The special situation of Southern Slovakia led the present government ... to the preparation of a draft-law, which would halt the lingual discrimination and national assimilation of Slovaks. We would like to create a situation in which we are able to provide protection for the members of the Slovak nation against the pressure of the foreign language. This draft-law threatens nobody, is directed against nobody. On the contrary this law provides an opportunity for the creation of lingual and social equality of every inhabitant of Slovakia.'

Thus, on the one hand, a nationalist government attempted to strengthen national unity through the promotion of a single-state language; on the other hand, Hungarian and other minorities sought to preserve their own cultural identity also through the means of language. In 1995 the outlook was one of increasing conflict between these two different perspectives. The Hungary-based Minority Protection Association delivered its verdict — that the new law violated not only the Slovak Constitution and bilateral agreements between Hungary and Slovakia, but also 'the spirit and principles of the latest international documents on the protection of national minorities'. The protest of

many of the 600,000 Hungarians living permanently in Slovakia threatened to complicate the ratification of a recent treaty between the two
countries. The European Union, which had recently issued a démarche
against the Slovak government because of perceived violations of 'common democratic practices', once again expressed its concern. At the
same time there was much popular support for the measure, with
demonstrators crying 'na Slovensku po slovensky!' outside the state
parliament. The prospects for any real agreement on the issue of
language rights seemed bleak.

In its desire to take decisive action to ensure the pre-eminence of the
Slovak language as a unifying force, the nationalist government had
produced a piece of legislation which was widely seen as being anti-
Czech, anti-Hungarian and even anti-English rather than simply pro-
Slovak. Criticism came from many different quarters during 1995–98
when strict attempts were made to implement the language law with
fines imposed on transgressors. And yet it can be argued that the actions
of the Slovak government were no more excessive than those of other
societies which have felt the need to make the association between
linguistic uniqueness and socio-cultural and political unity (and therefore independence) in this way. The idea of a people's individuality and
identity residing in its language is very old. Language may be seen as a
link not only with a glorious past but with a cultural authenticity that
can be protected under some form of language planning by nationalist
governments.

Language planning—in Fishman's terms the 'organised pursuit of
solutions to language problems'—is likely to include codification of the
target language through dictionaries, grammar and pronunciation
guides, the aim of which is to stabilise and strengthen the selected
language model and its elaboration through style manuals. Language
legislation is the ultimate means of formalising such processes, making
it mandatory (rather than a question of style) to use a chosen code or
individual expression. Such planning and legislation are not the preserve
of ultra-nationalist political parties. In 1983 a new law concerning the
'enrichment of the French language' was passed by the French National
Assembly, following on from an earlier piece of legislation known as
the 'Bas law' in 1975. These two laws combined made certain French
(rather than foreign) expressions obligatory in official correspondence,
state contracts and directives from ministries, and stipulated that French
should be the language of communication in certain specified contexts.
Fines were imposed for violations of the laws, for example on an
American airline which had distributed English boarding passes to
French passengers.[1]

Predictably, both laws have proved to be unworkable and have had
no apparent effect on reducing the amount of foreign words and
expressions assimilated by the French language. Loopholes in the
legislation have been easy to exploit, while the French government has

remained unwilling to extend the scope of the law to cover exempt areas such as the names of commercial signs, businesses and trademarks. The failure of language legislation in a highly developed Western European country has acted as a clear warning to others. Sixteen different Language Amendments were introduced in the US Congress between 1981 and 1990, aiming to establish English as the nation's official language — none has reached the stage of a congressional vote even in committee.[2] In Latvia a new language law aimed at establishing Latvian (rather than Russian) as the language of private commercial transactions is about to be redrafted. Even though the 1957 constitution of newly-independent Malaysia stipulated that Malay would be the national language, with English keeping the status of an official language for ten years only (after which it would be phased out altogether), English still has an important role within the country.[3]

All of this suggested that the actions of the Slovak government were likely to end in failure. Yet it was not difficult to understand why the Meciar government adopted such measures. The newly independent state was torn between past and future. Prior to 1989, totalitarian repression backed up by the stabilising force and the military might of the Soviet Union served to eliminate any doubts. But after independence in 1993, Slovakia faced a genuine dilemma whether to face eastwards or westwards — towards the vanishing certainties of the past or the uncertainties of the future. The desire for modernity, expressed by most ordinary Slovaks, also brought with it turmoil and unrest, threatening the national unity which was seen as so important to the fledgling state. Progressive measures deemed to be unsuccessful are still likely to be followed by an opposite reaction looking backwards towards the stability of communist rule. This situation has become a familiar one in many other countries in the region: since 1989, Poland, Hungary and Bulgaria have all alternated between governments of reform and 'socialist' regimes consisting mainly of ex-communist politicians.[4] The Meciar government used language as one of the means of establishing some degree of control over the forces of change — controversial alterations to the criminal code and stricter laws governing the right of assembly have been others. From the outside, such measures may have seemed unnecessary — after all Slovakia has been at peace, with treaties signed with Hungary and its other neighbours — but under the surface fears of ethnic conflict, as in the former Yugoslavia, have remained.

The irony is that such measures tended to bring conflict closer. There was a sharp reaction from the Hungarian minority within Slovakia, from the Hungarian government in Budapest, and from outside commentators in a number of European capitals. By 1998, when the next round of general elections were held, Slovak society had become deeply disturbed. Nationalist politicians insisted that Hungarian objections to the 1995 law revealed their underlying treachery and disloyalty to the nation. As one representative put it: 'Our Hungarian compatriots are against learning the language of the country where they are living. Why? Because of the hope of joining Hungary.'⁵ But already changes were taking place. Many ordinary Slovaks had become government critics and had begun to listen to the opinions being expressed by the outside world. The language law was an issue that had succeeded in dividing society and had brought the country into disrepute. The prospect of international isolation was unappealing. In September 1998 the voters decided that they had had enough, and Vladimir Meciar's government and the Slovak nationalists were defeated. The language law remained, but the new governing coalition renewed a promise to make provision for the languages of ethnic minorities through separate laws. At the time of writing the future still seems uncertain, but the presence of Hungarian minority representatives, in government for the first time ever, is likely to ensure a more balanced piece of legislation in the near future. In so far as Slovakia has moved under parliamentary control to a more plural society, so the danger of the fragile disunity has receded.

Various conclusions — three in particular — can be drawn from the Slovak experience of attempting through legislation to influence linguistic change. The first is that attempts to set a barrier to defend one's language can prove impossible to implement. The failure of language conservation policies in countries such as France illustrate the first of these points very clearly: in the French case, language legislation was drawn up with a purely negative purpose — that of resisting the advance of English 'loan' words and expressions being assimilated into French. Recent events in Slovakia mirror this failure.

Secondly, 'negative' legislation which imposes restrictions on a minority language will intensify divisions in society, and in extreme cases contribute towards actual conflict. It is also likely to give minorities further ground for rallying to their cause. The actions of recent Turkish governments, for example, in restricting the language rights of the Kurdish minority have arguably made conditions more favourable for the Kurdish independence guerrilla movement in its struggle against Ankara's attempts to unify the nation. It seems likely, therefore, that faced with the possibility of growing divisions in their own society, ordinary Slovaks decided in 1998 to reject the nationalist message in favour of greater tolerance of existing diversity.

Thirdly, while such legislation is unlikely to succeed (except within a totalitarian society), legislating in order to clarify language rights is an entirely different proposition. It may actually be beneficial in a divided society by providing space for majority and minority languages to exist. That has been the experience (it is said) in Malaysia where legislation originally designed to be anti-Chinese and anti-English has not only rejuvenated the Malay language but cleared the air for a multilingual, multi-ethnic society to live peacefully together. Given honest and open debate among parliamentarians, laws can enable ethnic groups to be aware both of their own language rights and those of others. If the new Slovak coalition government decides to follow this path, then a language law which initially threatened harm may ultimately be of service to the whole of society.

1 See J. Flaitz, *The Ideology of English: French Perceptions of English as a World Language*, Mouton de Gruyter, 1988.
2 See J. Crawford (ed), *Language Loyalties*, University of Chicago Press, 1992.
3 A. Pennycook, *The Cultural Politics of English as an International Language*, Longman, 1994, pp. 191–7.
4 See, for example, R.J. Crampton, *Eastern Europe in the Twentieth Century*, Routledge, 1997.
5 *Slovak Spectator*, 8 January 1998.

Ghana: Un Beau Voyage in the 1990s?

BY DENNIS AUSTIN

LOOKING at the political wilderness of Africa, can we see any inclination towards parliamentary democracy as a remedy for ethnic conflict? What is certainly visible is communal violence of such intensity as
to threaten the actual existence of some of the continent's 53 states.
The worst are spectral entities which survive only de jure in international law; they lack any capacity to meet the expectations implied in
the promise of independence. Others are despotically ruled on the
assumption that, since there is no consensus, force must hold the state
together. Hope, therefore, trots on a short lead. Yet there are a small
number of countries which now manage ethnic conflict within democratic structures. Being rare, they are worth examining. They are not of
course so solidly democratic as to be immune from collapse, nor so
firmly rooted in constitutional rule as to occasion surprise should they
lapse into dictatorship. Nevertheless, they are peacefully governed by
leaders responsible to elected parliaments. They are: Senegal, Botswana,
South Africa, Ghana. Nigeria has returned to civilian rule within a new
federal framework that is (so to speak) still on probation. Others, such
as Tanzania, might be listed as proto-democracies under governments
which intend, or say they intend, to move in the direction of reform
although words are poor substitutes for deeds.

Alas that we need to be wary of intentions! But all too often the
pledge to democratic government ceases to have meaning and becomes
no more than a sequence of variations on the past: different kinds of
dictators, other forms of brutality. Many governments are fixed to the
treadmill of earlier years, more fearful of the consequences of change
than of the cost of repression.

The exceptions are of particular interest since they mark out a
separate path. They trust the people as voters and govern through
parliaments in place of armies or parties. They do so not because society
is free from divisions of language, religion or historical antecedents but
because they are willing to believe that ethnic quarrels can be managed,
even perhaps diminished, through constitutional provision, parliamentary debate and contested elections. Of the four states, Botswana makes
constitutional provision for multi-party elections which have been held
freely and fairly although power still rests with the Botswana Democratic Party which has been in office since independence in 1966. South
Africa is important to the continent as a whole, its leader admired on
the world's stage. It is still, however, in the infancy of its post-apartheid

years, its society beset with communal hatreds, and no one can foretell what effect they may have on existing structures of democratic control. Senegal has a long history of political tolerance within a parliamentary framework but continues to be faced with secessionist claims in the province of Casamance. Ghana, independent since 1957, is today a democracy bred out of dictatorship, and has shaped its politics from a divided society, and we may usefully ask, in the general context of this inquiry, why and how it reached this position.

The fortunes of the West African republic have always attracted attention. For many years Ghana was seen as a model of what a progressive colonial society might become. Its citizens were sensible, amiable, willing to learn and responsive to colonial guidance. In the 1950s several commentators hurried to Accra to interpret what was happening, some sensible, others schooled in political sociology when, in Wittgenstein's phrase, 'language goes on holiday'. Then, suddenly, events went awry. Communal violence took hold of rival parties and the movement towards self-government was interrupted. After independence, the country stumbled into single-party dictatorship, followed by military rule, and Ghana ceased to be of interest for a time, eclipsed by greater tragedies elsewhere in the continent.

The politics of the republic reached a low point in the 1970s and early 1980s when society appeared to be disjoint. Regional dissent was growing, the urban population was restless, farmers were disgruntled, and a military government sat in Accra. The effect could be seen in the disassociation of many groups of citizens from the authority of the government. It was as if society was fleeing the state as one more affliction like the weather or witchcraft or rapacious politicians. The consequences were serious. Professor Naomi Chazan travelled through the rural areas, and in her interesting *Anatomy of Ghanaian Politics* concluded that the state was suffering variously, 'a loss of salience, distinctness and pre-eminence'. She observed that while 'its existence as a de jure political entity might be unquestioned, its capacity was very much open to doubt'. The 'internal dissipation of the state meant that even the continued existence of the state shell had to rely increasingly on external props' without which the country might face 'total disintegration'.

The verdict was extreme and proved to be unjust, but Ghana was certainly at a low ebb. Local centres of power, traditionally based, were pitting their authority as autonomous 'statelets' against the government. In the 1980s, however, the international world turned to Ghana again as a model for economic reform. The catchphrase was 'structural adjustment' whereby the World Bank and IMF, in exchange for large injections of capital, sought to move the country towards the new Jerusalem of a free market economy. Society suffered, the government (under Fl.Lt. Rawlings) at first resisted, then yielded, and there was a gradual recovery of the economy. In 1991–92 political parties were restarted and began not only to restore hopes of democratic rule but to detoxify the poison of ethnic hostility. To understand fully what had taken place, we need to go back in time.

Past times

The Gold Coast — to use the former name — came into existence at the beginning of the twentieth century. Like all but a handful of African countries it was a created state. There were no Gold Coasters or Ghanaians in history. The territory emerged as part of the partition of Africa by European powers, its northern boundary drawn in arbitrary fashion at the 11° parallel. There was a southern Colony area of local chiefdoms, a central Ashanti Kingdom and a northern Protectorate of scattered communities: a common pattern. In 1919 the state was enlarged by the addition of the western part of Togoland as a prize of war carved out of the former German colony, the French establishing a separate Republic of Togo to the east. (The effect was to divide those who spoke the local language, Ewe, by a new international boundary.) The modern name 'Ghana' was taken after independence from a mediaeval savannah state in the region of the Niger River.

That there was a predatory character to partition has long been recognised. The European powers were vultures descending on an already wounded continent, injured by slavery, plundered by concessionary companies. We should be cautious, however, in passing judgment. All empires have been predatory and most people have been governed by other people. How may states in past centuries have been dismembered by stronger neighbours? The notable aspect of the division of Africa was its totality. No territory was spared. Abyssinia escaped for a time after its defeat of an Italian army in 1885 but that was avenged in 1935–36 by Benito Mussolini. The Gold Coast was one victim among many.

But if modern Ghana is a contrived state, the ethnic make-up of its peoples remains historically rooted. One must remember that Africa is immensely old, fern-dark and ancient. We are all, it seems, descendants of an African Eve. The history of Africa's traditional rulers — kings, emirs, chiefs and clan elders — recedes into the past, marked out by migration and conquest beyond the reach of recorded history. The European intrusion was a comparatively recent phenomenon, preceded by others across north Africa: Arabs, Romans, Greeks, Phoenicians. The slave forts along the West African shore, now serving their time as tourist attractions, were established from the sixteenth century. There were slave raiders during these early years into what is now northern Ghana, and the beginnings of an Ashanti Kingdom, graced by the title 'Empire', whose myths and legends are still recited today. *Wukum apim, apim beba* is still the emblematic motto of Ashanti: 'if you kill a thousand (of us) a thousand more will come.' The warrior Kingdom under Otumfuo Asantehene in the capital Kumasi was all powerful, feared and aggressive. Had it not been for the imposition of British rule in the south, Ashanti might have extended its control to the coast, although not acceptably, if the rivalry of subsequent years is an indication: to be feared is rarely to be loved.

Nationalist years

Move forward to the 1950s, to the heyday of Ghanaian independence and a new country seemed to appear. A change of name, a flag, a national anthem, a People's Party, a charismatic leader, country-wide elections and the achievement of self-government: surely a bright future beckoned? When looked at closely, however, the picture darkened. What began in hope continued under party dictatorship, military rule and regional disaffection. Nationalism in Ghana as throughout Africa proved to be an elusive concept. The winds of change certainly blew strongly across West Africa in the 1950s, but within a decade or two they seemed almost to have blown themselves out. There was civil war in Nigeria, and a growing list of broken-backed states throughout the continent.

The fact is that Ghana in 1957 was not the nation-based state its new leaders proclaimed it to be. There was a strong pluralism at local level and a communal rivalry which threatened unrest. Regional protests evoked their own nationalism and the central government in the capital was nervously aware that post-colonial unity was much less assured than anti-colonial sentiment. The voting figures in the last election before independence persuaded the British to transfer power — they were by now more than willing to quit — but the divisions within society could be seen in the pattern of majority and minority groups. The governing party led by Nkrumah was the southern-based Convention People's Party which, possessed of all the spoils of office, secured 71 of the 104 seats in the National Assembly and 57% of the vote. Against the CPP were locally-based parties appealing to communal sentiments, plus that perennial feature of Ghanaian politics, those who represented the narrow élite of professional men and women opposed to Nkrumah. There was a Northern People's Party, an Ashanti Liberation Movement, a Togoland Congress whose leaders wanted integration with the neighbouring republic, a local ethnic party in the capital (Ga Shifimo Kpee), dissident movements in the south and the Ghana Congress Party of the intelligentsia. The joint opposition demand was for federation; the more fanatic among the Ashanti wanted separation and backed their claim with violence. Rival supporters murdered and fought for control of local strongholds until Nkrumah, prodded by the last colonial Governor, yielded to the demand for elections. They were held under strict security control and independence followed nine months later.

Within a year or so, the opposition was broken, suppressed by harsh laws including a Preventive Detention Act applied by administrative order. An armed rebellion in the Volta Region was extinguished by the army and the prisons began to fill. Democracy too was stifled. The colonial government had tried in its final days to lay a foundation for constitutional government — a legislative council transformed to a parliament, an executive council changed to a cabinet, national elections, judicial independence and a professional administration — but the new party leaders were impatient of such restraints. Their slogan was 'Freedom', their desire was 'Security'. They turned instinctively to an imposed order and if that meant injustice, so be it. The point was made explicit by Nkrumah in his *Autobiography* who believed that 'even a system based on social justice and a democratic constitution may need backing up during the period following independence by emergency measures of a totalitarian kind'. What followed, alas, was neither freedom nor justice and was certainly not democracy. After a decade of declining fortunes Nkrumah, too, became a victim. In 1966 he was ousted by a military coup. Thereafter disaster followed disaster. In 1969 the army tried to restore some semblance of constitutional rule by holding elections. In came the Opposition only to be removed three years later by a second coup. The army was divided and further conspiracies ended in the public execution of senior officers. There was a brief return again in 1979 to civilian government under a Northern leader but already a new hero had appeared (Fl.Lt. Rawlings) who is still there today though in more democratic guise. Having seized power in 1979 Rawlings withdrew from office, then returned in 1981 to govern through an appointed military council until 1992 when he stood, successfully, for the office of President.

How can one account for this sad train of events? There were three culprits: ethnic rivalry, the colonial legacy and economic collapse. The simplest, and most immediate, cause of failure was economic deterioration.

Economic failure. It was glaring. By the end of the 1970s the country was close to famine. The rains failed, there were tropical fires, the world price for commodities (cocoa and palm oil) fell, and when the IMF offered help, the conditions it imposed were so harsh that a special Alleviation Programme had to be implemented. At the height of the crisis, farmers withdrew their produce from market, imports almost ceased, inflation soared, the currency was worthless. All the familiar sayings were now seen to be true: 'An empty rice bowl gives democracy a hollow sound', or 'Bread without democracy is hard but democracy without bread is fragile'. The fate of Ghanaians at this time, however, was to have neither rice nor bread nor democracy.

From the end of 1981, when economic troubles grew thick and fast and Rawlings staged his second coup, the authority of the new government started to falter. The coup leaders were ready to be brutal but the state itself began to weaken as the economy grew worse. It was now that structural adjustment programmes were devised by international agencies and overseas donors. Because the IMF and World Bank looked askance at the corruption of African regimes, they sought to administer funds through other channels. During the 1980s some US$ 8 billion were transmitted to Ghana, but not solely through the government in Accra. Relief agencies funded by the Commonwealth and UN began to act independently. The instruments they employed — not only of course in Ghana but throughout Africa — were non-governmental organisations which multiplied across the country. By the end of the 1980s there were over 300, displacing so far as they could the service role of the state. Like a latter day version of indirect rule, their activities bolstered local sentiment. It was as if the state was being by-passed across a range of services from child care and famine relief to health and agriculture. Many of these locally-based organisations which were financed by overseas agencies — quasi-professional, quasi-voluntary — strengthened communal interests to the detriment of state control. Not until the 1990s did the central government fully establish its authority, through a network of elected councils, over what was loosely described as a novel form of civil society. Rawlings too regained popularity as the economy began to take strength from the harsh medicine administered under international direction. It became better managed and better financed until today the streets are paved, children fed, markets replenished and taxes collected. Argument still continues about the relative success of the structural adjustment imposed over a decade under World Bank/IMF programmes, but few Ghanaians today would deny their daily lot has improved.

Colonial legacies. The colonial past has been a frequent target of criticism. It was, say its detractors, unhelpful to its nationalist successors: worst, it was inadequate. One can see why it is abused. At the level of high theory, the colonial state cut a poor figure. It was certainly a long way from the Hegelian state — that 'hieroglyph of the reason which reveals itself in actuality'.[1] The fact is that in the mild, lazy days of colonial rule, prior to the brief period of nationalist awakening, the lives of most Ghanaians were not national but local. They acknowledged the authority of the District Commissioner and took their grievances to his court or to the Native Authority, but few beyond the larger towns had any concern for what was happening nationally. In Hegelian terms, the colonial Gold Coast was an 'immature state in which the citizen was conscious of the state, if at all, as external to him. His interests were civil and economic not political; he felt himself a participant in public affairs only as the subject of his Prince'.[2] A policy of indirect rule — the form of control which placed emphasis on the authority of chiefs — reinforced local loyalties: hence the charge brought by nationalist politicians that colonial rule had colluded with 'tribalism'. The plain truth, however, was that many Ghanaians remained ethnically divided. The Ashanti were generally regarded with suspicion, the Ewe were held to be clannish, the south was divided between rival chiefdoms, and smaller communities in the north, such as the Konkomba and Nanumba, were frequently at odds in what could only be called tribal warfare.

And perhaps, after all, colonial rule had been too brief and too shallow to prepare its citizens for national government? The political class in Ghana was poorly schooled for the burden of self-rule. The contrast may be seen in comparison with India. Gandhi reached England in 1888 to train as a lawyer at about the time the partition of Africa was beginning to be agreed. The Indian Congress Party had been formed in 1885, and was to have over 50 years of political apprenticeship before independence in 1947. The Convention People's Party in Ghana was formed in June 1949, in office in 1951, and independent six years later. Pandit Nehru at independence was an experienced politician of a mature rooted party, Kwame Nkrumah was prime minister in 1952 almost before he was a politician. The difference was not only in the number of experienced leaders and skilled administrators but of institutions, beliefs and the depth of the colonial experience.

Ethnic conflict. Colonial rule is dead and gone but the older past survives. How could it be otherwise? The extent to which Ghanaian society can recapture aspects of its traditional past may be open to doubt, but the affections, loyalties, beliefs and customs, the daily life of towns and villages, together with the languages of local society, are still there. Travel out from Accra and its Ga-speaking community to the Akwapim hills, and the language changes to one form or other of the Akan group of dialects; further inland it will be Asante; north across the Volta Lake the visitor will hear a variety of different tongues; east of the river Volta he will be among Ewe-speaking chiefdoms. Each language marks out a kinship group. They are the pedigree of local nationalities. 'We are Ghanaian,' men say, 'but we are also Dagomba or Mamprussi or Ashanti, Fanti, Nzima, Ga and Ewe.' And some at least will dream of a larger local autonomy. The state is a kaleidoscope of historically distinct communities. The sum of each community constitutes the nation-in-making.

In the early days of agitation for self-government, it looked as if a new social group was taking shape which might cross ethnic divisions to provide a unifying nationality — class moderating ethnicity, ethnicity tempering class — much as Professor Plumb's 'consolidating classes' of Restoration England offered a base for parliamentary institutions at the end of the seventeenth century. The new class in Ghana was formed from the semi-educated, literate-in-English, traders, schoolteachers, clerks, pastors, goldsmiths and cash crop brokers who constituted a middle stratum between the better educated élite of the professional class and the unlettered majority. The appeal of self-government propagated by these new leaders was broad enough at first to take the country into independence, but the pull of local interests and sentiment remained even against the patronage of office, partly because the spoils of government could not secure everyone's advantage. Even in the run-up to independence, the notion of self-government began to be redefined. Claims were made by a number of different 'selves' on the grounds that if political freedom were being promised, why should Ashanti or the North or the Ewe region of the Trust Territory not be free to decide its own future? Kinship was an enduring bond. Indeed, when trouble came at national level to challenge the authority of the government, successive leaders took refuge among their own immediate kin: Nkrumah drew round him members of his local Nzima community, Fl.Lt. Rawlings turned initially to his Ewe supporters after he seized power in 1981.

Modern Ghana may look secure today but we also know from the breakdown of authority in Russia and Yugoslavia how modernisation can be relocated. Theories of political development which assume a closer national integration at state level have had to take account of renewed ethnic ambitions which are nonetheless modern for being based on the past.

The return to constitutional government

The problem stemming from ethnic rivalry was simple to state — how best to translate social diversity into political pluralism. The solution was difficult since it required concessions of both principle and practice. The government in Accra had to learn to relax its control without fear of local disaffection; opposition groups had to accept the authority of the state without fearing the loss of their identity. There was a learning curve to absorb, away from fear to trust, from central control to provincial autonomy and from authoritarian rule to democratic government. In the early years after independence, single party rule and a certain licensed cruelty towards opponents of the regime held the country uneasily together. Military governments followed the same track. And neither was successful. Politicians were venal, soldiers brutal, and when economic hardship came, the country began to fall apart. During the 1980s Rawlings turned to morality. He vowed to cleanse political society by revolutionary means, not party or parliament but methods closer to Cuba, Libya and the socialist ideology of the Third World. The chosen instruments of control were local Defence Committees for the Revolution. They too failed, and it was when the economy grew worse that Rawlings came under pressure to move towards market liberalisation.

The economy was forced into shape with international help. A solution to local disaffection could only come from within. One answer was not to suppress regional unrest but to rechannel ethnic loyalties by subdivision. The changes were introduced piecemeal. A western Brong-Ahafo region (based on anti-Kumasi sentiment) was taken out of Ashanti; the North became three separate regions; the South was similarly divided, and the capital became a region on its own. The divisions did not end ethnic disquiet but they moderated its capacity to oppose. Communal voting is still evident, and Ashanti remains hostile to the central government, except when an Ashanti is in charge; the Volta region still goes its own way, except when an Ewe is President. But there are now strong counter-weights to any overall dominance.

And there has been a change, if not in bloc voting, then in attitudes among the leaders. Throughout the 1990s, despite the cries and the tantrums, Ghana moved through a time of transition from bad to better. The government under Rawlings became less triumphalist, sobered by events. The opposition, based in Ashanti, grew less recalcitrant. The readmission of a limited democracy began to draw the country together. Elected regional and local councils replaced the quasi-military committees through which Rawlings had tried to revolutionise society. Political parties, each with a solid ethnic-local base, issued national programmes, newspapers were allowed a greater freedom, the courts resumed the rule of law and a consultative assembly met to draw up a parliamentary-presidential constitution for the Fourth Republic. Elections were held, and if evidence were needed of the changes taking place, it could be found both in the voting patterns and in the stand taken by party leaders. In 1992 Professor Adu Boaten, an Ashanti, stood as Presidential candidate against Rawlings, an Ewe, and lost, whereupon his Patriotic People's Party claimed malpractice: the register of electors had been badly carried out and the government had used its authority to secure the result it wanted. On these grounds the opposition parties refused to take part in the ensuing parliamentary election. The consequence was that Rawlings' National Democratic Congress won 189 seats out of the total of 200: a de facto single-party-government. Four years later, however, presidential and parliamentary elections were held again, and Rawlings won his second term in office with 57% of the vote against his Ashanti opponent John Kuffuor's 40%. But the opposition now contested the subsequent parliamentary election and won 64 seats. A pattern was set: the opposition wins in Ashanti, Rawlings is given overwhelming support in his Volta region, the rest of the country is divided.

There had been a change. Why? Where did the credit lie? And what does it say about the hidden contest between ethnic loyalties and democratic hopes?

1. A major instrument of change was the unlikely figure of Fl.Lt. Jerry Rawlings, born of a Scottish father and Ewe mother, married to an Ashanti, an Air Force pilot, and very much a hero of his time; an ideologue turned pragmatist who was much concerned to help the poor and contemptuous in his early years of old-style parliamentary rule. He was also quite ready to shed blood under the guise of necessity, as in 1979 when he first seized power from senior army commanders and ordered their execution. He allowed elections to be held but watched and waited, and in December 1981 intervened again—this time, it

seemed, for good. When in the seventeenth century in England Andrew Marvell observed the progress of Oliver Cromwell, a continuation of military government seemed indispensable:

> But thou, the War's and Fortune's son
> March indefatigably on.
> And for the last effect
> Still keep thy sword erect:
> Besides the force it has to fight
> The spirits of the shady night,
> The same arts that did gain
> A power, must it maintain.

But not for Fl.Lt. Rawlings in Ghana in 1990. He was fully prepared to march indefatigably on, but he also convened a Consultative Assembly, created his own political party and stood in the two presidential elections. Parliament has displaced revolution?

2.   The opposition too shifted its ground. Its leaders did not abandon their hostility to Rawlings, but they moved away from earlier demands for federation to an acceptance of regional diversity. They now have a base of support in Ashanti and, given a fair contest, can put together a following not by ideology or party programmes, but by the patient stitching together of local loyalties to local leaders.

3.   The likelihood is that both sides have concluded that the alternatives to parliamentary democracy do not work. The past has been too painful, the cost both of suppression and of rebellion are too high. In effect, they have accepted arguments used by Kofi Busia who believed that 'social realities suggest that the proper approach to the problem of tribalism in Africa is to accept the fact of pluralism'.[3] Ethnic associations were 'not necessarily incompatible with the building of a democratic nation and may even afford better prospects for democracy in consonance with group interests . . .: tribalism, whether it is manifested by an ethnic group large enough to be a region or only by a small one occupying a village, offers opportunities in local self-government'.

4.   Economic recovery was basic to political reform. Ghana became a exception to the often dismal effect of IMF and World Bank remedies. The country suffered terribly at first. Rawlings had to convince himself and to persuade those around him of the need to keep steadily to the required measures of reform, but the price is there to see today and society has benefited. With the programme of aid came international pressure for 'good governance', although what effect that had is unclear. The linking of free markets and free elections, however, may have chimed with Rawlings' own acceptance of the advantages of change.

5.   Marxist socialism became discredited after the collapse of the Soviet Union. That too may have helped to wean Rawlings off his earlier

beliefs. Parliaments and contested elections became the model of respectable politics, spawning a number of façade democracies across the third world; but behind the façade in Ghana went a genuine attempt to return to constitutional government.

And during these difficult years Ghanaians learned to respond to the different claims of nationalism, ethnicity and democracy. In the early 1950s nationalism seemed to be very much the Zeitgeist that its devotees believed it to be. Yet within a brief span of time many Ghanaians turned back to the familiar ties which determined their local allegiance. They did so partly as the result of the decision to hold elections for a democratic National Assembly, for at local level many communities remained wary of their neighbours and suspicious of the nationalist rhetoric voiced in Accra: they cast their votes for their own kin. Over the ensuing half century, however, they began to adopt a more pragmatic middle course between the pretence of an undivided unity and the dreams of communal self-rule. They moved towards a broad central ground of politics. They also expressed their disapproval of dictatorship by turning out to vote as often as they were allowed to do so. (The exception proved the rule. When Col. Acheampong, leader of the second coup, held a referendum in 1978 for a fraudulent scheme of Union Government, few bothered to vote and those that did tried to vote 'No'.)[4] The compromise arrived at in subsequent elections was to return ethnically-based candidates to parliament within a national or regional framework of party organisation. Men and women queued patiently under a tropical sun to record their choice between local rivals, but however strongly influenced by ties of ethnic origin they accepted, over time, the authority of the state. The compromise was both pragmatic and idealistic. It endorsed a national homology which had not been accepted earlier, namely, that between all Ghanaians there was a sufficient ground of political agreement to support constitutional rule. The conclusion to be drawn is important. When not bullied by party ideologies or soldiers, ordinary electors in Ghana have showed that democratic institutions can be used by regional-ethnic interests to produce a national consensus. The compromise was — still is — fragile, as any relationship is bound to be between the emotional pull of ancestry and the practical necessity of government, the essential require-ment being that the framework of a free political society should be assured.

Conclusions

Can it be assured? Democracy and ethnicity are uneasy companions. One requires unity, the other preaches division. The mistake in Ghana over the past 50 years was to try and enforce unity, first by single party government, then by military rule. The effect, paradoxically, was to turn Ghanaians in on themselves. Repression brought a surface compliance and a bogus unity. Ethnic-based parties, on the other hand, led only to the wilderness of separation: *yeate ye ho* was the Ashanti party slogan: 'We are drawing ourselves apart': but in fact there was nowhere to go. We wrote earlier of a learning curve away from distrust to an acceptance of the state on the basis of plurality, a learning that has been difficult and may still be insufficient for we do not know whether the tutelary democracy which colonial rule tried to provide in its closing years can strike local roots.[5] Can oaks be transplanted to where palm trees grow? Do they not need favourable conditions of economic growth, and will the twenty-first century provide that success? Can one be free and democratic and hungry? There is no end to such questions, and no answers. Yet it is critically important, not only in Ghana, to find forms of government that can meet the needs of ethnically-divided, would-be democratic countries, a search which has so far proved difficult. The emphasis has to be not only on institutions but on the abstractions of justice, civil liberties, the absence of torture, freedom of expression — all the benefits urged by the richer democracies on poorer less liberal societies. Ghana has travelled some distance along that learning curve, and over the next decade or so may continue to find a working arrangement between parliamentary rule and ethnic divisions. Its leaders must also, more immediately, face an election in the year 2000 in which Rawlings is barred under the 1992 constitution from standing. But if all goes well, and democracy survives, then Ghanaians may properly salute the Flight Lieutenant in his retirement in words used as the title for this account.

> Heureux qui, comme Ulysse, a fait un beau voyage,
> Ou comme cestuy là qui conquit la toison,
> Et puis est retourné, plein d'usage et raison,
> Vivre entre ses parents le reste de son aage!
>
> (Happy is he who has made a great voyage, like Ulysses
> or the one who seized the Fleece, and then returned,
> full of experience and wisdom, to live with his kindred
> for the rest of his years).
> Tr. from Joachim du Bellay (1522–60). *Sonnets.*

Summary of findings: Ghana

1. Ethnic quarrels in Ghana reflect the contrived nature of the state, artificially constructed by partition in the nineteenth century.
2. Elements of modernity (education, roads, trade, communications) have brought society together, offering a national framework of control; but in the early years before independence in 1957 nationalism was more anti-colonial than patriotic in temperament.
3. Moreover, nationalism became recast in ethnic terms when the prospect of self-government drew near. There were many 'selves', regionally and ethnically defined.

4. Parliamentary institutions of a tutelary nature were introduced in the closing years of British rule. They had a twofold effect (a) they focused attention, nationally, on the government in Accra, (b) they encouraged, through elections, local sentiment.

5. The problems of independence led to party dictatorship followed by military rule and economic collapse. Ghana turned to the IMF and World Bank for help.

6. There was misery and pain in the early years of recovery (1980s) but a learning curve was followed. Attempts to unify the country by coercion had failed and Ghanaians learned to compromise: the state accepted the need for diversity, ethnic factions admitted the necessity of state control.

7. New political parties drew on traditional sentiments; ethnic interests were expressed by locally chosen candidates in regional and national elections. Parliamentary rule was shaped from diverse ethnic groups. Democracy was bred out of dictatorship.

8. Much credit is due to Fl.Lt. Rawlings, re-elected as President in 1996, as well as to Ghanaians (of different stripe). Hence the conclusion that, like Ulysses, they have achieved *un beau voyage*.

Appendix

The strength of Ashanti sentiment can be seen in the following extract from a debate in the National Assembly during the last years of colonial rule. Ashanti members wanted an increase in the number of seats from 21 to 30, a demand backed by both government and opposition members from the region, They lost the debate and the Ashanti protest gathered pace from that date in November 1953.

B.F. Kusi [ex-CPP]: If in 1900 we had the support of all sections of the country we could have fought the British Empire and driven the British away and it would have been unnecessary for us today to agitate for self-government . . . Another point is sentiment — (interruption). Yes, I will explain that to you — All Ashantis express the sentiment that Ashanti is a nation and that fact has been accepted. We are not a region at all; we should be considered as a nation . . . Population alone does not make a country.

Krobo Edusei [Ministerial Secretary to Ministry of Justice]: I have got mandate from CPP members in Kumasi to ask for 30 seats. As I have already stated, this matter cropped up during the Coussey Committee meeting and the only compromise which was arrived at was that Ashanti should be given one-fourth of the representation . . . We are not asking for more: we are asking for 30 seats . . . we Ashantis are not preaching tribalism or anything of the sort; we are only agitating for our legitimate right . . . and, Mr Speaker, with your permission, I am going to read to Honourable Members one of the most important telegrams that I have received: KROBO EDUSEI, ASSEMBLY, ACCRA —

LIVING AND DEAD GODS AND ALL SPIRITS OF ASHANTI EXPECT YOU
TO PROVE YOURSELF TRUE DESCENDANT OF WARRIOR AMANKWATIA
SECURE THIRTY SEATS FOR ASHANTI HISTORY AWAITING YOU ALSO
— G.K. ADAI . . . We are loyal! Our chiefs are humble to the government
. . . But this is a demand which is being made by the whole Ashanti
nation . . . We do not want to cause any riot; we do not want to secede
from the Colony; we want to march abreast with them.

Atta Mensah [Ministerial Secretary to the Ministry of Communications
and Works]: It has been suggested somewhere that the intention of
Ashanti in asking for these thirty seats is that should Government refuse
to accede to our demand we would break away to form a federal
government. Such false and malicious statements . . . are most unfortu-
nate. It is not our intention whatsoever to wreck the smooth unity
which Ashanti has contributed in a large measure to build. On this
question of delimitation, as I have said, there is no difference of opinion
as far as the CPP and the [Opposition] are concerned in Ashanti.
Among the rank and file of the CPP, among the leaders of the
[Opposition] in Ashanti, among the rank and file of the Ashanti Youth
Association, from the Chief to the *ahenkwaa*, from the common man
to the aristocrat, there is no division on that issue, that is, our demand
for 30 seats.

C.E. Osei [Representative of the Asanteman Council]: Ashanti's position is 25% of the total seats . . . The Transvolta Togoland area which
has eight seats now will have an increase to 13, the Northern Territories
from 19 to 26. (Some Honourable Members: By population) — What do
you mean by population? Look here, my friends, there is no Government that can stand because it has population alone; it must have
money backing it . . . (Some Honourable Members: Shame! Shame!)
(Uproar) — You must be prepared to buy our good will. (Uproar).

W.E. Arthur [CPP Rural Member, Colony]: I want to remind my
brothers from Ashanti that they were not taking part in the administration of this country in the early days and it was only as late as 1946 —
if I am correct — that they were invited to take part in the Government.
And so I should not claim too much. (Mr Krobo Edusei: 'Talk sense!')
I am talking sense, Mr Speaker, they must understand that Ashanti is a
conquered territory. (Interruption) (Some Honourable Members:
Shame! Shame! Shame!) (Uproar).

Nana Boakye Danquah [Akyempimhene, an important Kumasi chief]:
On a point of order, Mr Speaker. The last speaker has said that the
Ashantis were conquered and I would like him to prove to this House
in what way or manner they were conquered. We were never
conquered.

Mr Arthur: We all know the history of this country and that:

Mr Bediako Poku [CPP]: On a point of order Mr Speaker. An expression has been made by the Honourable Gentleman who just sat down that Ashantis were conquered. If Ashantis were conquered, he should know that the Ashantis were not conquered by Fantis! (Uproar).

Mr Arthur: If he insists I will prove that it was conquered, and it was through the efforts of the people of the Colony that King Prempeh I — (Interruption).

Mr Speaker: What has that got to do with this debate?

---

1 'The state must be treated as a great architectonic structure, as a hieroglyph of the reason which reveals itself in actuality'. *Philosophy of Right*, trans. by T.M. Knox, Oxford, 1965, p. 288.

2 Hegel, translator's *Foreword*, p. xi.

3 K.A. Busia, *Africa in Search of Democracy*, Ch. VII, 'Tribalism'. Kofi Busia was Professor of Sociology in the University of Ghana, Leader of the Opposition, then Prime Minister 1969–72.

4 When the voting returns were manipulated, the Electoral Commissioner fled in protest to neighbouring Togo. Acheampong was overthrown by his fellow officers. The following year, 1979, he and they were executed publicly by Rawlings' Revolutionary Council.

5 Hegel's comment on Spain has some bearing on the problem: 'Napoleon wished to give the Spaniards a constitution a priori but the project turned out badly enough. A constitution is not just something manufactured; it is the work of centuries, it is the Idea, the consciousness of rationality so far as that consciousness is developed in a particular nation. No constitution, therefore, is just the creation of its subjects. What Napoleon gave to the Spaniards was more rational than what they had before, and yet they recoiled from it as from something alien, because they were not yet educated up to its level.' op. cit., p. 287.

Nigeria: Federalism and Ethnic Rivalry

BY MARTIN DENT

THE politics of Nigeria offer a fascinating spectacle of a country of over a hundred million people in search of a national identity. Its leaders have always struggled to combine a sense of 'being Nigerian' with the perspective of strong regional local loyalties secured by ethnic and religious ties, a problem that has troubled successive governments since independence in 1960. If there is a solution, it must lie with federalism shaped to local sentiment and the early hope of a federal democracy within the rule of law. Yet within a few years of independence the reality was different. Three over-mighty regions — North, West and East — were each under single party control, each drawing on majority, ethnic loyalties. Two military coups occurred in 1966. In the first, on 14–15 January, a group of Ibo officers overthrew the civilian government. In the process the Federal Prime Minister, Abubakar Tafawa Balewa, the Northern Regional Premier, Ahmadu Bello Sardauna of Sokoto, and the Western Regional Premier, Samuel Akintola, were murdered, as were four out of five Northern Senior Officers and two Westerners. In the second coup in July/August 1966, led by Northern officers and men, the head of the Military Government, Major General Aguiyi Ironsi was killed, as was the Governor of the Western Region. About two hundred Ibo officers and men were murdered in the barracks by Northern soldiers. Nigeria teetered on the verge of disintegration in this period of doom and destruction. When the Eastern Region attempted to secede, to establish a Biafran republic in eastern Nigeria, civil war ensued until a new political order was established under General Gowon. The long, bitter conflict ended in January 1971.

Military failure

Such was the sombre background to the decade of Nigeria's independence. For a time, radical Nigerians were obsessed by the idea that a strong man would arise who would enforce their own doctrines upon the majority of the population, but they soon found that the officers in power would not accept their advice. It is a tragic commentary on this fallacious desire for military dictatorship that, even when the Ibo population in the East had been decimated in the military coups which toppled the Ironsi regime, Ibos and other radicals still sent each other Christmas cards with the caption 'the year of the soldier'. Tai Solarin, the radical Yoruba headmaster and critic, greeted the first military coup with the acclamation 'here we are, General Officer Commanding Sir (i.e. Ironsi), 35 million people on parade waiting your word of command'. Nine years later, however, he criticised the military regime of General Gowon with the words: 'This is the beginning of the end.' In fact, neither comment was either justified or true.

From bitter experience Nigeria has learnt of the follies of military rule and at long last attitudes have changed. The last military ruler, General Abacha, the worst and the most tyrannical of all the military heads of state, died of sudden seizure in June 1998. Had he not died, there was every likelihood that he would have perverted the political process for a return to civilian rule by using his power and patronage to have himself chosen as presidential candidate. Under his successor, General Abdul-Salam Abubakar — a plain, honest soldier — the country moved rapidly through a succession of elections for local government councils, state legislatures, state governors, the two houses of the federal legislatures and finally the presidency. Given the opportunity, Nigerians go willingly to the polls, and the country has returned with relief to an elected civilian government under a democratic constitution. The new President, General Olusegun Obasanjo, is the one military head of state who had voluntarily given up power in 1979 to make way for an elected civilian ruler. (Obasanjo was later victimised and imprisoned under General Abacha.) The wheel has turned full circle and Nigeria has come back to the constitutional pattern of government with which it had set out on its adventure of independence in 1960. This time, however, the constitution is presidential, and in place of three regions at the time of independence there are now 36 states. The long period of rule by heads of state from the North (who ruled for 35 of the 39 years since the independence) has been replaced by the rule of a Yoruba from the South. Obasanjo, however, has at least as much support in the North as in the South; he won more votes there than in his own Yoruba area, having steadfastly refused to adopt the role of a tribal hero.

Debt

The legacy of military rule has been harsh, not least through the accumulation of external debts which have oscillated around $33 billion for the last seven years. Nigeria has been more harshly treated than other countries in Sub-Saharan Africa and has paid a rate of interest some 3% higher than the average for the region. The country has benefited from only a small amount of the low-interest loans offered to some countries under the International Development Association Scheme, and has been left with the majority of her multilateral international debt still owed to the World Bank at interest rates of half a per cent above the commercial rate. To add one injury to another, the absence of IDA loans has been taken by the World Bank as a reason for refusing Nigeria the debt remission possibilities of its 'Heavily Indebted Poor Countries' initiative.

Nigeria's bilateral debt to other countries is about $14 billion, the largest single creditor being the United Kingdom. So far, Nigeria has been refused remission by both the World Bank and the Paris Club of bilateral creditors. Only the private creditors have helped Nigeria through part of its colossal debt burden. In 1992, after an all night bargaining session between the coalition of private bankers' representatives and the Nigeria Minister of finance, Alhaji Abubakar Alhaji, the bankers agreed to an 80% remission of Nigeria's $6 billion overdue interest in exchange for Nigeria giving them $2 billion of bonds which she has promised to honour. So far, Nigeria has kept the promise, with only one rescheduling.

Federal unity

Nigeria's elected government is at three levels: that of local government, the state and the federal level. Nigeria is the only African state to have a federal form of government, with the possible exception of Ethiopia, which now has a novel form of ethnic federalism, and Tanzania, which preserves a kind of federal relationship between the islands of Zanzibar and Pemba and the much larger entity of the mainland. Federalism has now become part of the country's political culture; it is not just a matter of the formal legal structure, but of the territorial pluralism which complements and mediates the ethnic diversity of Nigeria. At the legal level, Nigeria lists three subjects of jurisdiction, a long list of exclusive control of the federal government, a shorter list of the control of the state governments, which also enjoy substantial powers, and joint or coordinate jurisdiction, where both central and state governments can cooperate, but where the federal laws and rules take precedence over those of the states. The bare enumeration of areas of jurisdiction would not of itself remove all the causes of doubt and possible conflict. There has been a 'cooperative federalism', whereby in areas under state control a degree of harmony is achieved through the voluntary agreement of states to follow the same general pattern as the central government and other states.[1]

In addition to these legislative provisions, Nigeria has developed administrative means to lubricate the interaction of the two great wheels of government, the federal and the state. Each of the 36 states in Nigeria appoints a liaison officer and staff to reside in the federal capital, to keep contact with federal ministries and to iron out any misunderstanding. In practice, the liaison officers spend much of their time chasing up payments due to the state from the federal ministry of finance. Such is the inefficiency of the financial process in Nigeria that, if reminders are not made in person, the amounts due may never be paid.

Conversely, the federal government had a presence at state level under the last civilian government of President Shagari. He appointed high level representatives known as Presidential Liaison Officers who were responsible for coordinating federal offices in the state, and for keeping an eye on the activities of the state government. In spite of the periodic rows and continuing suspicion in some states, the channel of communication with the President was valuable, although Nigeria has never developed the complicated procedures for intergovernmental relations typical of Canada, nor has it any equivalent to the Bundesrat in Germany to give the state governments a say in the formation of federal laws. Nigeria has always had a tradition of vibrant local identity focused upon traditional Native Authorities and their modern successors. The local government reform of 1975 produced a new concept of local government as the 'third arm of federalism', a more or less uniform pattern of elected local government councils being set up all over Nigeria. These councils have subsequently been freed of the control of state governments (which in the past have frequently removed councils and chairmen, more or less at their whim), and their funds now come direct from the federal government. Ten per cent of Nigeria's total revenue has been allocated for this purpose. Recently, a system of directly elected 'strong government chairmen' has been set up (somewhat similar to the United States' 'strong mayoral system') who appoint their own executive councillors from among those elected. Local government, which has for a long time been in some decay, may thus recover and become a valuable focus for local identity.

In historical research there is a prejudice against consideration of the counter-factual. It is rightly considered foolish to examine what might have happened as opposed to what did happen. In the study of federalism, however, it is helpful to see what might have happened had Nigeria's constitution and political arrangements not been federal. The situation is analogous to that of those who complain about the side effects of the various remedies for malaria. Quinine may itself cause its own kinds of fever, Mepocrine may turn you yellow, Lariam may affect your eyes — but these dangers are as nothing compared to the effects of malaria, which the patient is likely to suffer if the prophylactic is taken. Federalism makes it difficult to get quick implementation of decisions and policies conceived at the federal level. Furthermore, particularly in the early period, it has at times exacerbated tribal tensions. However, in casting up the balance we have to envisage what disasters Nigeria would have suffered had she been governed as a unitary state. This was the case during the disastrous interlude between General Ironsi's proclamation of the end of federalism in his decree of May 1966 and his overthrow and death two months later, on the occasion when he had ventured to spend a night outside Lagos. The successor government of Colonel (as he then was) Yakubu Gowon immediately restored federalism. Had Nigeria not been governed for almost all of its political history under a federal constitution, it would very probably have fallen into the danger of large areas and groups seeing themselves as the victims of a kind of predatory internal colonialism, where their collective prospects and their identity would be under threat. The response would then have been a revolt — as among the Ibo population in the 1960s — which could only be put down by military force. This is illustrated by the examples of the Sudan after the failure of the Northern-based government to establish and maintain full federalism, and of Ethiopia where the termination of Eritrea's federal status produced the longest civil war in independent Africa.

The first demand for federal protection from the perceived threat of domination came from the North in the early fifties. The region had a bare majority in terms of total population, but a very considerable minority of people with educational qualifications at every level. The heritage of the policy of indirect rule established by Lord Lugard was the preservation of the Islamic polity of the far North which was the political centre of gravity of the region. This involved dominance by the Fulani power-holders and the Hausa civilisation in which both Hausa and Fulani participated. The Kanuri people of Bornu had been in armed conflict with the Fulani caliphate of Sokoto in the last century, but they too made common cause in politics before independence in defence of a common heritage. Even the non-Muslim, non-Hausa, inhabitants of the North identified to a large extent at this time in the cause of Northern self-defence, for they found the ethos of its administration attractive. The writer has a vivid memory of a Tiv sergeant in the military police in 1976, who had been sent to prepare the National Museum Heritage hut, standing in front of the picture of Lord Lugard in the section for rulers of Nigeria, and saying with emphasis 'Great man Lugard, he made us Northerners'. The Tiv people are neither Hausa-speaking, nor Muslim, and lack the tradition of Emirate rule, but none the less many of them at that time regarded themselves as more of the North than of the South.

The demand for separate status at the federal level was not confined to the three regions and the major ethnic groups, the Hausa, the Yoruba and the Ibo, who were each the political centre of gravity in their regions. The minority peoples in the North, the West and the East soon began to agitate for their own separate regions. The United Middle Belt Congress under J.S. Tarka won a large and vociferous majority among his own people, the Tiv, but in all three regions these minority tribal aspirations were opposed and partly suppressed by the regional party in power. Only in the mid-Western area of the region did the minority achieve their own separate 'Mid-West' state under civilian rule, for which they voted with a majority, said to be just over 100%. So popular was the cause of separate states that when Nigeria's continuance as a nation state was threatened by extreme regionalism before the outbreak of the civil war, it was the minorities which saved Nigeria's unity. In the process, they won for themselves separate states through

Gowon's decree issued just before the Biafran secession. He broke up the three regions and substituted twelve states, thus ensuring the support of most of the minority peoples in the former Eastern Region, who then backed the federal government against the Ibo.

It was Chief Awolowo the Premier of the Western region and leader of the (Yoruba) Action Group party, who had first taken up the general cause of federalism as the best political system for Nigeria. He did this with the dual intention of safeguarding the position of the Western region, while at the same time winning the support of the minority peoples in the North and the East. His view was that every ethnic group of any size should be given its own state, whereas Gowon's creation of 12 states introduced a more limited federal structure. Instead of one state in the North, he created six and divided the East and the West into three states each. The 12-state structure of Nigeria was confirmed by the victory of the federal government, helped by the insistence of the two 'middle regions (the Mid-West and the Middle Belt under J.S. Tarka) that a full federal power was essential at the centre to avoid the break-up of Nigeria into separate regions.[2]

After the civil war the remarkably generous welcome to the Ibos on their return to Nigeria owed a great deal to the Christian convictions of Gowon. He certainly copied Lincoln's example of 'binding up the nation's wounds'. The presence of a federal structure gave the Ibos a state of their own and this had considerable effect in helping their rapid reintegration into Nigeria. It was in marked contrast to the situation in the United States following the civil war, where the defeated Southern states were kept under martial law for a number of years and only readmitted with their own elected state government to the United States federal structure ten years after the end of the war.

The 12 states created by Gowon were subsequently subdivided several times by successive decrees of military governments. They now number 36. This is by far the greatest multiplication of numbers of states in any federal system. The Nigerian capacity to subdivide both states and local government units is like the subdivision of the cells in a growing biological entity; there seems to be no end to it, for each local area or group thinks that it can enhance its status and its wealth by getting a state or local government council of its own. The danger is that this endless subdivision, if left unchecked, may make federalism itself unworkable.

Federal character

This tendency has been further encouraged by the new post-civil war doctrine of 'federal character', which has become a most important guide to the distribution of jobs and resources among the ethnic communities of the 36 states. It implies a system of equal shares for each unit, both for each state at the federal level and for each local government area at the state level. Each separate unit receives a proportion of its share of the distributable pool of federal finance under this principle. This is a powerful incentive to demand the creation of more states. On the other hand, the doctrine of federal character is a way of guarding against the danger of one advanced ethnic group, with a large number of qualified people, getting an over-large share of government jobs and patronage, and it has helped to prevent the extreme discontent of less advantaged people.

The bare bones of federal character were laid down in the requirement under the 1979 Constitution that there must be a representative from every state in the federal cabinet, among senior civil service posts and senior army officers, and representatives of every local government area in every state executive. This doctrine has been reaffirmed in the 1999 Constitution under which General Obasanjo has been elected President, which also established a special commission to enforce the federal character by equal distribution of senior posts among indigenes of all the states in the senior ranks of the civil service, the para-statals and the diplomatic service. A parallel commission has the task of ensuring equal representation of states in the armed forces, both at the officer rank and among the other ranks. If this provision were to be enforced rigidly, the result would be disastrous, but the doctrine has subsequently spread in practice to other matters: for instance, the pass mark for secondary education entrance was higher for better educated Christian areas of Kaduna state than for the Muslim areas which had fewer pupils in primary schools. A similar attempt to apply quotas to university entrance to help less well qualified areas led to acute quarrels over the performance of the all-Nigerian Joint Admission and Matriculation Board.

A corollary of the federal character doctrine has been the creation of states of roughly equal population, and a similar search for units of equality of population among local governments within states. In this respect Nigeria is almost unique among federations. The requirement of equality of population in local government areas produced a great dispute in Benue-Plateau state, under Governor Gomwalk, in 1969–70. Plateau state had a number of fairly small local government areas, while Tiv local government area constituted about half its population. Since a policy of equal shares for each local government area must result in the Tiv getting far too small a share of many government benefits, the answer was obvious — break up Tiv into three. This was the policy followed by Gomwalk. In this matter, as with many other disputes in Nigeria, the political and the administrative became intermingled.

The process of state multiplication continued under civilian and military control alike. The only attempt to recreate larger units came under General Abacha, when the government proposed the division of Nigeria into six 'zones' — the North East, the North West, and the Northern Minorities, the East, the West and the Southern Minorities. The plan was never implemented in any institutional form, and there is no mention of zones in the 1999 constitution. The only use of the concept today is as a geographical basis for the sharing out of appointments to the six major posts in the central government — the Presidency, the Vice-Presidency, the President of the Senate, the Senate Majority Leader, the Speakership of the Houses of Assembly, and the House of Assembly Majority Leader.

Absence of ethnic nomenclature

A great advantage springing from the structure and nomenclature of the Nigerian federal system has been the absence of direct tribal reference. A federal system that calls its constituent parts by ethnic names is asking for trouble. Yugoslavia before the second world war had attempted to create a number of units of a regional kind, in place of the three largest units, Serbia, Croatia and Slovenia; Tito reverted to these three ethnic names in addition to the other three republics of Bosnia, Montenegro and Macedonia. The assumption created by this ethnic nomenclature was that all major groups of Serbs should be in Serbia and that all major groups of Croats should be in Croatia, and that Kosovars should have no place in the republic of Serbia, in which their province was incorporated.

Nigeria avoided this danger by using the geographical areas as surrogates for ethnic identities, although no one doubts that the inhabitants of five of the states in the former West are overwhelmingly Yoruba, those of five in the former East are overwhelmingly Ibo, and those of nine in the former North are overwhelmingly Hausa/Fulani, while some others have a large Hausa share in their population.[3] The remaining states consist of a number of smaller ethnic groups. It seems that only the comparatively new state of Akwa Ibom exactly corresponds to just one ethnic identity, the Ibibios. Ethnic identity is very often the language of the market place, but in federal matters it is not to be mentioned and, like sex in polite conversation, it is usually described by a synonym.

Representation

It remains to examine the important area of representation, which is one of the major themes of this collection of studies. We are faced with a paradox. The creation of a state within the federal system may arouse expectations and emotions (generally seen elsewhere in the world) in the further demand for sovereign independence. On the other hand, the ability to channel off disruptive demands for separation into demands for separate units in a federal system is immensely valuable. (Were it possible to achieve this in Kosovo, in Chechnia, among Turks in Cyprus or Tamils in Sri Lanka and in other situations of division, it might help to avoid a number of armed conflicts.)

In order to create the sense that a state, within the federal system, really belongs to local people, it has to have its own legislature as well as its elected governor, appointed executive council and state apparatus. A local MP is also a great advantage. However, when one comes to look at the actual records of Nigerian state legislatures one is in for a disappointment. For the most part, state Houses of Assembly have sat for a very short period each day and confined themselves to discussing issues of prestige foreign to the real interests of their constituents. A House of Assembly, for instance, whose Hansard the writer examined for months of April, May and June 1985, spent an average of only one hour and a half in session on the relatively few days when it met.

This was typical of many state legislatures during the second republic. As one or two state legislators have admitted, it is doubtful if they really took their task seriously. The performance of the two federal houses were rather better, but even they often met for an hour or so to fulfil their constitutional requirement to sit for 200 days each year and then adjourned. In the first 18 months of civilian rule, they passed only 11 laws, among them being four for the budgets and appropriation bills. Listeners to debates of the Senate might find the camaraderie of members of rival party members amusing and excellent for the cause of national unity, but the substance of debates was at times theatrical rather than practical. For instance, the government's bill to establish an Open University for Nigeria met with opposition from senators of all parties—urged on by Vice-Chancellors of existing universities. It was denounced as an elitist institution alien to the interests of the mass of poorer people and was thrown out by a large majority. The Nigerian sitting next to the writer in the visitors' gallery observed: 'It will be all right in time; the government will get some influential big man to beg the key senators and it will pass easily.' This is exactly what happened two years latter.

The concept of serious debate on matters of government is in no way alien to Nigerian political culture. The word 'shawara' in Hausa, derived from the Arabic, is a powerful one and means serious discussion at a suitable gathering in order to get advice on best policy. Other Nigerian peoples have similar traditions. Among the Tiv, for instance, consultation is highly valued, and from colonial times onwards the practice was established of the administrator meeting in formal discussion with a large gathering of clan and kindred heads which came to known as the *Ijiir Tamen* (The Great Judgment). Other Nigerian peoples have an equal respect for the function of solemn consultation in public or private gatherings. Even during military rule, the desire to have prestigious bodies for consultation was often expressed by 'Leaders of Thought Conferences', whose members (nominated by government) included a fairly wide range of popular politicians as well as senior civil servants.

Where there is some political leadership in the assembly, Nigerian gatherings have been more industrious and more purposeful. In the Constituent assembly elected indirectly to consider the draft constitution for the return to civilian rule in 1979, debate was serious and well informed — lasting for between four and five hours each day, with very few weekdays off — and this disciplined performance may have been due to the presence of a chairman who was appointed by government with the mandate to get the business completed. Even this responsible body came to a dead halt in 1978 over the 'Sharia' clauses, relating to the procedure for the courts at the federal level to hear cases on appeal relating to Muslim personal law, when nearly all the Muslim members walked out. Only the decisive intervention of General Obasanjo, the military Head of State, induced the Muslim members to return and finish the business. Sharia law remains an explosive issue.

This may indicate that there are valuable elements in the British parliamentary heritage, where the ministers participate in the debates of the legislature and give some structure and coherence — an advantage lost in the wholesale adoption of the United States model by Nigeria. Some alternative means of bringing in an element of government leadership needs to be found. The role of the House and Senate majority leader also has to be better defined, together with the means for coordinating the executive and the legislature.

Issues for debate

Debate has often been far more concentrated on subjects which could probably be better dealt with elsewhere. The formula for allocation of the large proportion of Nigeria's revenue collected at federal level and distributed to the states has come back again and again for debate. Admittedly, the issue is one of vast importance to both federal and state governments, for the proportion of the total revenue collected at federal level and allocated to states is far higher than in any other federal system of government because of the overwhelming importance of oil revenue which accrues to the federal government. This contentious issue has been constantly reviewed and has taken a high proportion of the time of government and legislature. It needs to be put to rest once and for all, either by devising a constitutional formula that will last a long time or by setting up an independent quasi-judicial body (like the Australian Commonwealth Grants Commission) for continuous review of grants to state governments. The equivalent Nigerian body under review in the new constitution is the Revenue Mobilisation, Allocation and Fiscal Commission, which can give advice but has no power to enforce its decisions on the government.

A further factor, which inhibited the role of the legislatures in the second republic, was the fact that they gave themselves outrageously large allowances, equivalent to about £50,000 per head in 1979. President Shagari had courageously vetoed their attempts to vote themselves large salaries but was outflanked by the allowance. It remains to be seen if General Obasanjo, as President, will be able to inculcate a more serious intent into the federal legislature, and into his own administration, to remove the sickness of corruption which has so far affected all Nigerian governments and greatly hindered the economic development of Nigeria. Gordon Brown, as Chancellor of the Exchequer, has tried to persuade the Nigerian government to give the IMF a place in the Nigerian Ministry of Finance but this may be too humiliating to accept. It may be better to reinforce Nigeria's own audit through the Public Accounts Committee with advice and support of outside professional auditors.

Federalism and ethnicity

It remains to examine how far federalism has helped Nigeria to reduce tensions between ethnic groups and states. Many of the accompanying characteristics of Nigerian federalism have their parallels elsewhere. Every head of government in Africa knows that he must practice balance among the constituent ethnic and other groups in his country and that in allocating cabinet and senior governmental posts he should take care of ethnic arithmetic. If he is sensible, he will also make room for local self-government. The reason that Nigeria, almost alone of African states, practices federal as opposed to unitary government is that the three major ethnic groups, the Hausa in the former Northern region, the Ibo in the former Eastern region and the Yoruba in the former Western region, are unusually large and possessed of different cultures. Each of them had developed a strong sense of tribal cohesion, and the regional identities fostered by the British made unitary government impossible. The first achievement of the federal system was to enable these regions to coexist in one Nigeria. The cohesion was broken by the trauma of the two military coups of 1966 and the massacre of Ibos in the North, which provoked the Ibo majority in the Eastern region (led by Ojukwu, the regional governor) to secede. Secession was ended by victory in the civil war and by generous reconciliation but the memory persists and the danger is not forgotten.

Gowon's state creation, and the subsequent divisions creating a country of 36 states, have changed the nature of federal politics, although many Nigerians still grumble about the alleged domination of the country by the inhabitants of a region other than their own or by one of the three big tribes. Suspicions of the North by Southerners are sometimes focused on the supposed activities of the 'Kaduna Mafia', a shadowy association of senior people connected with the old Northern region. These grumbles are no longer open conflicts, though they could become so if one of the major groups felt itself permanently excluded from power. If, for instance, the first civilian President had been another Northerner, the Ibos and the Yoruba might have headed a movement of Southern dissent. The federal government has so far adopted a wise policy of fair shares, akin to the traditional doctrine of 'Eat and give to your brother' but the threat of violence in never far away.

The conflicts which Nigerian federalism now has to address are more local. The Ogoni in the South-East of the country — aroused by the passionate eloquence of the late Saro-Wiwa — protested violently against the pollution caused by the activities of the Shell Oil Company whose pipes were above and not below ground and whose flaring of natural gas at the drilling point caused considerable distress. At the same time, they complained bitterly of the unequal distribution of oil revenue which, under the old dispensation, left only 5% to the area of origin, a grievance shared by all the oil producing peoples in the Delta area. This has been remedied under the new constitution, which provides 13% of the Distributable Pool to be allocated on the principle of derivation, a financial correction which may help to heal the wounds among the disaffected peoples of the area. Ogoni's share of Nigeria's oil production is only about 3% but the extra revenue, if properly administered by the state and locally elected authorities, may help to remove the sense of grievance. In this and many local conflicts, several of which have resulted in violence as between local Muslims and Christians, there is a great need for reconciliation between communities, states and the federal administration. The return to democratic parliamentary rule is not a guarantee but a persistent hope that Nigeria can live at peace with itself.

1   Despite the presence of strong conservative Islamic feeling in the North, no state government has sought to reinstate Muslim criminal law or Muslim law of evidence. Both were replaced by codes shortly before independence. If an attempt were made to reintroduce them, it would be contrary to the secular basis of the constitution.

2   The writer was privileged to play some part in the debate, when Tarka announced that his delegation would quit the September 1966 Constitutional Conference over the issue of state creation and confederation. The writer pointed out that a confederal system had been tried in America in the years immediately after independence but subsequently abandoned in favour of full federal power at the centre

3   *Yoruba-speaking*: Oyo, Ogun, Oshun, Ondo, Ekiti. *Ibo-speaking*: Imo, Anambra, Enugu, Ebonyi, Abia. *Hausa-speaking*: Kano, Jigawa, Sokoto, Bauchi, Gombe, Katsina, Kebbi, Zamfara, Yobe and several other states with a substantial Hausa minority.

Lebanon: Patterns of Confessional Politics

BY ANDREW RIGBY

PRIOR to the 1970s Lebanon was a relatively peaceful society, held together by a tolerant coexistence between different religious communities. It was an unusual example of a democratic Middle-Eastern state. Then a long seventeen-year war brought about its collapse. A Hobbesian state of violence, 'a war of every man against every man', reduced the country to a despair that saw something like 2% of the population killed by its fellow citizens — 100,000 died and more than twice that number wounded and maimed. By 1990 over a million Lebanese had been uprooted from their homes. Not until the Ta'if Accords of 1989 were signed did the hope revive of a communal peace and a democratic order, and it is pertinent to ask not only why the state disintegrated but in what sense can there be a renewal of the former democratic consensus.

The problems are immense. If Lebanon were an island in a distant sea, the ethnic and religious make-up of its population would still pose difficulties. In fact, Lebanon is a small state sandwiched between Syria and Israel which, hating each other, have looked for allies among Lebanese society and have fought their battles by proxy among its citizens. External peace, therefore, is a precondition of internal order, but it is by no means the only requirement for parliamentary rule over its divided people.

The country is mountainous behind a narrow coastal strip, its society a complex of communities of ancient origin. The state itself dates from 1920, as a creation under French protection after the world war, becoming a republic in 1926. In order to create a viable homeland for the Christians and to weaken the Arab threat from Damascus, the boundaries of the state were extended beyond the Mount Lebanon heartland to encompass the mainly Muslim coastal area from Tripoli down to Tyre and to the Beka'a Valley to the east. The establishment of Greater Lebanon delighted the Maronite community, but it came at a price. There was now a sizeable proportion of Muslims, many of them deeply disaffected from the new state. Whereas in 1913, out of a total population of 415,000, Mount Lebanon had a clear majority of Christians (nearly 80%) and even of Maronites (58%), the 1932 census of Greater Lebanon showed a very different picture. The Maronites constituted only 30% of the total, the Sunnis 22% and the Shias 20%. In the years following, this balance was to tilt further in favour of the Muslims due to differential birth rates and emigration by Christians.

The establishment of Greater Lebanon marked the end, therefore, of the old order based on a close association between a Maronite majority and a Druze (Shia Muslim) minority centred on Mount Lebanon. From its inception, the new state was marked by division over its legitimacy: nearly half of the population was deeply resentful of its arbitrary incorporation in a Christian dominated state. Furthermore, whilst the Maronites enjoyed a political hegemony under the French, the emerging modern capitalist economic sector was largely concentrated in the hands of the more urbanised Sunni Muslims and Byzantine Christians (Orthodox or Catholic). As such, the economic and political centre of the new state shifted from Mount Lebanon to Beirut.

Despite these trends, the political ascendancy of the Maronites was never in doubt so long as the French were there to support them. In 1941, however, Lebanon was occupied by Allied troops, and the Free French under British pressure promised independence which came in 1943. For the Maronites, the loss of direct French patronage brought into sharp relief their dilemma: how to maintain their political ascendancy and their safe refuge as a Christian minority in the Middle East without the direct presence of their French patrons. The solution was enshrined in the 'National Pact' of 1943, concluded between the Maronite President, Bishare Khoury, and his Sunni Prime Minister, Riad al Sulh. The essence of the agreement was a recognition of the fundamental rights of the different communities. The seats in the Chamber of Deputies were distributed in proportion to the numerical strength of the communities, the two senior political posts being shared between representatives of the main communities, the President a Maronite and the Prime Minister a Sunni. The National Pact extended and consecrated this system of the confessional distribution of public offices, while enabling the Maronites to retain control over the key political, security and military positions. The division of power was based on the relative population of each sect as in the 1932 census, which had the Christians at 52% of the total population and the Muslims at 48%. As a consequence of these figures, the agreement stipulated that the Christians should have six representatives at any given level of government to every five Muslims. These same proportions were to be observed throughout all levels of the country's administration. In addition, the Prime Minister was to be a Sunni Muslim; the Speaker of the Chamber, a Shia Muslim; the Minister of Defence, an Orthodox Christian; the Minister of the Interior, a Druze; the Commander-in-Chief of the Armed Forces, a Maronite Christian.

The Lebanese consociational system

The key features of this political system reflected the consociational model developed by Arendt Lijphart in his *Democracy in Plural Societies* published in 1973. The main elements were: government by 'grand coalition'; the mutual veto or 'concurrent majority' rule; proportionality as the principle of representation; and a high degree of autonomy for each community to run its own internal affairs.

Government by 'grand coalition'. As we have seen, the bedrock of the system institutionalised after 1943 was an accommodation between the political elites of the different communities, in particular the leadership of the Maronites and the Sunni Muslims. As David McDowell observed, 'Lebanon was governed by a consortia of interests and power brokers that reflected the composition of the political establishment, but not necessarily the electorate'.[1]

The mutual veto or concurrent majority rule. Despite the historic suspicion between the political leaders and despite the opposed orientations towards the wider Arab region in which Lebanon was embedded, they had a common interest in sustaining the National Pact from which they derived the lion's share of political power. One of the prime conditions for sustaining the agreement was that they should avoid disruptive issues that might drive a wedge between them. When this pattern of conflict avoidance was ignored, the consequences could be disastrous, as in Lebanon's first civil war of 1958. One of the understandings of the National Pact, therefore, was that Lebanon would pursue an essentially neutral and non-aligned course in relation to foreign affairs. A corollary of this was that although each had external allies and co-religionists, no community should seek external assistance in pursuance of their domestic interests. Lebanon experienced its first civil war when this rule was broken by President Camille Chamoun who invited in American marines to help him suppress what he perceived as the Arab nationalist threat to the Lebanese state. This was widely viewed as a breach of the 1943 accord and Christians joined with Muslims in demanding that Chamoun quit office.

Proportionality as the principle of representation. The founding fathers were convinced that the country's vertical cleavages between different sects must be acknowledged and accommodated within the political system if the state was to survive. The ratio of 6:5 Christian:Muslim was reflected within each constituency, the number and religious composition of the deputies reflecting the demographic weight of each community within the electoral district . In so far as representation was based on religious grounds, there was little incentive to establish cross-confessional ideological parties. The system of multi-member constituencies, however, did encourage elite cooperation across the communities. By the 1960 election, the country had been divided into 26 constituencies, eleven of them uniconfessional, from which 99 candidates were to be returned. (Given the agreed ration of 6:5, it was necessary for the number of representatives to be in multiples of eleven.) Within the Tripoli constituency, with its predominantly Sunni Muslim population, there were four Sunni seats and one Greek Orthodox. Each constituent eligible to vote had five votes to cast, one for each seat.

Hence, to ensure election each candidate had to compete for votes not only within his own community but in the other communities as well. Invariably, this resulted in the formation of lists of candidates from the different communities, each person on the list having an interest in persuading his bloc of voters to vote for the whole list. Under this system there was pressure on candidates to form cross-confessional alliances in order to increase their chance of election, the real competition being within the communities. Thus, given that cabinet seats were filled by proportionality, any candidate seeking a cabinet seat would attempt to defeat an incumbent from within his own community rather than from another.

Confessional autonomy. The Lebanese political system was created as a means of preserving some degree of national unity through accommodating the depth of religious feeling, particularly amongst the Maronite Christian community. Such feelings permeated not only every aspect of political life but key areas of personal and social life. Thus, personal status laws and the institutions through which they were applied remained exclusively under the control of the religious leaders of the country's seventeen officially recognised sects. Indeed, sectarian affiliation itself was and is determined by religious law. As might be expected in such circumstances, the different confessions developed their own welfare and education services over the years to cater for their co-religionists, the central state adopting a minimalist role in such spheres. It has been estimated that up to 70% of school children in Lebanon passed through schools of their own confession, barely meeting those of another faith. Moreover, the communities tended to be endogamous. As late as 1970, marriages between different Christian communities still accounted for less than 10% of all Christian marriages, whilst Muslim-Christian partnerships were, and remain, statistically insignificant.

The collapse of consociationalism

The consociational model embodied in the 1943 National Pact may have been a necessary condition for the establishment of the state, but it could not ensure its persistence. Indeed, it can be argued that by the 1970s those same factors that acted as a source of stability had begun to exacerbate divisions and hastened the collapse of a political system that had lost legitimacy in the eyes of significant sectors of society. At the core of this collapse was the failure of the political elites to reform a rigid political system when confronted by fundamental pressures from both the domestic and external world. The division of power within the political system was based on the numbers of each community, but by the 1960s it was clear to most Lebanese that this power-sharing system was based on demographic myth. Differential rates of population growth had produced a clear Muslim majority within the country, their numbers supplemented by the influx of 130,000 Palestinian refugees following the establishment of the State of Israel and the resultant war of 1948–49.

Moreover, within that Muslim majority, the most rapid population growth was amongst the economically deprived, socially excluded and politically marginalised community — the Shias. They became increasingly disaffected as the power-sharing arrangements appeared ever more clearly a cynical device whereby other communities and their elites might cream off the spoils of office and privilege. Hence, from Muslims in general, but from Shias in particular, the demands to reform the system grew ever more strident.

Resentment at their relative political exclusion amongst Shias was compounded by their growing sense of economic injustice as a consequence of Lebanon's laissez-faire uneven socio-economic growth. This had led to the concentration of economic activity in Beirut and the neglect of outlying rural areas, especially in the south where there were heavy pockets of Shia small farmers and peasants. The living conditions of these impoverished folk were made more difficult by the Palestinian presence in the south and Israeli bombardments and incursions across the border. Many of them migrated north to Beirut in search of security and employment, where they joined thousands of others in the slum areas that became known as the 'Belt of Misery'. Removed from their villages of origin, made increasingly aware of the social and economic injustices that permeated Lebanese society, and sensitive to the unrepresentative nature of the political establishment, the occupants of the Belt of Misery were obvious targets for political reform movements led by a new generation that began to emerge with the aim of mobilising the Lebanese dispossessed. The political system could not accommodate such movements in so far as they challenged the confessional foundation upon which the state was based.

For many within the Maronite community, such demands for reform were to be resisted at all costs. They were seen as movements intended to establish Muslim domination and the defeat of the Maronite project of sustaining a homeland in the midst of a hostile Arab world. Already, by the late 1960s, with the Cairo Agreement of 1969 allowing the Palestinians free rein in the south of the country, there was a virtual 'state within a state'. Following the expulsion of the Palestine Liberation Organisation (PLO) from Jordan in 1970 and its relocation to Lebanon, this external presence was even more intrusive and, from a Christian perspective, threatening. In this way, external factors exacerbated internal divisions within Lebanon, a process which was to intensify as communal groups with cross-border ties sought out foreign sponsors to support them in their domestic power struggle. Such foreign patrons within the region and beyond were only too willing to sponsor Lebanese clients in pursuit of their own regional and global interests. The country became entangled in the regional conflict between Israel and the Arab states, the different parties fighting out a proxy conflict on Lebanese territory.

What had become increasingly apparent by the early 1970s was that the Lebanese political system was too rigid and too unresponsive to cope with the demands being made upon it. In the words of Michael Hudson: 'Increasingly, the uneasy (elite) agreement on the key question of distribution of power among sects within the elite cartel came to be challenged both on the elite and mass levels . . . Lebanese society was becoming mobilised behind a variety of political identities and ideologies other than sect. Members of the elites were not immune to these currents, and so conflict broke out at elite level, within as well as between sectarian communities. The resulting deadlock and immobilism prevented the Lebanese government from undertaking reforms that might have mitigated the rising tensions.'[2]

The result of these rising tensions was that two broad coalitions began to form. On the one side was a conservative alliance, which became the Lebanese Front, determined to preserve the status quo, and on the other the coalition that constituted the Lebanese National Movement demanding reform of the existing political system. Once the civil war commenced in earnest, particularly after the PLO joined the fight in December 1975, the cleavages became ever more intractable. In this 'retribalisation', each faction developed its own militia, invariably backed by one or more external patrons which then proceeded to 'cleanse' the territory they claimed and to run it as their own fiefdom. By the spring of 1976 sectarian demarcation lines were established throughout the country. As Deidre Collings described it, 'Ultimately, the war developed an insidious life of its own as the militia-run "war system", dominated by those with weapons, patrons and a vested interest in Lebanon's continued destabilisation, became firmly entrenched.'

Peace initiatives during the civil war and the Ta'if Accord

There were numerous efforts at peace making, but it was not until late in 1990, when the 1989 Charter of National Reconciliation (Ta'if Accord) began to be implemented, that peace of a kind returned to Lebanon. The peace initiatives had failed on three counts. Firstly, the initial efforts were fruitless because neither side was prepared to compromise. During the early months of the war a National Dialogue Committee was established following pressure from Syria, but it proved to be a dialogue of the deaf. Each party was committed to its own agenda: the Maronites demanded the restoration of law and order, the Muslims demanded constitutional reforms.

Secondly, by the time the ageing elites were prepared to compromise they had lost the ability to implement their agreements. As the war continued, counter-elites within each community emerged, controlling their own militias. Eventually the conflict between the different communities was laced with bloody conflicts between different factions within the communities, and power accrued to those most skilled in the use of violence.

A third reason for failure was the malign influence of external actors. By 1976, just one year into the war, the basic outline of a peace settlement had been reached between the Maronite President Frangieh and the Syrian Foreign Minister, which became known as the Constitutional Document. This became the template for all subsequent proposals for reforming the power-sharing arrangement in Lebanese political life. The Christians agreed to relinquish some of their power in return for assurances from the Muslims that the confessional system would remain, albeit with a changed ration of representation from 6:5 in favour of the Christians to equal representation. At a subsequent series of Arab summit conferences, it was resolved to establish an Arab Deterrent Force which would assist the Lebanese government in reasserting its authority, not least in the task of disarming the various militias. The assumption was that if the Lebanese government had a force capacity far superior to that of any of the militias, then it would be in the position to enforce its rule and implement the agreed reforms. Unfortunately, such a force had to be composed of troops drawn from a representative number of Arab states. This in turn required harmonious relations between the Arab states, and by the late 1970s the Arab world was being riven asunder by President Sadat's overtures to Israel which culminated in the Camp David Agreement. A further fault-line open up in the Arab world with the Iran–Iraq War and Syria's open support of the Iranians against the rival Baathist in Baghdad.

For all these states, each embroiled in its own conflict, the civil war in Lebanon presented an opportunity for them to pursue their own agendas through the manipulation of one or more domestic factions. In turn, their Lebanese clients were eager to obtain the sponsorship of external patrons in support of their own military and political programmes. There developed a situation in which proxy wars were superimposed on the domestic conflict taking place within and between the different confessions. As the war continued, the number of domestic actors involved in the conflict grew, as did the number of external patrons. In such a situation, no peace proposal stood any chance of being implemented.

Not until the late 1980s did circumstances in the region become more supportive of peace in Lebanon. Egypt had been welcomed back into the Arab fold, the Iran–Iraq War had come to an end, and the collapse of the USSR had left the United States as the sole super-power, so rendering a US-sponsored peace proposal possible. In May 1989 a Tripartite Arab High Commission from Arabia, Morocco and Algeria was established. At the end of September it convened a meeting of Lebanese deputies in Ta'if, Saudi Arabia, where they were presented with a draft agreement which they subsequently endorsed.[3]

The Ta'if Accord contained no surprises. It was based on the established consociative principle of the need to share power in order to regulate the conflict of interest between the various sects. As such, it did not mark any radical departure from the National Pact of 1943. At its core was the recognition that if Lebanon was to survive, then all the various communities had to agree to live together and to acknowledge that coexistence required the sharing of power and that no single sect should seek a monopoly.[4] The proposals left unchanged the established distribution of the top three offices of President (Maronite Christian), Prime Minister (Sunni Muslim), and Speaker of the Chamber of Deputies (Shia Muslim). However, they did require a substantial transfer of executive powers from the President to the Cabinet, which was to be presided over by the Prime Minister rather than the President. The powers of the Chamber of Deputies were to be increased with the requirement that the selection of Prime Minister by the President should be taken only after binding consultation with the Chamber. The authority of the Speaker was also increased through the extension of his term of office from one to four years to match the length of each parliament. Within the legislature, the confessional balance was to be equal numbers of Christians and Muslims. To allow for this parity, the number of seats was increased first from 99 to 108, and subsequently to 128. Electoral district boundaries were to be redrawn, to make them larger and more communally mixed, while the principle of decentralising administration to regional department was affirmed.

The Accord also proclaimed as a national goal the eventual abolition of political sectarianism. As a step in this direction it urged that the principle of a fixed ratio of confessional representation amongst the ranks of the civil service should be abolished except for the appointment of the heads of the ministries which posts should be equally distributed between Christians and Muslims. It also called for the eventual removal of any statement of confession on identity cards. To oversee this proposed process, a National Committee, chaired by the President, was to be appointed.

With regard to foreign policy the Accord moved beyond the equivocation of the 1943 Pact (which referred to Lebanon as a country with an 'Arab face') by affirming that Lebanon was 'Arab in its identity and association'. It also recognised the reality of its 'special relationship' with Syria. Thus, it was acknowledged that the assistance of Syrian troops would be required if the Lebanese state was to 'extend its authority over all the territory of Lebanon', which would also involve the disarming and dissolution of the militias. The Accord made reference to the eventual redeployment of Syrian troops, but not to their withdrawal, anticipating an eventual agreement between Beirut and Damascus as to the number and location of those Syrian troops that would remain.

The Ta'if Accord aimed to lay the foundation for a new and independent Lebanon—a second republic. But it was interpreted and implemented to suit Syria's interests. As Joseph Maila has observed: 'The Ta'if Accord's implementation effectively ended the violence in

Lebanon. It restored a certain peace to the country . . . But it failed to ensure Lebanon's independence. Lebanon's peace was achieved at the price of its independence.'[5]

Post Ta'if: the second republic

The Maronites became increasingly fearful that Lebanon, their erstwhile haven, was becoming little more than a province of Syria's authoritarian and repressive regime. Believing that the 1992 general election was a sham, pushed through by Syria for its own purposes, they boycotted it in large numbers. The election itself, however, revealed the old pattern of electoral malpractice in favour of the traditional political elite within each community.[6] In the years following this first postwar election, the feelings of frustration and marginalisation within the Christian communities grew stronger. Some of their more powerful leaders were in forced exile or in prison; they have become more inward-looking and have emigrated in increasing numbers. The traditional elite and former militia leaders have proved incapable therefore of breaking out of the narrow confessional pattern of politics. This was most graphically illustrated by the wheeler-dealing of the 'troika': the Maronite President Elias Hrawi, the Sunni Prime Minister Rafiq Hariri, and the Shia Speaker of the Chamber of Deputies Nabil Berri. A particular feature was the persistent squabbling over constitutional prerogatives which had been stripped from the presidency by Ta'if, whilst Hrawi struggled to retain what executive powers he could.

While the political leaders continued to behave as if the state was their own patrimony, the economic gap between the haves and the have-nots continued to widen with a regressive taxation system, inadequate welfare provision, increasing public debt and budget deficits, waste and corruption throughout the public sector. Disgust at the venality of the politicians became widespread. For example, a report from the Central Fund for the Displaced of February 1999 revealed that former officials of the fund had misappropriated scarce resources earmarked for the return of mainly Christian families displaced during the war. Such malpractice helped to explain why, in spite of spending millions of dollars, only 35% of the displaced have returned to their homes. Socio-economic unrest began to rise, as evidenced in particular by the 'Hunger Revolution' led by Sheikh Tufayli, a former Hizbullah leader in the Baalbeck region.

The response of the Lebanese authorities to the upsurge of social unrest and political protest was repression. The army was used to break up protest demonstrations and strikes; political activists continued to disappear into detention in Syria without charge or trial. The media and the labour unions became particular targets of the regime's wrath and broadcasting stations were closed down, allegedly for their roles in fomenting sectarian passions. The government also intervened to topple elected leaders and replace them with pliant allies.

The result was a deepening of disaffection felt by large swathes of the population. Writing in 1997, Karim Pakradouni painted a grim picture of the Lebanese postwar experience: 'The Lebanese can feel the essence of the social contract gradually slipping away day by day, as the electoral system becomes an appointments system, the liberal economy becomes a network of monopolies, and the democratic order turns into a police state.'[7] He predicted that if these trends were left unaddressed, then the country would be driven into a political impasse that could quickly deteriorate once more into sectarian conflict. He characterised these anti-democratic trends as the 'Arabisation' of Lebanese politics. Perhaps a more apt description would have been the 'Syrianisation' of Lebanon. With 35–40,000 troops in Lebanon, in addition to its ubiquitous intelligence personnel, Syria continued to manipulate Lebanon's divisions to suit its own interests and to legitimate its presence as the necessary arbiter between the sparring sects. But sectarian politics also suited the interests of the old members of the Lebanese political cartel and former warlords, and that in turn was reinforced by the social fabric of traditional patron-client networks, clan and sectarian loyalties that still permeate many dimensions of Lebanese life. It is a mutually reinforcing set of relationships.

Conclusion

Those who call for a secular democratic state often fail to take account of the depth of religious feeling in the lives of so many Lebanese. The big problem is not so much how to eliminate sectarian loyalties, but how to depoliticise such aspects of identity, so that a civic consciousness can emerge based on a shared Lebanese identity and sense of national interest. How might such a process be advanced?

Salim el-Hoss, who succeeded Rafiq Hariri as Prime Minister in December 1998, has made a number of specific proposals which include the following: the creation of a single electoral district in order to encourage the formation of cross-community political parties; the direct election of the President, without reference to religious affiliation, along the lines of the French or United States model; the use of referendums in order to involve the public in more active citizenship roles; administrative decentralisation; an active anti-discrimination policy, and the promotion of uniform history books throughout the educational system.[8]

Whilst proposing such institutional changes, el-Hoss has questioned how much can be achieved by such methods, imposed from above, without a grassroots force for change from below. Are there any grounds for believing that such pressures might become a significant factor in the political development of Lebanon? There are a few. Prior to the long civil war, disillusionment with the traditional political system was becoming widespread, particularly amongst the educated middle classes of all communities. Cross-community political movements were beginning to emerge and the trade unions were becoming stronger. Then the civil war broke out, and with it came the retribalis-ation of Lebanese political and social life. But even during the depths of the civil war it was clear that the overwhelming majority of Lebanese wanted peace, coexistence and national unity. Many had the courage to articulate such aspirations in mass demonstrations and by other means throughout the war. The trade unions remained to the fore in maintaining and proclaiming a non-confessional stance. In recent years there have been signs that this trend has begun to re-emerge, driven by frustration with the consequences of inequitable and uneven economic development, and disgust at the corruption of a self-seeking political class subservient to their Syrian overlords.

Political changes in Lebanon have also given grounds for hope. The appointment of the former army commander, General Emile Lahoud, as presidential successor to Hrawi in November 1998 was welcomed, particularly by the Maronite community which felt that here was a man who might be prepared to stand up to the Syrians. The following month Prime Minister Hariri resigned and was replaced by Salim el-Hoss, one of the leading critics of the corruption and quarrelsome sparring of the 'Troika'. He has been forthright in the call for a secular state and a political life free of sectarian loyalties. These appointments, and sub-sequent dismissals of corrupt officials, were generally welcomed throughout the country. After nine years, the consolidation of the Ta'if Accord may have begun.

At the time of these changes a Lebanese public opinion poll revealed that fighting corruption was the most important priority for people after the implementation of Resolution 425 of the United Nations and the withdrawal of Israeli troops from the south. Hopes that this might become a reality were raised in May 1999 when the newly elected Prime Minister of Israel, Ehud Barak, reaffirmed his electoral pledge that he would withdraw Israeli troops from Lebanon within a year of his taking office. If this were to happen it would be an immense step on the path towards a regional peace settlement.

When Syria disarmed the militias after the civil war, it left Hizbullah in the field as a reminder to the Israelis that there could be no peace along their northern border until they agreed to the return of the Golan captured from Syria in 1967. If Israel did withdraw from the Lebanon, however, then not only would the destruction wrought upon Lebanon by Israel cease, but Syria's rationale for maintaining such a heavy military presence in the country would be undermined. If Syria were to withdraw, in the context of a regional peace process, the position of the old political leaders and warlords in Lebanon would be weakened once they had lost their Syrian patrons. The opportunity would then be there for the emergence of a new generation of forward looking political leaders to challenge the old guard.

In the context of such progress torwards a regional peace front, and corresponding changes in the domestic political arena, the space would open up for the development of a more inclusive sense of Lebanese identity. It would need to be based not only on a consciousness of the differences between the communities but also the awareness that it is through the embrace of such diversity that a shared sense of what it means to be Lebanese can be constructed. The prospect is optimistic but not unreal. It envisages the establishment in the future, as once in the past, of a more tolerant society. A secular democratic state would then promote citizenship under parliamentary laws without specific reference to communal or religious identity. That may happen. But, to return to where we began this account, the future must also be conditional on developments beyond Lebanon's domestic control.

1   D. McDowell, *Lebanon: A Conflict of Minorities*, 1986.
2   M. Hudon, 'The Problem of Authoritative Power' in N. Shehadi and D. Haffar Mills (eds), *Lebanon: A History of Conflict and Consensus*, Taurus, 1988.
3   In August 1990 the Lebanese Chamber of Deputies passed the constitutional reforms contained within the Accord, but its full implementation had to await the Iraqi invasion of Kuwait, which ended Baghdad's support of General Aoun's 'war of liberation' against what he perceived as Syrian domination and enabled Syria, as a member of the anti-Iraq coalition, to obtain the green light from the United States to go ahead and crush the resistance.
4   See H. Krayem, 'Lebanese Civil War and the Ta'if Agreement' in P. Salem (ed), *Conflict Resolution in the Arab World*, American University, 1997, p. 425; and L. Maila, 'The Ta'if Accord: An Evaluation' in D. Collings (ed.), *Peace for Lebanon*, Lyane Reinner, 1994, p. 35.
5   Ibid., p. 41.
6   For details of the 1992 election, see A.R. Norton and J. Schwedler, 'Swiss Soldiers, Ta'if Clocks, and Early Election: Towards a Happy Ending' in Collings, op. cit. For details of malpractice in the run-up to elections in 1996, see *MEI*, 530, 19 July 1996, p. 12.
7   K. Pakradouoni, 'Arabising Lebanese politics', *MEI*, 550, 16 May 1997, p. 22.
8   S. el-Hoss, 'Prospective Change in Lebanon' in Collings, op. cit.

India: Democracy and Dissent

BY ANIRUDHA GUPTA

INDIA'S democratic political system has long been a matter of bovine pride for many of its citizens, just as it has been an object of suspenseful wonder to outside observers. How can India run a democratic politics when the country is plagued by caste, community and cultural divisions? Its society is not only fractious — it is also poor. More than 40% are illiterate and under-nourished, and the least favoured among its people seem doomed not by lack of talent or enterprise but by circumstance of birth. The fact is, however, that Indians do not accept the familiar saying, commonly heard in Asia, that 'an empty rice bowl gives democracy a hollow sound'. They believe that they can retain a sense of national unity, improve their living standards and protect India's different communities by exercising their franchise in a truly open political system. This alone perhaps explains why democracy in India appears less fragile than in most post-colonial states. As in other aspects of Indian life, belief has triumphed over realities.

How else does one explain the enduring Indian paradox of democracy and dissent? Not, certainly, by attributing its survival to the gods since Indian deities are proverbially wayward. They do not submit to any particular destiny. Should one try and establish a connection between democracy and India's slow rate of growth — a majestic Hindu rate of about 3.5%? Both have been slow moving and erratic. If so, that would refute those who argue that countries with a low level of economy need authoritarian regimes in order to provide a necessary political order for development. They point to the Asian dragons — or tigers — of the Far East under narrowly-based elites which have used strong-armed measures to pull their states out of the slough of poverty, and (it is said) by transforming their economies have made their politics less resistant to political change. India has not experienced any comparable phase of rapid growth although the economy reached a long term annual rate of 5% in the 1980s. By and large, however, democracy and slow growth have gone hand-in-hand in India whereas the economics — and the politics — of East Asia have faltered.

But is India a genuine democracy? Perhaps there is more façade than substance in a state which keeps its civil society under duress and its citizens under tight control? 'In national politics,' said Lloyd and Suzanne Rudolph, 'the police have acquired a reputation as the instrument of a lawless state or of state violence. They are charged with the torture and illegal detention of accused persons, the rape of poor women who are suspects or witnesses, the widespread use of "contract killings" to remove opponents to local political notabilities or inconvenient elements, the incapacity to control lawless gangs in several northern states and to deal with the increasingly frequent train and bus robberies, and finally, failure to deal with terrorism in Punjab.'[1]

Failure has meant the deployment of a large number of police and paramilitary forces in counter-insurgency operations which, instead of abating the violence, have seen it escalate. By 1990, state troops and the police in Punjab had killed over 5,000 'suspected terrorists'. In Kashmir, the tally of dead exceeded 3,000 by the early 1990s, and from a permanent low-level conflict grew in intensity by the end of the decade. The army has also been killing and capturing insurgents in the dozen or so small states of the North-East for over twenty years. The point made in the Introduction has certainly been true for India that as 'governments turn to emergency methods of control, suspending constitutional rules in favour of coercion, meeting force with force . . . the institutions of a free society are eroded'.

The state apparatus of coercion has also acted from time to time in a partisan way during bouts of ethnic violence. Indeed, both the police and army have been accused of fostering communal conflict. A vivid account of police behaviour during the communal riot in Bombay (1992–93) can be found in an inquiry conducted by a group of independent scholars. A couple of years later, a senior police officer of Uttar Pradesh completed a study on the 'Perception of police neutrality during communal riots'. From a survey of ten major riots, he reached the conclusion that 'no riot can last for more than 24-hours unless the state administration wants it to continue'. He also discovered deep anti-Muslim bias — an institutionalised bias — within the police force itself.[2] A similarly disturbing trend can be detected in the junior ranks of the army, particularly among those recruited from the caste-riven villages of northern India. The frequent deployment of armed forces in local conflicts has caused great resentment in this section of the army. In the wake of 'Operation Blue Star' to force Sikh militants from the Golden Temple in Amritsar (June 1984), over 2,000 Sikh army personnel mutinied. Around 600 soldiers of the Sikh Regiment's 9th battalion broke into the regimental armoury and drove through the cantonment town of Ganganagar, firing indiscriminately. Two days later 1500 Sikh soldiers stationed in Ramgarh (Bihar) attacked the armoury, killed their commanding officer and set off for Amritsar. Ultimately, the rebels failed: some were shot dead while others were meted out severe punishment.

That is the dark side to ethnic/communal disorder. But there are also strong counter-forces which give Indian politics a more cheerful and hopeful aspect. Some examples may be given.

1.   Military intervention has been kept at bay. Despite local mutinies and ethnic unrest, the army's loyalties to the central government — of

whatever political colour—have never come into question. Commissioned officers (observes the author of a recent study) 'will never instigate a coup against the civilian government. Their professional training and historical traditions demand they remain in the barracks'.[3] In brief, the army has affirmed its attitude of political neutrality. It insists that politics and the military do not mix: they are 'immutably different and separate, and the military is and should be outside politics'.[4]

2. Secularism has not yielded to militant Hinduism. The fear lurks behind many arguments that there is a concerted campaign against Muslim, Christian and other non-Hindu communities and that the organic link between secularism and democracy, if strained beyond limits, will destabilise constitutional government. A majoritarian Hindu state (it is said) will lead India to disaster under a new (Asian) version of fascism. The fear is undoubtedly real, but how well-founded is it in practice?

Whatever militant Hinduism and the Bharatiya Janata Party, together with its extremist associates may bring about, neither the aims nor the practice can truly be called fascist. Pre-war European movements emphasised the primacy of race and ideology: Hinduism, by contrast, holds that all religions have equal validity and that no race or nation has the right to impose its laws on others. Admittedly, that may not be the case in practice, since Hindu traditions have given rise to many injustices, the worst among them being the institution of caste and untouchability imposed on Hindus. But the important aspect to note is that caste, as a practice and an institution, has come to be contested by Hindus themselves of both upper and lower caste origins. It is in this sense that the present Prime Minister Atal Bihari Vajpayee's assertion that Hinduism cannot but be secular holds a great deal of sense. It reinforces Professor D.E. Smith's interpretation that Hindu tolerance is indeed a living tradition which has contributed vitally to the establishment of a secular democratic state in India. He adds: 'There is the doctrinal assertion of the essential oneness of all religions, to which many educated Indians (and not only Hindus) subscribe as a self-evident truth. More important, however, is the general attitude of "live and let live" toward all manifestations of religious diversity. Therefore, when questioned about the theoretical basis of India's secular state, a large majority of the Indian leaders of all persuasions will immediately relate it to the Hindu tradition of tolerance.'[5]

3. A more serious charge is that the politics of Hindu-based parties threatens Indian democracy in respect of minority interests. The destruction of the Ayodhya mosque in December 1992 can be seen as a significant pointer to the triumphalism of the BJP whose rapid advance to power in the 1990s does have an uncanny, disturbing resemblance to that of the Nazi party in Germany in the 1930s. From 17% of the

vote and 85 seats in the Lok Sabha in 1989 it climbed to 33% and 182 seats in 1998. The call by BJP leaders for a restriction of minority rights, of Muslims and Christians in particular, justifiably worried other parties. One can understand why the BJP campaigned for a Hindu state to replace India's non-descriptive, multi-secular constitution, and it has not been alone. We can note, briefly, other pressures. There is the effect of a theocratic environment in the south Asian region, the fact that — barring India — all other governments in the region have officially proclaimed themselves to be defenders of a majority faith: Islam in Pakistan, Bangladesh and Maldive, Buddhism in Sri Lanka, Hinduism in Nepal. Such proclamations have a malevolent influence on the psyche of India's majority community. The basic moves of the Indian nationalist movement were predominantly Hindu. Gandhi's *Ramdhun* (praise of Rama) and stress on *Sanatan Hinduism* dismayed a number of Hindu and Muslim leaders who turned away from Congress; the Mahatma's mixture of religion and politics widened the gap between Hindus and Muslims in the years following the first Non-Cooperation Movement in 1920–21. At grass roots level, what has mattered is not philosophical discourse but the day to day well being and security of the towns and villages of the northern Indo-Gangetic Valley; but they also retain a very strong historical memory of Muslim rule. The political agitation of colonial times then set the two communities on a collision course, delaying and blocking negotiations for constitutional reform. When Partition came in 1947, Muslims belonging to the Punjab and the North West Provinces (Uttar Pradesh and Bihar) migrated to Pakistan, but an equally large number stayed back in India, giving rise to new strains and tensions in Hindu-Muslim relations.

Yet despite all the stress and the violence, the democratic ethos and institutions of post-independent India have not only survived but taken root. This in itself constitutes a conundrum the like of which has not been seen elsewhere. An impossibly fragmented society, riven by innumerable castes, tribes and communities, pulling and clashing against one another, having to suffer the violence which flares up, sometimes on limited single issues, sometimes in periodic conflict, in a country of almost a billion people — yet united and governed largely, though not efficiently, by democratic means.

How should one account for this persistence of democratic rule, and how does it bear upon so great a diversity? One can throw up one's hands, note the ferment, and repeat the witches' chant of 'Double, double, toil and trouble, fire burn and caldron bubble' which comes close to mirroring the grand Indian muddle of India's democracy. We can in effect leave the question unanswered. But there are some tentative answers that are worth exploring.

Caste, ethnicity and religion are the three major clusters of identity in Indian society. But these clusters are not exclusive and they are antagonist to one another. Thus, religious denomination provides a broad umbrella to those who come under, say, Hindu religion; but caste and its numerous subdivisions make it impossible for the generic Hindus to act as a single unit. A Hindu fanatic who raises a scare about Muslims or Christians may face in turn a caste backlash if he does not belong or turn to the right caste in a social dispute. Caste divisions may also support different sides among warring groups as between Hindus and Muslims. This encourages numerous splits and combinations in the political field. For instance, the BJP's emphasis on religion during the 1988 election campaign attempted to rally support from different Hindu caste groups. Not only did this campaign fail, but it encouraged a process of enlargement of caste solidarity among those who considered the BJP a political front of Baniyas and Brahmins—the two castes considered the most exploitative and unjust oppressors in Hindu society. 'Who constitute the governing classes in India?' asked Babasaheb Ambedkar, undisputed leader of the *dalits* in the 1950s. And he supplied the answer himself—Brahmins and Baniyas. The former, he declared, 'enslaves the mind and the Baniya enslaves the body. Between them they divide the spoils which belong to the governing classes. The Brahmins as a class demand and extract, among other privileges, the right to sleep with the wives of others. The Banians exploit poor, starving and illiterate Indians'.[6] No wonder that Dr Ambedkar for the Scheduled (Harijan) castes and Mohamed Ali Jinnah for the Muslim League found themselves sharing a common platform against Gandhi's upper caste Congress movement.

The writer recalls the Jinnah-Ambedkar amity of the pre-partition days with a purpose. Both feared that the Congress, as a successor of the British, would harm Muslim and Harijan interests. Both maintained that the Congress did not represent the country: that it was actually a 'Hindu body'. Such a successor to the Raj would (they thought) inflict irreparable harm on the interests of both Muslims and Scheduled Castes. When no plea for constitutional safeguards was guaranteed, Jinnah called for the Partition of India and Ambedkar asked his followers to quit Hinduism and embrace Buddhism.

Interestingly, the associations of Muslims and lower caste (dalits) re-emerged in the 1980s. In her anxiety to win back the Hindu vote which she had lost in the 1977 election, Mrs Gandhi began to play the Hindu card in a big way. The move alienated the minority lower caste parties at a time when extremist Hindu factions had begun to call not only for the destruction of the mosque at Ayodhya but for the enactment of a common law code (putting an end to Muslim rights) and the banishment of Urdu as an official language. Fear of Hindu extremism, together with the perception that Congress was incapable of resisting its appeal, persuaded Muslims to seek alliances with regional and caste organisations which had long tried to resist upper-caste Congress hegemony. By the time of the critical 1989 election, Congress had forfeited the support, once readily given, of several aggrieved groups in its northern heartland of Hindi-speaking constituencies. The BJP gained ground; rival parties like the Janata Dal, with a strong regional base, drew a growing support; caste parties — notably the Bahujan Samaj Party of the Scheduled castes — began to organise. There was a sea-change in the politics of UP and Bihar, the two largest states of the Union which sends 120 MPs of the 550 members in the Lok Sabha. In both states, Congress was reduced to the margins of politics. The Janata Dal replaced Congress in Karnataka and Orissa; Kerala and West Bengal stayed predominantly Communist. The effect of this changing kaleidescope of alliances brought unstable government at the centre but it also made impossible any return to single party dominance.

Against this background of elections and shifting party fortunes we can justifiably conclude that democracy gives voice to a multiplicity of ethnic, regional and religious demands, and in doing so places them together within a parliamentary framework of control. One can go further and say that only in this way can a continent-wide democracy survive, and only through democratic usage can the diversity of India be held together.

Constitutional safeguards

1. We wrote earlier of a 'democratic ethos' and one may question whether the framework of government in India would hold fast if it were not for a consensus among all political groups to accept 'the rules of the parliamentary game'. (The rules have, however, to accommodate ill-tempered behaviour among Lok Sahba members.) There is great respect, too, for the courts and the judiciary. Politicians and parties may be corrupt or immoral (and many are both), but they do not violate or exceed the limits of constitutional governance. They may indulge in shady deals, and even keep private armies of criminals, but they must vacate their office and positions of power if the judiciary finds them prima facie guilty of specific charges. This willingness to abide by parliamentary rules, and to accept the authority of the courts, is true of all parties and leaders — Saffron-clad supporters of Hindutva, defender of castes, and red-flag upholders of communism. If democracy needs safeguards, it is well served in India not only by a political culture favourable to parliamentary government but through the protection of its laws under the constitution of the republic.

2. The framework of constitutional rule has held despite repeated crises including separatist movements among Kashmiri Muslims and Punjabi Sikhs. During the late 1980s and early 1990s the character of India's democracy in Punjab often seemed more martial than legal and constitutional. The attack by the Indian army on the Golden Temple in Amritsar, and the subsequent assassination of Mrs Gandhi by members of her Sikh bodyguard, unleashed a wave of violence. Sikhs were hunted down and killed by Hindu mobs in New Delhi and the Congress

government enforced street controls on the Punjab as police and para-military forces butchered Sikh militants.

Despite such violence, however, successive governments in New Delhi tried to move back to constitutional ways and to arrive at solutions which restored a civilian administration in both Punjab and Kashmir. It was the BJP—the party which preached the virtues of *Hindu Rastra* (Hindu Rule)—which called for reconciliation with the Sikh Akali Dal movement. By 1990 an Akali Dal revival was able to win the state elections and form a non-Congress ministry in Amritsar. The BJP led government in New Delhi allowed full freedom to the Akali government to help Sikhs stay within the Indian Union. It instituted an inquiry into police excesses and the killing of innocent Sikhs during the Emergency and included an established leader of the Akalis in the coalition government at the centre. The guidance followed was simple: force when necessary, compromise where possible.

So too in Kashmir when successive Indian governments have faced a perplexing challenge to its authority. Armed conflict across the dividing 'line of control' between India and Pakistan, and attacks by local insurgents, have put Kashmir and Jammu on a very different footing within the Union. Attempts at negotiation seemed doomed, particularly when Kashmiri Brahmins—the caste to which the Nehru family belong —were forced to flee as 'internal refugees' to India. Ultimately, how-ever, even in Kashmir, civilian politics were restarted. Farooq Abdullah and his National Conference party won a majority of the seats in the 1992 elections and were able to form a civilian government in Srinegar after a gap of eight years or more. Once again, the BJP shifted its ground. In opposition, it had argued that Article 351 of the Constitu-tion, which guaranteed special privilege and status to Kashmir and Jammu, should be abolished; once in office in 1998, it maintained its neutralilty in Kashmir politics and attempted to forge a tactical alliance with the National Conference in order to strengthen its own position at the Centre. Unity, not by force but through negotiation, has kept the Union intact.

3. Federal unity: neither centralisation, as attempted by Mrs Indira Gandhi's Congress, nor the weak shifting coalitions of her successors, has destroyed the balance of unity and autonomy implicit in the union. Federalism is the essential ingredient since it enables the centre to govern within the constitutional space guaranteed to the regional states of the union. As democratic politics grew in maturity, so rigidity and extremism gave place to the not wholly attractive bargaining of a competitive politics, defined by region, caste and community, and enlivened but never swamped by ideology. The communists in West Bengal and Kerala, who had denounced Nehru as a tool of Anglo-American imperialism, joined the game to become experienced parlia-mentarians; those who turned to violence over grievances rooted in

religion or caste or language were assuaged by reforms and by changes to the pattern of state boundaries; movements in the North-East which threatened secession drew back from separation. In this evidence of shifting loyalties and positions of advantage, one can reasonably see the BJP tempering its Hindu zeal in order to endorse, if not to embrace, an Indian-style secularism. Compromise and opportunism! But both are necessary if democracy is to replace the politics of *Danda* (the stick) and if it is to withstand outbreaks of communal-religious violence. There is no fixed jigsaw of pieces, only an ever-changing pattern of people defined in a thousand different ways. The democratic result may be confusion and uncertainty, as in the aftermath of the collapse of the coalition government in April 1999, but that is the cost of union in what is, after all, that contradiction in terms — a democratic empire within a subcontinent.

How can we reach any conclusion, except by repeating that a democracy can override successive political crises once the institutional structures of parliamentary rule and judicial authority are accepted — freely accepted — by the political class, however divided its support may be among the people at large. India since 1947 has come close to breakdown through ethnic and religious violence, but has so far maintained intact the democratic barriers which guard its national unity. The remaining danger today is perhaps hubris, the pride of arrogance which can bring nemesis. Nuclear weapons are now the prized token of a government which proclaims its military strength in order to hold aloft its democratic credentials. The question is, whether the saving graces of compromise and caution will once again rescue India from itself.

In October 1999 India went to the polls again in its third election in three years. The results — 'a triumph for federalism' according to Arun Jaitley, spokesman for the BJP — brought a shift from the centre to the regions. The distribution of seats October 1999/March 1998 was: BJP 296/253, Congress 134/167, United Front (state parties) 42/98, Independants 65/25. Atal Behari Vajpayee was reappointed BJP leader and Prime Minister of a 25-party National Alliance government.

---

1   I. Lloyd and S. Rudolph, *In Pursuit of Lakshmi*, Bombay: Orient Longmans, 1987, p. 223.

2   See F. Agnes in J. Magquire et al (eds), *Politics of Violence: From Ayodhya to Behrampada*, Sage: New Delhi, 1996; C. Jeffrelot, 'The Politics of Processions and Hindu-Muslim Riots' in A. Basu and A. Kohli (eds), *Community, Conflicts and the State in India*, OUP: New Delhi, 1998; D. Austin, *Democracy and Violence in India and Sri Lanki*, RIIA Pinter, 1994.

3   A. Kundu, *Militarism in India*, Viva Books: New Delhi, 1998, p. 193.

4   S.P. Cohen, *The Indian Army*, OUP: New Delhi, 1990, p. 176.

5   D.E. Smith, *India as a Secular State*, Princeton University Press, 1963, p. 149. For another recent and very refreshing discussion of the impact of religion on Indian society and politics see G.J. Larson, *India's Agony over Religion*, OUP, 1995.

6   Quoted in A. Shourie, *Worshipping False Gods*, ASA: New Delhi, 1997, p. 14.

Malaysia: Dilemmas of Integration

BY DAVID SEAH

MALAYSIA has managed its plural society relatively well despite the problems of integrating its three major communities.[1] There is an absence of ethnic unrest and the population of mixed origins intermingles without fear of violence within a firmly controlled federation. The achievement has not been without cost (as we shall see), nor without careful recognition of the problems of diversity, remembering the insurgency by (some) Chinese in 1947, 'Confrontation' with Indonesia and the communal riots of the 1960s. The mixture of Malay, Chinese and Indians is of long standing from the years of British rule and colonial exploitation, an ethnic pattern which continues today and has to be managed. There was no way of putting the clock back once Malaysia had come into being, first as the independent Federated Malay States in 1957, then as a larger federation in 1963 through the addition of the East Malaysian states of Sabah and Sarawak. (Malaysia initially included Singapore until its expulsion in 1965.) The policies adopted in respect of ethnic problems have been largely those of the United Malays Nationalist Organisation (UMNO) whose leaders have always taken pride in the country's strong economic growth and orderly political succession through democratic elections. In 1993 Mahathir Mohammed announced that Malaysia would be a 'developed country' by 2020. The present intention is to put the country at the cutting edge of information technology, having a new administrative capital at Jayaputra, a new international airport, and a 'Multi-Super Corridor', a Silicon Valley equivalent. The aim has not been dwarfed by the recent economic downturn.

Behind these bright hopes and aspirations, the basic elements of the federation have not altered significantly. Malaysia remains a multi-racial society. The constitution, however, interprets the term 'Malay' in an ethnic sense, implying the possibility of creating a relatively homogenous community of language, religion and culture through a strategy of integration. The objective is far from being attained, not least because of the tendency to switch the description 'Malay' from an ethnic to a racial category in accordance with popular sentiment, thus excluding Chinese and Indians. If assimilation is not achieved, the question has to be asked whether there will be political and economic room to accommodate the diverse racial groups. Will they be given or allowed to find the required autonomy to meet their aspirations? And how much state control should be exercised as the country moves forward socially and economically?

These are the implications and questions examined here. The extent to which the recent imprisonment of Mahathir's once designated successor, Anwar Ibrahim, affects the country's democratic credentials also remains to be considered. The fact that Anwar had to be charged in court does reflect the restraints on the Prime Minister's power. So, too, was the appointment of a royal commission of inquiry into the treatment of Anwar in police custody.

Problems of definition

Always confounded by controversy, pluralism demands both tolerance and understanding. The Malay constitute the dominant group, yet it is not easy to say who they are. Defined as a racial group, the Malay include all those who live in the vast archipelago and have the physical traits of the Mayo-Polynesians. Defined as an ethnic group, however, they are those who belong to a discernible cultural community: they speak the Bahasa Malay language, practice the Islamic religion and adhere to the customs of their community. These three qualifications have generally been accepted since independence, the consequence being that a non-Malay-by-race can be regarded as an ethnic Malay if he or she fulfils the criteria. But not all the Malay-by-race are fully accepted as, for example, the Balinese who are influenced by Hindu beliefs and the Bataks in northern Sumatra who are Christians or animist and whose culinary traditions include dogs, an animal with which Muslims do not like to be associated.

These broad distinctions need to be refined. Part of the Malay peninsula population is of recent immigrant origin: nearly 10% of the workforce, including a number of illegal settlers, comes from outside (mainly Indonesia). There is an argument for culture (*Kulturkreis*) which sees Malaysia as part of the island archipelago within which migration becomes an internal movement among the same people. The non-Malay, therefore, are 'outsiders', even if some (e.g. the Babas or 'Straits Chinese' in Malacca) have been partly assimilated or (like the Indian Muslims) can trace their lineage in Malaysia back over some five hundred years.

There are no simple boundaries between such categories. Even the all important *Malay Annuals* (*Sejarah Melaya*) gives Iskander Shah (Alexander the Great) as the founder of the Malacca Sultanate, centuries before the arrival of Islam. There is indeed an element of universalism within Muslim-Malay culture, a cosmopolitanism implicit in Mahathir Mohammed's book *The Malaya Dilemma* (1970) which stresses the beneficial effect of inter-racial and inter-religious marriage. The first Prime Minister, Tengku Abdul Rahman, was partly Thai; Mahathir's grandfather came from Kerala in southern India. Balancing this outward looking element, however, is an innate and strong rural conservatism particularly among the northern states which differ in outlook and customs from Johore and the south.

A useful pragmatism helps to soft pedal ethnic and racial differences but they cannot be ignored. Some politicians have urged that the constitution be restated to emphasise Malaysia as a 'Malay country', and there are certain fundamentals associated with the Malay community. Islam is the official religion, although Malaysia is not an Islamic state: the idea of a non-Muslim Malay is taboo, and there is no provision for the shedding of one's Islamic beliefs. There is a Sharia court which handles matters of faith and enjoins the laws, norms and customs of Islam, including the required fasting, prohibition of alcohol and the forbidding of what is known as 'close proximity' between unmarried partners. Such rules of identity have implications for other groups in Malaysia's plural society in which there is a variety of faiths — Islam, Confucianism, Taoism, Christianity, Hinduism, Sikhism.

Colonial rule of pluralism

The effect of British rule was profound — so too were the consequences of its withdrawal. The British were vigorous in promoting the growth of different groups under local customs, the only areas of direct control being Penang and Malacca (and Singapore prior to 1946). Elsewhere, the policy was that of indirect rule using the traditional authority of the Sultans. Other policies aimed at maximising development through economic specialisation and a division of labour. The Malay remained as farmers while their brighter sons were recruited into junior administrative positions. The Indians were deployed as rubber tappers and are still to be found on the estates. The Chinese came as traders and subsequently expanded into tin mining and local industries, a role which led to their concentration in urban centres. Thus there came about in Malaya the features that T.S. Furnivall described in 1956 in his *Colonial Policy and Practice* when he wrote of Burma as a 'plural society'. Its essential characteristics were the presence of different ethnic groups with no common purpose or will. Each lived separately and had their own semi-formal sources of jurisprudence, communication and information, while subscribing to the overall policies of British rule. Integration was absent except in the market place and the colonial economy.

Such a social and economic setting made the presence of an external power essential, and as long as colonisation remained, the management of pluralism was extremely simple. The views of the Malay Sultans, and of Indian and Chinese leaders through their clans and secret societies, were invariably enforceable through their respective communities, and these subterranean channels of authority strengthened the plural nature of society since each community was self-regulating. But Malaya remained the land of the Malay — and of the Sultans under British rule.

Pluralism as a *political* issue developed at the tail end of colonialism. The thought of having to interact with each other dawned on these semi-segregated communities once the idea of independence took shape.

There needed to be fresh thinking not only among the Malay population but among both Chinese and Indians how best to shape a new political future.

Insurrection and independence

Although many segments of the Chinese and Indian communities retained a strong affection for their homelands, others looked for new loyalties, and some turned to revolution — there was a communist-driven, pro-China uprising after the end of the second world war. The decision was traumatic and made the management of inter-community relations immensely more difficult, not least by persuading political leaders that communism and Chinese chauvinism were inseparable. The insurrection also forced the government — first the British, then the UMNO leaders — into adopting harsh measures of control. The uprising numbered some 10,000 insurgents, and weeding them out required large resources of men and material in jungle skirmishes over months of fighting against the Chinese-led Malayan Communist Party (MCP). The insurrection also raised concerns about the loyalty of the Chinese for, apart from the communists, there was a smaller wealthier group of Chinese who favoured a continuation of colonial rule.

On the other hand, there were several Chinese leaders who saw the need to join the Malayan nationalists in order to sustain an independent state. They were well aware that the Malay would play the key role in any democratic settlement — numbers alone would ensure that, and the new Federation of Malaya Agreement in 1947 did in fact ensure Malay dominance. The United Malays Nationalist Organisation won the first election and was in office at independence a decade later. Nor were the minority communities initially granted a broad citizenship. By 1947, for example, three-fifths of the Chinese population had been born in the country but only one-fifth (c. 500,000) were granted full citizen rights. It remains the case, however, that compromise won the day. The UMNO secured the support of the Malayan Chinese Association and the Malayan Indian Congress to form an inter-communal Alliance Party, and a government was formed which was representative of each community. The key positions of Prime Minister and Deputy Prime Minister were in Malay hands, the Finance Ministry went initially to a Chinese. Integration was still far distant but there was now a working accommodation between all three communities.

The establishment of the wider Federation of Malaysia raised other problems. Many groups in the two overseas states of Sabah and Sarawak claimed indigenous status. So a new definition was announced, that of Bumiputra or 'Prince of the Soil' to enfold Malay, Orang Asli, Durums, Kadazans and Dyaks among whom the Malay remained dominant within the federation, a dominance in all sectors — political, constitutional, electoral. Dr Mahathir has been Prime Minister since 1981 and his three predecessors were all Malay. The constitution avows to protect the overall interests of every community on an integrationist programme, but there are flaws in the thinking behind such ideals. Muslims of Indian and Pakistani origin, for example, are accepted as 'Malay' along with those who can claim Bumiputra identity, but there is a reluctance to accept on an equal footing converted Chinese Muslims who exist in a sort of limbo, neither full members of their own community nor regarded as Bumiputra. It is not that there are no Chinese Muslims—there are many in China—but the change to Islam in Malaysia requires a change of mind set on both sides.

The constitution favours the Malay. Article 153 obliges the government to give special privileges to them in respect of licenses (from petty hawking to operators of heavy haulage machinery), educational opportunities and positions in public service. Similarly, Article 89 makes it clear that Malay access to reservation land will be protected. The practical effect is a form of affirmative action in the interest of the Malay. It is not one of assimilation but centrality. Suhaini Aznam put the matter succinctly in the *Far East Economic Review* in June 1991: 'The Chinese and Indians see Malaysian culture as comprising equal facets of all three races, with minor contributions by the other minorities of Sabah and Sarawak states. The Malays see it as being based on their culture, a force holding firmly in the centre with additions from Chinese and Indian culture . . .'

The government is also caught in this dilemma of perception. It wants to encourage assimilation while ensuring that the benefits go to the Bumiputra. The result underlies the racial subtext to the policies of pro-Malay affirmation action so that what emerges is a very watered-down form of integration. The ambivalence and bias can be seen in the New Economic Policy of 1966–90 and in its present modified form of the 'New Development Policy'.

Riots and the NEP

Serious communal riots took place in 1969 following the first all-Malaysian general election. The UMNO Alliance Party suffered a significant reduction in support when compared with the 1964 election. The Alliance won 66, down from 89, of the 104 mainland seats, and 49% of the poll against the earlier 58%. The beneficiaries were communal-based parties including a pan-Malay Islamic Party. (UMNO also lost the state elections in Penang: there was stalemate in Selangor and Perak.) Rioting then broke out between Malay and Chinese in Kuala Lumpur and Selangor, and a State of Emergency was imposed.

The New Economic Policy was introduced after the riots in order to try and redress the relative poverty of the Malay population and to encourage the growth of an entrepreneurial class among the Bumiputra. The aim was to increase their share of the local stock capacity from 4 to 30%. The premise was that the Chinese, and to a lesser extent the Indian minority, had chalked up a disproportionate share of the wealth of the country. In 1990, therefore, the name was changed to New Development Policy, the intention being not simply to redistribute wealth but to promote economic growth among the Bumiputra. The problem for the non-Malay was again one of perception. Such policies were seen as unfair, particularly when applied to the key sector of education. A study (published in 1998 by Boo Cheng Hau) of the 1985 Fifth Malaysian Plan looked at the declared aim of giving the non-Bumiputra and Bumiputra targets of 44 and 55% access to tertiary education and found that the actual outcome was a 31:61 ratio; a staggering 94% of diploma courses, and 66% at certificate level, were from the Bumiputra. Yet the indigenous Orang Asli, though ethnically within the Bumiputra category, were not similarly rewarded.

Other consequences have followed. Some of the licenses were bought by non-Malay from the Malay. In order to secure contracts, the non-Malay also appointed Malays as directors of enterprises which were then said to be 'Malay owned'. These arrangements came to be called 'Ali-Baba schemes', not to idolise the thief in the *Arabian Nights* but to describe the supposedly harmonious relationship between Bumiputra and non-Malay. A new Malay elite has in fact been created, though small in number: whether its equity ownership will be raised to 30% remains to be seen. A related problem is the extent to which the non-Malay will be forced out of the market and whether there will be sufficient jobs for the new class of educated and semi educated Malays.

Looking back over the years since independence, neither assimilation, nor the lesser aim of accommodation, has greatly succeeded. The majority Malay community has been unenthusiastic and, if only for that reason, the government has not sought to force the pace of integration. One index of success might be a shift in the pattern of religious belief or an increase in the use of the Malay language but the data presently available offer no evidence either way.

Control measures

In response to the postwar communist insurrection, the colonial government introduced the Essential Regulations Proclamation in 1948, giving the administration enormous powers over the movement of people. The Emergency brought not only the banning of the Malayan Communist Party but the strengthening of the powers of the state over arrest and detention. Curfews and police checks became frequent; detention could be extended up to 12 years. The most ambitious part of the Emergency was the relocation of the rural population living in pro-Communist settlements to fortified and rezoned areas, known as New Villages, which could then be placed under curfew. Newspapers were vetted and a license had to be obtained for printing.

The main community to suffer from these restrictions were the Chinese, including those who had committed their future to the new state. Three-quarters of the New Villagers were Chinese, as was the bulk of those detained. The insurrection had forced many to make a decision on political loyalty between the Malayan Communist Party and the UMNO led alliance. No other group was faced with so dramatic a choice. Not until 1960 was the State of Emergency lifted, and it took the MCP nearly two decades before it declared an end to the struggle. The institutional mechanisms of the Emergency were never wholly removed. At best they were modified. The Internal Security Act of 1960 replaced the Emergency legislation, but the government continued to rely on force, including preventive detention, and freedom of movement and action was restrained by amendment of Articles 150 and 151 of the constitution pertaining to civil rights.

While the intention behind such measures was to ensure stability, they can also be seen as an attempt by the government to manage a plural society through stringent laws approved by parliament. They were, in a sense, a paraphrase of Furnivall's concept that control was needed over and above the rights of separate communities. What had been thought necessary under colonial rule was now reinterpreted by nationalist leaders. There was a requirement, for example, whereby all non-governmental groups and individuals had to show that their actions were not endangering political stability, a requirement imposed by the government which decided whether agitation, in one form or other, was a threat to national security within the terms of the legislation. There was also a prohibition of 'communal words' which might cause ill-feeling between ethnic groups. When the riots in Kuala Lumpur took place in 1969 they were met promptly by enforcement of an Emergency as provided by the 1960 Act.

It has proved to be a durable political instrument. It was invoked to detain the ex-Deputy Prime Minister Anwar Ibrahim. The main victims have been those whose views are known to differ significantly from those of the government, not only on communal grounds (although party leaders are quick to discover an ethnic cause) but among students, civil rights groups and disgruntled workers. The Tasek Utara dispute was a case in point. In 1974 a group of Malay squatters were evicted from an illegal site and a number of university students took up their cause; the agitation snowballed when impoverished farmers also challenged the government in Baling. After the police had arrested several students and teachers, Dr Mahathir declared that communists had subverted a Chinese university-based organisation although the popular perception was that it had been Malay activists who had begun the agitation. The government then introduced the Universities and University College Act (1975) which clamped down on Malay and Chinese students alike. Malaysia continues to be a constitutional state under parliamentary rule but it is well armed with non-democratic powers.

Ironically, such measures may indeed bring communities together if those who are aggrieved jointly challenge the authorities by collaboration across the ethnic-racial boundary. There are also associations like the Law Society and the long established human rights organisation, 'Aliran', which have stood out against the government. One of the founders of Aliran, Chandra Muzaffar, is a converted Indian Muslim who reflects many of the characteristics of an assimilated Malay — analytical, sober-minded, issue-orientated. He has sided with Anwar and has found his tenure as a university professor discontinued, the penalty (one must suppose) not for defending human rights but for entering politics on the 'wrong side'.

Bridging the divide

To eradicate communal conflict and to bridge ethnic-racial differences will be far from easy. The task involves many facets — a redistribution of wealth, a shift in location between rural Malay and urban Chinese, a change of values and assumptions and a meeting of religions. There is, for example, a commonly held view that non-Malays, because of their immigrant origin, are more concerned about material comforts, whereas the Malay are content with a more placid life-style. How is that likely to change? There is no simple way forward. Nevertheless, there are certain features of the attempt to ameliorate racial and ethnic differences over the past half century which are worthy of note by way of conclusion to this brief account.

1. The elements of ethnic/racial discord were always openly acknowledged, as was the awareness of the danger if it were badly handled. The benefits of collective inter-ethnic action were similarly recognised, and in this respect the UMNO Alliance was a notable achievement since it allowed all the major groups to act as a team. That most of the positions of power went to Malays need not be interpreted as unfair.

2. Two simultaneous approaches have been adopted: creating an ethnic Malay group comprising all racial groups, allowing for some accommodation of differences in the short run; and uplifting the economic conditions of ethnic Malays, most of whom are of Malay race. There have been obstacles on both sides. The Chinese and Indians find assimilation difficult; the Malay are not very willing to accept those who do not seek assimilation. Such problems lead to absurdities as when a Malay minister criticised Anwar's wife for being a Chinese brought up in a Malay family. Politics may do much but they cannot change attitudes.

3. When we look back to 1942 (the beginning of the Japanese occupation) and the intensity of ethnic and racial animosities then and during the riots of the 1960s, we can say that the present prognosis is a good deal more favourable. Malaysia's neighbour may point the way. Thailand had a policy hostile to Chinese, then changed course towards integration to the point where a Chinese could be regarded as a Thai if he took a Thai name, accepted Buddhism and adopted Thai customs

and language. The process of assimilation was remarkably successful, helped by the fact that many Chinese were nominally Buddhist and were happy enough to use both a Thai and a Chinese name. Some have held the office of Prime Minister, others are prominent in business: they are Chinese who are officially accepted as Thai. The problem in Malaysia is likely to be of longer duration because of the threshold of Islam — at a time and stage when Islam is marked by significant intellectual interpretation. The present religious fervour may very well slow the pace of conversion and, therefore, of integration.

4.   Class and economic values are rising in importance. The Mahathir-Anwar dispute is a conflict of belief as well as a struggle for power. The battleground may become one not of ethnic dominance or racial animosity but of politics and class. Recent street demonstrations against the government may not be within the strict rules of parliamentary government but they have been a lively testimony to Malaysia's quest for democracy. Mahathir has talked of the country facing a conspiracy of external powers but, if true, it gives added weight to the surmise that the economics of class will begin to override race and ethnicity, not least in relation to development. Already Malaysia has many of the attributes of a developed society, and in the modern world (which Mahathir is keen to join) of Information Technology, transnational finance and parliamentary democracy, who can say what will unite or divide the people of Malaysia in future years?

---

1   Population: 14 million, Malay 54%, Chinese 35%, Indian 10%, others 1%. Federation of 13 states: Peninsula Malaysia 85% of the pop. 40% of the total area: East Malaysia (Sabah and Sarawak) 15% of the pop. 60% of the area.

Dealing with Difference:
Four Models of Pluralist Politics[1]

BY RICHARD BELLAMY

PLURALISM of ideals, interests and identities are inescapable features of contemporary polities. This plurality arises in large part from the very dynamics of modernity. New technologies have extended functional differentiation and specialisation, augmenting the complexity of modern economies and societies. The tasks of governments have multiplied and become increasingly complicated as they seek to regulate ever more diverse areas of social life, each with its own peculiarities (and norms). Individuals, too, have to juggle the conflicting demands and values of work, family, friends, locality, gender, ethnicity, religion and so on. Though cultural diversity is sometimes portrayed as the product of atavistic attachments that have curiously, if occasionally disturbingly, survived into today's globalising world, modernising processes have also enhanced polyethnicity and multiculturalism. Greater labour mobility, for example, has resulted in states containing significant immigrant populations. The weakening of the state's capacity to control either the economy or security within a global environment has also encouraged well-established national minorities to seek greater autonomy, as can be seen in the growing assertiveness of the regions within the European Union.

Such pluralism makes politics necessary whilst sometimes rendering it virtually impossible.[2] Differences of opinion and interest provide the content and rationale of democracy, yet can become so great that participants cease to feel members of a common polity bound by shared purposes. In such circumstances, citizens talk past rather than to each other. That proves especially likely in the case of cultural differences, when people may literally speak different languages and have opposed perspectives that affect their views and behaviour across the whole range of human activities. Because the diversity of cultures is but one aspect of the heightened pluralism of modern societies, however, it is also subject to and further complicated by other sources of plurality. Granting political autonomy to different cultural groups displaces but does not resolve the problem of pluralism. The new units will almost certainly contain cultural minorities themselves, whilst their members will disagree fundamentally on many issues, including how they relate to different cultures. People may share a 'world view' or culture, yet divide over what its fundamental values are, how they should be ranked, their justification and their bearing in particular cases. Neither Christians or Muslims, workers or capitalists, socialists or conservatives, the French or the British speak with one voice on all matters. Clashes between inherently or contingently incompatible values, modes of reasoning, interpretations and types of claim arise amongst all cultures, ideologies and classes.

Thus, plural societies produce divided loyalties that unsettle the theory and practice of politics. From the allocation of health care to the implementation of environmental regulations, almost all policy decisions confront people with seemingly impossible choices between the incompatible yet equally reasonable commitments of different spheres of their lives and the rival claims of different values. Many public policies involve such a variety of normative considerations and factual information that people may disagree about not just how conflicts might be resolved but also their very nature and the relevance of the various elements involved. The tensions created by such disputes are undoubtedly less when those involved feel part of the same political community. However, many of these discussions involve disagreement about the internal and external boundaries of the polity. The contested legitimacy of state intervention in the market and the home, for example, and the undermining of state sovereignty by the increasingly international and trans-state character of most social and economic processes, mean that the issues of who can decide and where are as deeply problematic as, and intimately related to, the questions of what may be decided and how. Once again, these considerations cut across cultural divisions and to some degree subvert them by creating transnational allegiances between particular cultural and subcultural groups. Debates about the future shape of the European Union display all these features, with views on the powers and organisation of the Union reflecting the diverse ideals and interests of different sections of the European population rather than being an accepted structure within which these differences get debated. The current antipathy to the EU of the British Conservative Party, for example, is more a function of its antagonism to certain forms of state interference than a dislike of Europe as such.

These preliminary points help place the management of cultural diversity in context. Some political science treats this situation as an aberration from the norm of homogeneous nation states. This simply is not true. Will Kymlicka cites recent estimates that 'the world's 184 independent states contain over 600 living language groups and 5000 ethnic groups'.[3] But as we have seen, multiculturalism is only one aspect of the challenge pluralism poses to liberal democracies. An adequate discussion of cultural diversity must take these other forms of plurality into account too. In what follows, four models of pluralist politics are examined. The first tries to abstract from people's differences in order to find neutral ground in a liberal constitution. The second seeks a modus vivendi between competing interests groups. The third employs group rights to segregate the various sources of pluralism into more or less homogenous units. The fourth gives voice to and recognises the different ideals, interests and identities of individuals and groups, whilst encouraging the negotiation of fair accommodations between them in ways that sustain and even reshape, but do not destroy, political community.

Each of these models embodies a particular view of compromise. For if disagreements turn on values and concerns that are incompatible and incommensurable (that is, of such a different nature that comparing them simply makes no sense — like trying to rank Einstein, Shakespeare and Beethoven), then concessions will be needed on all sides as they construct common ground. The constitutional neutralists seek compromise by trimming the issues that divide us from the political agenda and settling on a supposed set of core political values on which we ought to agree. Interest group pluralists try to split the difference through mutually advantageous trade-offs. Consociationalism and group rights attempt segregation, giving each group autonomy within its domain and a mutual veto to prevent incursions. However, the argument here is that only negotiated agreements offer genuinely reciprocal compromises that are mutually acceptable and hence legitimate, fair and stable.

Constitutional neutrality: compromise by trimming

The archetype for this model is the separation of Church and State, with its proponents regarding the liberal solution to the European religious wars of the sixteenth and seventeenth centuries as the paradigm for resolving all pluralist conflicts.[4] The idea is to demarcate the scope and nature of politics through agreement on a set of basic political liberties and rights. These principles form the core values of the polity and the medium for discussion. They provide the preconditions for politics and are supposedly independent of the broader interests and ideals people may hold and wish to pursue. The constitution thereby avoids reference to any particular vision of the good. Its purpose is to provide a neutral framework within which all may thrive on an equitable basis with others. Each individual has an equal chance to press his or her views so long as the arguments employed and resulting policies do not interfere with the liberty of others to do likewise. This procedural fairness allegedly removes all legitimate grounds for complaint that one's concerns or opinions have been ignored or harmed. Thus, religion gets placed in the private sphere and religious arguments removed as irrelevant to political debate. Churches may freely form and organise their own affairs as they wish, but they cannot insist the state punishes dissenters and heretics or officially promotes their beliefs. Much as neighbours of opposed ideological convictions might preserve neighbourly relations by restricting their conversation to gardening and sport and so manage to cooperate in baby sitting circles and other matters of common interest, so such a neutral constitution preserves social peace and enables differing groups to coexist and collaborate in support of public goods. Contentious opinions can still be expressed, but only in private arenas such as pubs and clubs or with friends and family.

Amongst the most influential defences of this approach is John Rawls' *Political Liberalism*. He sees the United States' constitution as the embodiment of this model. He argues that its multi-ethnic and immigrant population is united by an 'overlapping consensus' focused on the institutions and rights of the American legal and political system. The consensus results from the 'method of avoidance', whereby citizens abstract from their substantive conceptions of the good and fix on the principles of justice necessary for their political coexistence and cooperation. The result, he claims, is to place the constitution beyond what he calls 'the fact of pluralism'. Indeed, he contends acceptance of such a settlement arises precisely because people recognise the difficulty of reaching substantive agreement in such circumstances, a dilemma he associates with the 'burdens of judgment'.

Leaving conveniently to one side the indigenous population which enjoys special rights and a certain political autonomy, the viability of this scheme remains questionable. Far from holding the ring for political debate, the basic liberties are themselves matters of deep disagreement. Thus, feminists contest the protection of pornography by the right to free speech; conservatives dispute the constitutional protection afforded to abortion; the bearing of the equal protection clause in matters such as schooling and affirmative action policy has provoked heated discussion; whilst the equal right of citizens to vote has prompted debate on almost every aspect of the political system — from the fairness of the current electoral system to the appropriateness of the existing powers and responsibilities of the different state and federal institutions. In all these cases, people's views of the political framework prove inseparable from both their deeper convictions and their specific opinions on particular policies. The interpretation of any right, its relation to other rights, its importance in relation to values, and its implications and relevance for any given case — these are all matters on which people can and do reasonably disagree.

Rawls, like other proponents of this position, sees the Supreme Court as a neutral arbiter of such disputes. However, pluralism means there is no neutral ground to retreat to. Such conflicts cannot be decided either a priori or through trimming away the supposedly non-political elements. Empirical analysis reveals Court decisions display much the same mix of contestable normative and empirical considerations as one finds amongst the general public.[5] At their best, courts try to act as a respected third party and to offer a compromise that fairly represents the respective claims of those involved but which long hostility, myopia or other factors hinder the disputants from reaching themselves. Such solutions are not uncommon in international disputes. But they are no substitute for the institutionalisation of compromise amongst the parties themselves. Not only does the process of negotiation ensure that people's positions do not get misrepresented, it also builds trust and reciprocity whilst giving the decision a legitimacy that few third parties have the authority to provide. It is to various strategies for political compromise that we now turn.

Interest group pluralism: compromise by trading

Advocates of interest-group pluralism regard constitutional norms as 'trivial' to the working of a pluralist democracy compared to the social rules and practices that arise from the very character of modern, dynamic societies.[6] The crucial determinant in their view is the distribution of power, interpreted as the capacity to control another's responses. Power so conceived rests on a variety of different kinds of resource and the relative share of them held by those involved. Their central claim is that liberal democracy depends upon and helps reinforce a distribution of different forms of power amongst a plurality of agents and agencies such that everyone enjoys a piece of the action. Democratic societies are in essence 'polyarchies', to employ Robert Dahl's term. To further and protect their interests, minorities need only enjoy the standard range of civil and political rights allowing them to freely associate and participate within regular, competitive elections. The nature of polyarchical societies is such that when conflicts occur, groups will always be able to force and reach mutually beneficial trade-offs with others.

Interest-group pluralists believe two features of contemporary societies favour this process.[7] First, there are different and competing sorts of 'political resource', from money and knowledge to status and access to political organisations. These resources are focused upon numerous 'strategic locations' of diverse kinds within different spheres of social and political life, from factories to the media, churches, education and so on, and give rise to a wide range of 'bargaining positions' within the economy, society and polity. As a result, influence, authority and control are dispersed amongst a number of different social groups and cannot be monopolised by any one of them or amassed at any single centre or organisation. Power does not breed power because influence or control in one area of life does not necessarily translate to another area. Second, people have multiple and occasionally conflicting allegiances to very diverse groups. They have attachments to work, neighbourhood, church, class, family, ideology. This multiplicity produces 'cross-cutting cleavages' whereby people may be opposed on certain issues but allies on others. There will be no consistent majority, merely a number of coalitions of minorities which vary according to the policy. Everyone will have the experience of being in a minority at least some of the time. Indeed, some supporters of a majority decision that favours them in one area will have other interests in different aspects of their lives that are adversely affected by it. Consequently, people will be disposed to compromise and to ensuring the fairness of the outcomes as well as of the procedures of decision making. To sweeten the pill still further, economic growth makes politics less zero-sum and enhances the likelihood of striking mutually advantageous bargains.

This model of pluralist politics is offered as a characteristic of all mature liberal democracies, although its proponents have most closely analysed the United States and Britain for confirmation of their thesis. Like constitutional trimmers, albeit for different reasons, they see the state as a neutral terrain where deals are struck between an ever changing set of coalitions amongst whom there is sufficient overlap for a consensus on the rules of the political game to prevail. Unfortunately, its supposed empirical grounding notwithstanding, it is as flawed an account of the adequacy of liberal democracy to accommodate plural-ism as the constitutionalist's. Interest group pluralism assumes a trader's compromise. When traders bargain, however, each looks out for them-selves, taking account of the interests of others only in so far as it affects what needs to be conceded. In other words, it offers a modus vivendi solution to resolving pluralist disputes. However, the strong need concede less to the weak than to the strong and the rich can out wait the poor. So the fairness of bargains and the maintenance of public goods assumes the distribution of power is itself sufficiently equitable to make equity the best policy. Otherwise, the different equilibria will vary in whom they favour according to the balance of power rather than the prevalence of needs and good reasons. Collective action problems will also arise whenever the recommended outcome is not an equilibrium, with privileged groups and individuals opting out or free-riding where possible. Clean air may be in the interests of all, for example; but, in this scenario, costly environmental regulations only get imposed on polluting factories if either neighbourhood groups and environmentalists can muster an equivalent political clout to the manu-facturers, or the costs to the polluters of continuing to pollute can be made similar to those falling on the polluted.

Interest group pluralists claim the distribution of power to be such as to obviate these potential difficulties. Critics dispute their analysis, noting how their focus on actual decision making ignores the ways social, cultural and economic factors may systematically bias the politi-cal system so that certain policy conflicts never get aired.[8] Far from being neutral, the procedures of the state can discriminate against certain groups and favour others. Some of these pluralists did concede that they had overlooked how the requirements of capital accumulation narrowed the policy options available to governments, and that some mechanism for democratising the exercise of economic power might be necessary to place workers on an equal political footing to their employers.[9] However, similar problems exist for a whole range of groups. Feminists have long argued that political meetings are often badly timed and located for women given their generally greater family and care responsibilities, and that many female concerns are dismissed as 'private' and hence non-political even when they are able to voice their views. Likewise, ethnic and cultural minorities have often found their worries are ignored or rejected on the grounds that they fail to fit the established political morality, including cases when this was not so. Thus, Tariq Madood has shown how the views of most British Muslims on matters such as the publication of *The Satanic Verses* and the separate schooling of women often parallel standard liberal ideas concerning the prevention of defamation or incitement and equal opportunities respectively. However, they have been consistently mis-described as fundamentalist rejections of liberalism rather than poten-tially constructive engagements with it.[10]

A trader's compromise also assumes one can always 'split the differ-ence'. That possibility implies that all values lie along a single dimension or have a single denominator, with competing groups all desiring more of a certain good. Interest group compromises can have this aspect, notably in the classic case of wage bargaining. But even here there may be quite distinct and potentially incommensurable values at stake, such as health or status, which prove less tradable. Many goods, such as integrity and identity, cannot be treated as mere preferences that one can have more or less of. Such conflicts tend to be more absolute, forcing a choice between either one or the other option. At the very least, traders may find themselves dealing in quite different currencies and have to negotiate conversion rates rather than taking them as read. This possibility becomes particularly tricky when cleavages are seg-mented and vertical rather than horizontal and cross-cutting. Differ-ences based on ethnicity, culture, language, gender and religion always possess this characteristic to some degree. They constitute a world view that orientates their holder's opinion over a wide range of issues. As Dahl admits, such matters prove far less tradable so that 'the prospects of polyarchy are greatly reduced'.[11] We shall see in the last section how this pessimism may be unwarranted, the result of his narrow view of the nature of pluralist politics. We must first, however, look at his favoured solution to such kinds of pluralism: namely, the segregationist gambit of group rights and consociationalism.

Consociationalism and group rights: compromise by segregation

Group rights and consociationalism aim at producing a mixture of autonomy and power-sharing amongst distinct national, ethnic, relig-ious or other cultural groups which share a state but have either partially incompatible demands or identify more closely with other group members than with the rest of the community. They seek to preserve a group's control of as many areas vital to its form of life as possible, to protect other aspects against damaging incursions, and to ensure the necessary collective decisions are consensual. It is not easy to draw the appropriate boundaries, however, since the criteria are frequently contested. Creating divisions and policing them may cause more harm than they remove.

Will Kymlicka has identified three kinds of group-differentiated rights: self-government rights, polyethnic rights and special representation rights.[12] These rights are not mutually exclusive, and many political systems contain a selection from each of them. Self-government rights are commonest amongst regionally-based national minorities, such as the Welsh and Scots, and can led to demands for secession. The basis of this demand is that a national culture instantiates the various goods and values intrinsic to the identity and well-being of those who share it. Allowing a degree of self-determination offers the best way to ensure this culture is not only preserved but develops in ways that reflect the evolving views of its adherents. Though such protection is especially warranted for minorities who fear being swamped by the majority culture, a regionally concentrated majority might also desire such a right so as to reduce the need to compromise with minorities. Though Kymlicka overlooks this possibility, self-government rights can also be established on a non-territorial basis, such as functions.[13] Territorially dispersed and non-nationalist cultural minorities can in this way belong to their own trade union organisations and even run their own education and health care systems.

Usually such groups seek polyethnic rights. These give exemptions from certain laws that disadvantage them, permitting Sikhs not to wear motor cycle helmets, for example, or Jews and Muslims to trade on Sundays. More controversially, such rights can also extend to such positive measures as an entitlement to deal with public authorities in a minority language or to have minority languages and religions taught in schools. These rights aim less at self-government than coexistence with and partial assimilation into the majority culture. Finally, special representation rights seek to equalise the say of minority groups within the legislative process. They may include a range of measures — from creating constituencies favourable to the election of representatives drawn from such groups, reserving a number of seats in the legislature for them, encouraging quotas within the established political parties or employing electoral systems (such as proportional representation) that favour the setting up of a group based parties, to directly or indirectly ensuring power sharing in the executive.

Polyethnic and representation rights offer protection for groups which by virtue of some set of shared constitutive characteristics are structurally disadvantaged by the prevailing social and political system in ways that devalue or undermine their exercise of individual rights. Non-cultural minorities can also benefit from them, as can groups that are a majority in the population yet structurally disadvantaged by past discrimination, notably women. Hence, these mechanisms have been taken up by women, gay, lesbian and disabled groups as well as racial, ethnic and religious minorities. Obviously, the legitimacy of such measures turns on the protected properties or beliefs being of significance to their possessors and not just the objects of irrational prejudice by others (though this may also be the case). They must also pass a minimal threshold of acceptability. Paedophiles, for example, are a structural minority who are justifiably discriminated against. These thresholds may be matters of dispute, as illustrated by debates over issues such as the acceptability of certain crude methods of slaughtering animals or of male and female circumcision.[14]

Such rights assume the relevant group to be relatively coherent and that the members all identify with the way they have been defined. For a potential tension exists between the protection of segmental pluralism and other forms of plurality within and across the segments. Members of most groups have other allegiances and may be almost endlessly divided into subgroups. Thus, Scots can be divided into men and women, Protestants and Catholics, Highland and Lowland, socialists and conservatives, to name but some of the obvious distinctions one might make. Privileging some differences over others will only work if those involved feel that particular division to be more encompassing or more important than the others or in some sense distinguishable from them. To continue the earlier example, giving Scotland political autonomy or even independence need not prevent individuals continuing to differ over matters of religion, ideology and the rest. Likewise, permitting Sikhs to wear turbans rather than helmets or official caps does not inhibit their freedom of action in other spheres. On the contrary, it can facilitate their involvement in activities from which they might otherwise have been excluded, such as the police or armed forces. But the granting of special rights does not always operate in such beneficent ways. Though the declared purpose of these rights may be to prevent erosion of group identity by external social and political processes, preserving a given group culture has internal implications for what its members may do. If a religious group is allowed to withdraw children from school before the age of sixteen, as the United States Supreme Court has allowed the Amish to do, then along with the children being able to help with harvests earlier, and having less exposure to the corrosive influence of the external world, will go a reduction in their capacity to leave the group or even criticise and develop its doctrine. Similarly, if Quebec is allowed to prohibit or limit the public use or teaching of English, then that has profound implications for the Anglophone community (and indeed for many Francophones) who desire an active engagement with Anglo-American culture.

These sorts of cases connect to a more general concern about the inherent conservatism of group rights. Critics fear they may entrench and possibly even impose a particular identity on groups to the extent that it reinforces majority prejudices and discourages their recognition by and engagement with the wider society. For example, some Asian groups argue that designating them 'black' involves just such an imposed and prejudicial identity. Even when polyethnic and special representation rights are voluntarily accepted and oriented towards inclusion, they do so on the group's own terms. Because such measures are not costless for those outside the group, they can create resentment, especially if they appear to withdraw the beneficiaries from a reciprocal recognition of the beliefs and attitudes of others. Supporters argue that group rights are simply entitlements that require no apology or concession. They are analogous to special rights for the disabled, say, compensating their recipients for structural disadvantages for which they have no responsibility. We should no more expect Sikhs to pay higher insurance premiums than ask wheelchair users to contribute to the costs of ramps. The analogy is inappropriate, however. Ethnicity or cultural indentity may be largely unchosen but their bearers usually view them positively and can partly shape them. Their claim is not only that they can contribute as much as others given the opportunity, but also that they add a new dimension that may change how we conceive existing roles and even add new ones. But although ethnicity and cultural identity are largely unchosen, their bearers usually view them positively and can partly shape them. Their claim is not only that they can contribute as much as others given the opportunity, but also that they add a new dimension that may change how we conceive existing roles and even add new ones. That additional dimension does entail mutual accommodation, however, and not just protection against interference.

Group representation and minority vetoes within legislatures pose parallel problems. Advocates of such measures concentrate on their role in unravelling the prevailing consensus, arguing that the presence of minority groups in legislatures and an ability to block certain legislation broadens the horizons of dominant groups by compelling them to adapt to different perspectives. But such adaptation is only likely to be genuine if it is reciprocal. Group representation risks insulating hitherto subordinate groups from any such necessity and may undermine the motivation of dominant groups to do so too. Worse, it can result in deadlock and acquiescence in an unjust status quo, particularly when buttressed by a veto. Whilst a veto may protect minorities against the passing of discriminatory laws, it can also be wielded to protect the perpetration of injustice. Tyranny can result from acts of omission as well as commission, as John Calhoun's notorious scheme for concurrent majorities to safeguard slavery in the American south demonstrated all too clearly.[15]

Worries about group rights entrenching exclusion and antipathy are particularly strong with self-government rights. They bedevil the main attempt to institutionalise this variety of pluralist politics, consociationalism. A model associated with Belgium, Switzerland and, in the past, Holland and Austria, consociationalism has four main features: a grand coalition or power-sharing executive, segmental autonomy involving either territorial or non-territorial forms of self-government, proportionality as a principle of political representation, civil service appointments and the allocation of public funds, and minority veto.[16] This political system combines self-government and special representation rights, and invariably establishes certain polyethnic rights too. It allows people to spend their whole lives within a given segment, from say birth in a denominational hospital, through education and employment in schools, enterprises and unions of a given religious persuasion, to burial in a church cemetery. In the process, segmental identity gets strengthened, but this adds to rather than detracts from the system's legitimacy if not, as we shall see, its stability. Consociationalism's success depends on the ability of elites within the Grand Coalition to deliver the acquiescence of their followers in return for a mutually beneficial carve-up of resources. It is the elites, not ordinary people, who interact and make compromises with each other.

Though Arend Lijphart, this system's most prominent advocate, claims consociationalism offers a universal panacea for 'deeply divided' societies, it favours conflicts of a certain kind. It works best when types of difference are focused on hierarchical organisations capable of defining and stabilising the beliefs of their members.[17] Religions typically have this character, with the clergy deciding church doctrine. So can ideologies when parties successfully establish themselves as their official guardians, as occurred with certain Communist parties. However, differences based on ethnicity or those associated with new social movements are rarely of this nature. As historical constructs of the human capacity for reflection and interpretation, they are internally contested and open to development. They are usually more informally organised and have less clear cut programmes. They are concerned not so much with a fair division of the spoils as with the shape and nature of the polity within which such resources get defined as well as distributed. Consociationalism survives in large part through hindering the development of groups around such divisions. It requires that differences be already organised politically and have an established leadership. Dissent within the ranks undermines the authority of the elites and questions the whole rationale for segmental autonomy and representation.

The extent to which consociationalism promotes peace between those divisions it does recognise may be doubted. Consociationalists hope a degree of group autonomy, either in the organisation of a region or in running certain services, will help minorities express and act on their differences within the context of a larger unit. They also believe such empowerment, combined with a guaranteed say in any national legislature, offers a way of transforming the thinking of dominant groups by encouraging them to look beyond their own assumptions and interests so as to take on board those of others. Far from fostering changes in the hegemonic culture, however, segmental autonomy may be perceived by the dominant group as a pragmatic concession that safely confines the minority to the ghetto. Meanwhile, as we have noted, segmental autonomy may prove even more intolerant than the wider community towards individual dissenters and those minorities that prove unable to organise themselves in this way. Minority as well as majority elites have few, if any, incentives to develop a spirit of compromise amongst themselves or their followers. Their power rests on emphasising their differences and extracting the highest possible price for any concessions. Ultimately, only instrumental considerations will prevent the various parties from going it alone. Thus, the size of the different cultural groups usually needs to be sufficiently similar to make governing without the others difficult. There usually also need to be further reasons, such as external threats or economic viability, that make secession unattractive.

A relationship based on purely instrumental factors rarely proves stable, since those concerned will always take advantage of any change to the balance of power. Many commentators have noted consociationalism's supposed successes rest on additional factors. Where consociational systems have survived, as in Switzerland, there has usually been a long history of elite cooperation, in the Swiss case dating back to the early modern period, and a greater popular consensus (evidenced in Switzerland by the national referenda), than consociational analysts have claimed.[18] When, as in Northern Ireland, elites are in many ways even more hostile than the general population they and their organisations can be positive blocks to rather than facilitators of mutual accommodation. In most cases, cross-cutting cleavages are also present and may lead to the passing away of the system, as has largely happened in the Netherlands and Austria. Indeed, Dahl contends that consociationalism has never survived unless accompanied by a measure of social and economic development sufficient to create elements of polyarchy. Unfortunately, evidence also points to consociationalism sometimes working to the detriment of the very background elements that allow it to operate. For the elite bias of consociational mechanisms diminishes popular interaction between the segments and so can fuel separatist parties. Though analysts dispute the gravity of the Belgium crisis, few deny that some such dynamic has been at work there.

Some critics of group rights and consociationalism ascribe their problems to their supposed illiberalism, itself often related to the very idea of differentiated citizenship. This criticism misses the mark. As Kymlicka and Lijphart respectively have shown, both these mechanisms have a solid liberal pedigree. Their justification lies in demands for equality and freedom through the removal of constraints that those concerned were not responsible for. Though additional difficulties arise through a small number of the groups so protected being illiberal, that is not the prime issue. By and large, protected groups do respect basic liberal principles. Liberalism is not what divides the Quebecois from their fellow Canadians or the Scots from the rest of Britain any more than it did the Norwegians from the Swedes. Aboriginal people employ contractarian reasoning not dissimilar to the liberal's and most cultures respect a not dissimilar list of universal human rights.[19] The problem, as we saw above, is that these principles can be nonetheless the subject of disagreement when discussing their relevance to any concrete case. A uniform constitutional status does not guarantee unity let alone unanimity amongst citizens when it comes to deciding how to exercise and apply those rights.

Demands for political autonomy arise when a group feels it is more appropriate to resolve these disputes between themselves rather than in conjunction with others. They believe that historical, functional, geographical, linguistic, cultural and other reasons make them a discrete demos. When the two groups can separate in ways that are not too costly to either, as occurred with Norway and Sweden and may happen with Scotland and England, it is hard to mount a principled objection to their doing so. However, separating off into relatively homogenous units is becoming ever harder in today's global and multicultural societies. An independent Scotland would still have to operate as a member of a transnational European Union and contain significant cultural minorities, including substantial English and Anglo-Scottish communities. Within this context, the chief defect of the segregationist approach is not its illiberalism so much as its doomed attempt to combine the two previous liberal strategies examined earlier, namely trimming and trading. Segregation is but a radical exercise in trimming away differences and keeping interference and the common public sphere to a minimum. The remaining interaction is supposed to be a pure matter of trading guided by a shared interest in mutual autonomy and the provision of such advantages as security from external threats. However, trimming can never produce consensus, nor trading fairness and stability, unless agreement and equity already obtain amongst the parties concerned. Pluralism makes such preconditions unlikely. The task of plural societies is to create reciprocal agreements in unfavourable circumstances. The next section proposes an alternative approach that grasps this nettle.

Democratic liberalism: compromise as negotiation

If liberal democracy employs constitutional trimming to reduce the grounds for mutual interference to a level where mutually advantageous trading can take place, democratic liberalism requires the negotiation of differences and the search for conditions of mutual acceptability that reach towards a reciprocal compromise that constructs common good. This approach draws inspiration from the republican tradition. Whereas liberals view freedom as a natural condition obtained through an absence of intervention, republicanism sees it as a civic achievement resulting from the absence of domination. A free society is one where citizens lack the capacity to dominate each other and where they can ensure the laws track their various interests and ideals.[20]

Trimmers attempt to define a shareable public sphere by a least-common-denominator approach, traders by appeal to mutual advantage. Both strategies try and get agreements by showing certain arrangements are in every group's or individual's interest. But that makes them highly vulnerable to free riding and defection because there are hardly any arrangements that someone could not gain from abusing. Freedom as non-domination, by contrast, is a common good. It benefits all but can only be achieved through the civic cooperation of all. It is a good that individuals can only know in common. As such, it is discontinuous with pre-political individual preferences. It emerges solely through membership of a polity where all enjoy equal status and collaborate to ensure the equity of the laws. Of course, individuals may sacrifice civic liberty in order to dominate others, but something valuable will have been lost in the process—the experience of living on equal terms with others and knowing you are valued for your true worth rather than because of the power and influence you can wield over your supposed admirers.

Given that multicultural conflicts are typically characterised in terms of struggles for recognition, a condition of civic liberty ought to be attractive to all parties in such disputes. However, the motivation to create such a society may still be absent if we can only fully appreciate the benefits of a free society when we live in one. As earlier republican theorists observed, where the conditions of civility are absent we need a Legislator to create an institutional context capable of promoting the appropriate civic virtues. Though Solons are undoubtedly in short supply these days, the facilitative role played by an independent third party in establishing the rules of the game is a familiar one in domestic and international disputes of all kinds, from squabbling neighbours upwards. This approach also emphasises that the crucial aspect of constitution-making is institutional design rather than the principled legal framework. Republicans take the idea of the body politic seriously. Just as a healthy physical constitution results from a balanced regimen that harmonises the different bodily passions and functions, so a healthy polity involves a balanced regime or political system that mixes the social interests and moral ideals in play, constraining the ability of any one to dominate another and motivating each to seek mutually acceptable compromises that reflect the concerns of those affected. The upshot of this republican strategy is a democratic liberalism that treats liberal rights as intrinsic to and products of democratic processes rather than the preconditions for them, as liberal democrats suppose.

The key disposition to foster is encapsulated in the republican formula 'audi alteram partem' or 'hear the other side'. This criterion constrains both the procedures and the outcomes of the political process. People must drop purely self-referential or self-interested reasoning and look for considerations others can find compelling, thereby ruling out arguments that fail to treat all of equal moral worth. They must strive to accommodate the clashes of preferences and principles associated with pluralism by seeking integrative compromises that view the concerns raised by others as matters to be met rather than constraints to be overcome through minimal, tactical concessions. In sum, trimming, trading and segregation must give way to negotiation.

Unlike trimmers, negotiators do not seek a pre-political consensus to constrain politics. Rather they aim at the political construction of compromise agreements that reflect, rather than abstract from, the particular attachments and circumstances in which people find themselves. Indeed, it is these specificities that make compromise possible by allowing the various feelings and arguments that lie behind people's preferences and values to be appreciated. Abstractly considered, ranking Beethoven over Shakespeare may be simply nonsensical, but on a given night I might be able to explain why I preferred going to a concert rather than a play. Political compromise standardly draws on these additional reasons to accommodate different and seemingly incompatible points of view. Unlike trading, however, negotiators must try for a mutually satisfying solution rather than one that just satisfies themselves as far as possible. Instead of viewing a conflict as a battle to be won or lost, the parties must see it as a collective problem to be solved. Finally, unlike segregators, negotiators employ group rights to promote engagement with the broader collectivity rather than to protect and withdraw groups from such involvement. So group representation rights may be necessary to ensure certain minorities reach a sufficient threshold to have a choice that people take seriously; but an interactive presence might be better encouraged through quotas within established parties, such as exists for women in many European countries, rather than separate constituencies, seats or parties. Likewise, vetoes are to be avoided as largely negative.

The mechanisms needed to realise this scheme will necessarily vary according to the complexion of the groups involved. Certain general rules of thumb nonetheless emerge. First, voting systems must involve as wide a range of voices as possible whilst encouraging reciprocal acceptance and accommodation. Second, though dispersing power can aid this process, it too should be subject to similar conditions. Third, and less familiar, review procedures are needed whereby both the decisions and the means whereby they were arrived at can be contested. To fix ideas, I shall close this section with an example of each of these techniques.

Plurality electoral systems, such as first-past-the-post, pose problems for minorities. Small parties are unlikely to be successful, particularly if a group if dispersed over several constituencies. By enhancing the power of the executive, minority influence is reduced within the main parties

Parties (% of the vote)	Policy or Candidate Preference Rankings
Party A (25%)	a b c d
Party B (30%)	b a d c
Party C (40%)	c a d b
Party D (5%)	d b c a

Source: A. Weale, *Democracy* (pp. 132–3).

as well. Unless the governing party's parliamentary majority is small — the exception rather than the rule given that a massive majority can be delivered by well under 50% of the total vote — there will be little or no need for the leadership to compromise even with their own supporters. Proportional representation appears the obvious solution but has difficulties of its own. Allowing the proliferation of single issue parties can militate against an appreciation of the concerns of the wider community. Government coalitions between such groups will tend to reflect a trader's rather than a negotiator's compromise. Party list systems make outcomes more proportionate to a party's share of the vote but do not necessarily guarantee that party representatives will more proportionately reflect the range of public opinions.

To get around these problems we need a voting system for selecting representatives and making policies in the legislature that builds in compromise to majoritarian decision-making. As Albert Weale has recently shown, 'Condorcet voting' has just this feature.[21] Under this system voters rank their preferences for candidates or policy options. The Condorcet-winner is the ranking that could defeat every other in a pair-wise contest (see Table).

Here a plurality vote would lead to option or candidate 'c' being chosen, having secured the largest number of first preferences. However, the Condorcet-winner is 'a' since it emerges as the majority preference when its ranking is compared against each of the alternatives. Weale observes that the combined consequences of issue-by-issue majority voting — technically known as 'the issue median' — coincides with the Condorcet-winner, as this procedure likewise involves finding those alternatives that command majority support. Thus, the Condorcet-winner 'both captures the idea of a majority converging around a compromise solution where there are divergent ideal preferences and it can be construed as the outcome of a procedure by which members of a political community take issues one by one'.[22] When there are three or more alternatives a Condorcet-winner may not exist, with pair-wise comparisons producing not an outright winner but a cycle. In candidate elections this result can be overcome by selecting the person who loses by the smallest margin(s) in one or more pairwise comparisons. Weale argues that in the case of issues, so long as these are discreet, so that voter preferences on one issue do not depend on the outcome of a vote on another, then sequential voting is acceptable as a way of breaking the cycle.[23] Though such methods do not guarantee that the compromise candidates so chosen will themselves possess the skills of negotiating compromises when legislating, Condorcet voting will also mean governments usually have to build majorities on many issues, making such attributes desirable.

Dispersing power to semi-autonomous political units can also give minority groups a voice and an element of control. Within differentiated societies, centralised and hierarchical ways of distributing power will be inadequate. Sheer size and complexity, as well as cultural and other differences, often render centralised decision-making inappropriate and inefficient: it overrepresents people unaffected by, or with scant interest in, the resulting policies, underrepresents those most involved, and pays insufficient attention to the peculiarities of particular enterprises, services and locations. Dispersing power amongst a variety of constituencies opens up spaces for undominated choice and allows the framing and/or implementation of laws to suit the particular needs of both a diverse public and a differentiated social system. The commonest form such dispersal takes is the creation of distinct territorially based tiers of government. As we noted in the last section, such schemes do not serve polyethnic groups well, nor do they always match the requirements of functional diversity. Typically, they also involve a devolution downwards of a discreet set of powers and so do not provide a share in centralised decision-making but rather remain subject to it. Thus, the territorial dispersal of power needs supplementing or even replacing by a more vertical organisation of sovereignty across a wide variety of domains: from the workplace to schools and hospitals. This manoeuvre allows the development of a multiplicity of demoi that reflect the range of our multiple allegiances and interests. As ever, however, the promotion of diversity has to be balanced by the maintenance of solidarity. Where cross-cutting cleavages exist, membership of these demoi can be expected to be heterogeneous and connections between the different domains will be made, so that the knock-on effects of decisions in one area for others will get factored in. Even so, the necessity for appropriately joined-up thinking will have to be formalised by connecting the various domains to more comprehensive decision making bodies. By sending representatives to a territorially based legislature, responsible for dispersing funds and regulating public goods, these diverse bodies will feed into central decision-making but be constrained by their respective rival claims. Such devices will be even more necessary in the case of segmental cleavages if the pitfalls of consociationalism are to be avoided. Denominational schools, for example, should still belong to a local education authority under a plural membership and participate in deciding regional funding priorities, teaching training, assessment and the setting of attainment targets for pupils.

Analysts of the European Union have commented on how the multi-level governance that emerges from such a dispersal of power has begun to characterise European decision-making. Policy increasingly involves negotiation and dialogue between a wide variety of actors and tiers of government. Joanne Scott, for example, believes the 'partnership' principle employed within Community structure funding can be interpreted in these terms. She argues that partnership shares power across different levels of government, with the Community recognising that member states are not single units and that actors outside the official public sphere also merit a political voice. Thus, it 'does not involve the parcelling out of limited pockets of sovereignty, but a genuine pooling of sovereignty'. In other words, it ensures that mixing of voices which is distinctive to the democratic liberal approach, promoting deliberation by dispersing power.[24]

Contestatory and revisory procedures are familiar in legal contexts, where the right to appeal adverse judgements is standard. The grounds in these cases relate to the propriety of the procedures, matters of law, and the reliability, relevance, suppression or discovery of crucial evidence. Appellants can question the fairness and appropriateness of their convictions and raise new issues that cast their actions in a different light. Similar mechanisms are being increasingly employed to contest political decisions.[25] Judicial review of the constitutionality or procedural correctness of legislation is now commonplace. Special regulators, such as Ombudsmen, have also been created for both legislatures and many publicly and privately provided services, from banking to hospitals. These sorts of institutions offer important checks on the majoritarian bias of almost any voting system. However, multicultural struggles frequently turn on the very rules of the political game. New political demands, and complaints that one's concerns are not heard, raise questions about such matters as the qualifications for citizenship (as in calls to extend the franchise), the composition of the legislature (as in debates over quotas for minorities), the forms and methods of political participation and debate (should it be consensual or adversarial, director or indirect, a plurality or proportional voting system and so on), and the location, scope and character of political decision making (federal or confederal, amongst workers, or only for politicians and so on). A democratic liberalism makes space for such constitutional questions to be contested as part of normal politics rather than as exceptional matters. The logic for doing so has recently been stated with admirable clarity by the Canadian Supreme Court in its ruling on the constitutionality of the Secession of Quebec. The Court observed how:

'A functioning democracy requires a continuous process of discussion. The Constitution mandates government by democratic legislatures, and an executive accountable to them, "resting ultimately on public opinion reached by discussion and the interplay of ideas" (*Saumur v City of Quebec*, supra at p. 330). At both the federal and provincial level, by its very nature, the need to build majorities necessitates compromise, negotiation, and deliberation. No one has a monopoly on truth, and our system is predicated on the faith that in the marketplace of ideas, the best solutions to public problems will rise to the top.

Inevitably, there will be dissenting voices. A democratic system of government is committed to considering those dissenting voices, and seeking to acknowledge and address those voices in the laws by which all in the community must live.'

One corollary of democracy so conceived was the constitutional confederal of:

'A right to initiate constitutional change on each participant in Confederation. In our view, the existence of this right imposes a corresponding duty on the participants in Confederation to engage in constitutional discussions in order to acknowledge and address democratic expressions of a desire for change in other provinces. This duty is inherent in the democratic principle which is a fundamental predicate of our system of governance.'[26]

Such discussions naturally have to be consistent with the prevention of domination by not denying the democratic choices of either the people left over, or any minorities the new limit may contain to be self-governing, in a manner commensurate with their numbers, but their availability is also necessitated by that goal.[27] In a pluralist society it is inevitable that the contours of politics will be in continual flux, and the legitimacy of any political system will ultimately depend on its being open to new developments and obtaining continuous democratic endorsement through referenda, conventions and more informal channels of public debate.

Some commentators fear that any recognition of pluralism must ultimately lead to the dissolution of the polity. But unity does not require uniformity. A political community based on negotiation and compromise ties a people together through a series of 'family resemblances' and affinities rather than a common identity.[28] This produces a deeper and more stable union than appeals to either a putative set of basic common principles or to mutual advantage are likely to generate, whilst still recognising diversity and difference.

Conclusion

Pluralism is not just a problem within liberal democracies, it challenges the very practices and ideals of liberal democracy. Liberal principles cannot be treated as a consensual framework within which democratic trading can take place. Nor can particular cultural differences be hived off into separate liberal democratic units. Rather, differences have to be continually and democratically negotiated with compromise not consensus as the goal. Instead of freedom from interference, the citizens of such a political system enjoy the civic liberty of non-domination which makes the politics of mutual recognition possible. Many find the endless negotiation that accompanies pluralism tiresome. For good or ill, however, it is the price one pays for liberty and diversity.

1   Research for this paper was supported by an ESRC Research Grant on 'Sovereignty and Citizenship in a Mixed Polity' (R000222446).

2   For the nature of pluralism see R. Bellamy, *Liberalism and Pluralism: Towards a Politics of Compromise*, Routledge, 1999, ch.1.

3   W. Kymlicka, *Multicultural Citizenship: A Liberal Theory of Minority Rights*, Clarendon Press, 1995, p. 1.

4   Despite differences between them, recent writers in this tradition include C. Larmore, *Patterns of Moral Complexity*, Cambridge University Press, 1987; J. Rawls, *Political Liberalism*, Columbia University Press, 1993; and B. Barry, *Justice as Impartiality*, Clarendon Press, 1995.

5   See R.J. McKeever, *Raw Judicial Power? The Supreme Court and American Society*, 2nd edn, Manchester University Press, 1995. For an analysis of the weaknesses of this strategy in the British context, see Bellamy, op. cit., ch. 7.

6   R.A. Dahl, *A Preface to Democratic Theory*, University of Chicago Press, 1956, p. 135.

7   For a summary, largely paraphrased here, see R.A. Dahl, *Democracy and its Critics*, Yale University Press, 1989, pp. 251–4.

8   The classic critiques are P. Bachrach and M.S. Baratz, *Power and Poverty*, New York: Oxford University Press, 1970; and S. Lukes, *Power: A Radical View*, London: Macmillan, 1974.

9   C.E. Lindblom, *Politics and Markets*, Basic Books, 1977; R.A. Dahl, *A Preface to Economic Democracy*, Polity Press, 1985.

10 T. Modood, 'Kymlicka on British Muslims', *Analyse und Kritik*, 15, 1993.

11 Dahl, *Democracy and its Critics*, p. 254.

12 Kymlicka, *Multicultural Citizenship*, pp. 26–33.

13 This possibility was key to English pluralists such as G.D.H. Cole and has recently been taken up by theorists of associative democracy. See P. Hirst, *Associative Democracy: New Forms of Economic and Social Governance*, Polity Press, 1994.

14 For these caveats see C. Offe, '"Homogeneity" and Constitutional Democracy: Coping with Identity Conflicts through Group Rights', *Journal of Philosophy*, 6, 1998, pp. 125–31.

15 J.C. Calhoun, *A Disquisition on Government*, Indianapolis: Hackett, 1958.

16 A. Lijphart, *The Politics of Accommodation: Pluralism and Democracy in the Netherlands*, University of California Press, 1968.

17 For this criticism see B. Barry, 'Political Accommodation and Consociational Democracy', *British Journal of Political Sciences*, 5, 1975, pp. 502–3.

18 H. Daalder, 'On Building Consociational Nations: The Cases of the Netherlands and Switzerland', *International Social Science Journal*, 23, 1971, p. 361.

19 J. Tully, *Strange Multiplicity: Constitutionalism in an Age of Diversity*, Cambridge University Press, 1995; S. Caney, 'Defending Universalism' in I. MacKenzie and S. O'Neill, *Reconstituting Social Criticism*, Macmillan, 1999.

20 This formulation of neo-Roman republicanism is from Q. Skinner, *Liberty Before Liberalism*, Cambridge University Press, 1997 and P. Pettit, *Republicanism: A Theory of Freedom and Government*, Oxford University Press, 1997. This section draws on Bellamy, op. cit., chs. 4 and 5.

21 A. Weale, *Democracy*, Macmillan, 1999, ch.7.

22 Ibid., p. 137 and pp. 146–7.

23 Ibid.

24 J. Scott, 'Law, Legitimacy and the EC Governance: Prospects for "Partnership"', *Journal of Common Market Studies,* 1998, 36, p. 181.

25 For the importance of contestatory mechanisms see Pettit, op. cit., p. 232.

26 Supreme Court of Canada, *Reference re Secession of Quebec*, 20 August 1998, ss. 68–9.

27 For the caveats see T. Pogge, 'Cosmopolitanism and Sovereignty' in C. Brown (ed), *Political Restructuring in Europe: Ethical Perspectives*, Routledge, 1994.

28 See Tully, op. cit. for this Wittgensteinian notion and its importance for a pluralist constitutionalism.

INDEX